RESTRICTED

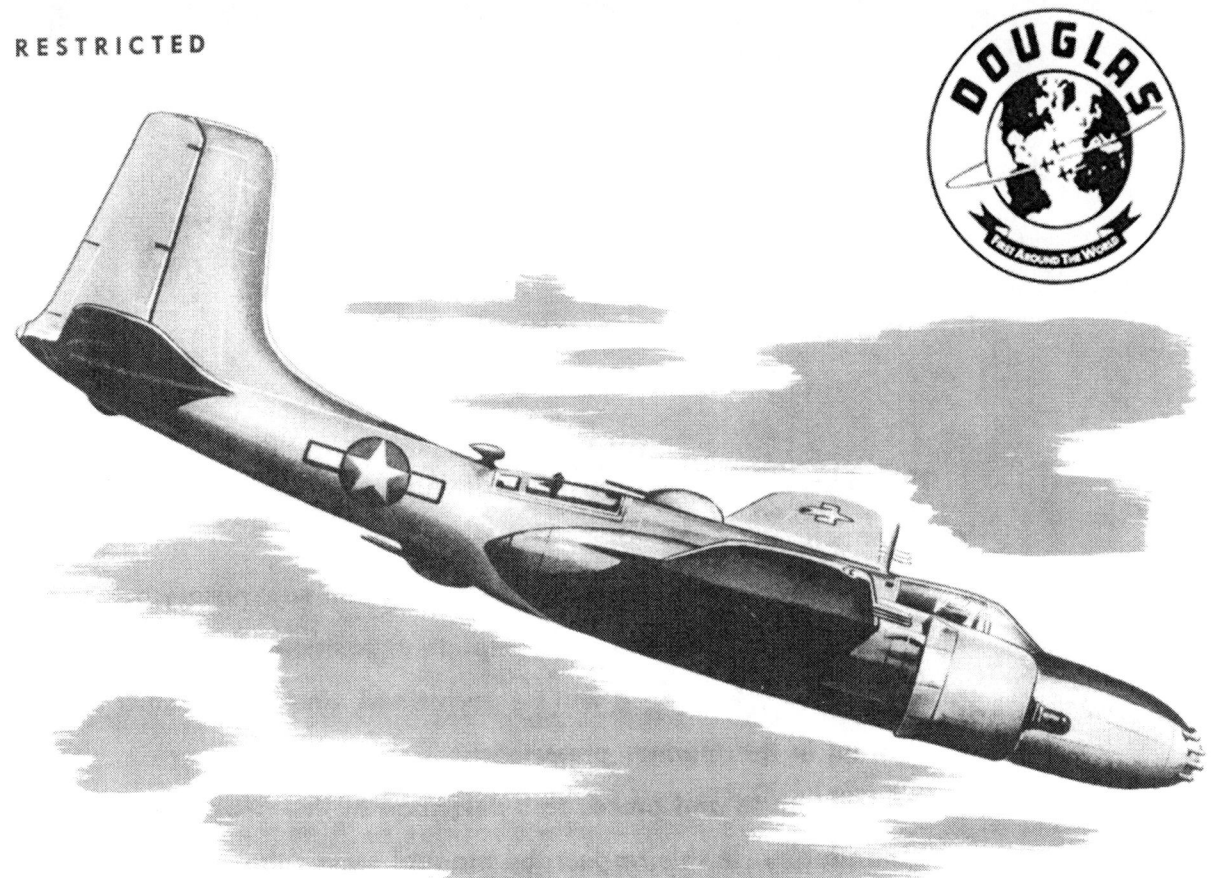

A-26 Invader

Pilot's Flight Operating Instructions

©2008-2010 Periscope Film LLC
All Rights Reserved
ISBN #978-1-935700-03-6
www.PeriscopeFilm.com

This manual is sold for historic research purposes only, as an entertainment. It is not intended to be used as part of an actual flight training program. No book can substitute for flight training by an authorized instructor. The licensing of pilots is overseen by organizations and authorities such as the FAA and CAA. Operating an aircraft without the proper license is a federal crime.

This text has been digitally watermarked to prevent illegal duplication.

RESTRICTED AAF MANUAL 51-126-1

PILOT TRAINING MANUAL FOR THE

CHECK TITLE PAGE FOR DATE OF THIS MANUAL

Invader A-26

HEADQUARTERS, ARMY AIR FORCES RESTRICTED

AAF MANUAL 51-126-1   **RESTRICTED**

PILOT TRAINING MANUAL FOR THE INVADER

This revised edition supersedes the original (blue cover) Pilot Training Manual for the Invader. All copies of the latter are rescinded.

Hq. Army Air Forces
Washington 25, D. C., 15 August 1945

The use and authentication of this manual are governed by the provisions of AAF Regulation 50-17.

BY COMMAND OF GENERAL ARNOLD

Ira C. Eaker
Lieutenant General, United States Army
Deputy Commander, Army Air Forces

Additional copies of this manual should be requested from:
Hq. AAF, Office of Flying Safety, Safety Education Division
Winston-Salem 1, North Carolina

INITIAL DISTRIBUTION REVISED EDITION: HEADQUARTERS AAF, 1ST AIR FORCE, 3RD AIR FORCE, AAF TRAINING COMMAND, AIR TRANSPORT COMMAND

RESTRICTED

T.O.P.—DAYTON, O.—NOVEMBER, 1945—2,000

INTRODUCTION

This manual is the text for your training as a A-26 pilot and airplane commander.

The Air Forces' most experienced training and supervisory personnel have collaborated to make it a complete exposition of what your pilot duties are, how each will be performed, and why it must be performed in the manner prescribed.

The techniques and procedures described in this book are standard and mandatory. In this respect the manual serves the dual purpose of a training checklist and working handbook. Use it to make sure that you learn everything described herein. Use it to study and review the essential facts concerning everything taught. Such additional self-study and review will not only advance your training, but will alleviate the burden of your already overburdened instructors.

This training manual does not replace the Technical Orders for the airplane, which will always be your primary source of information concerning the A-26 so long as you fly it. This is essentially the textbook of the A-26. Used properly, it will enable you to utilize the pertinent Technical Orders to even greater advantage.

COMMANDING GENERAL, ARMY AIR FORCES

RESTRICTED

THE A-26 *Invader*

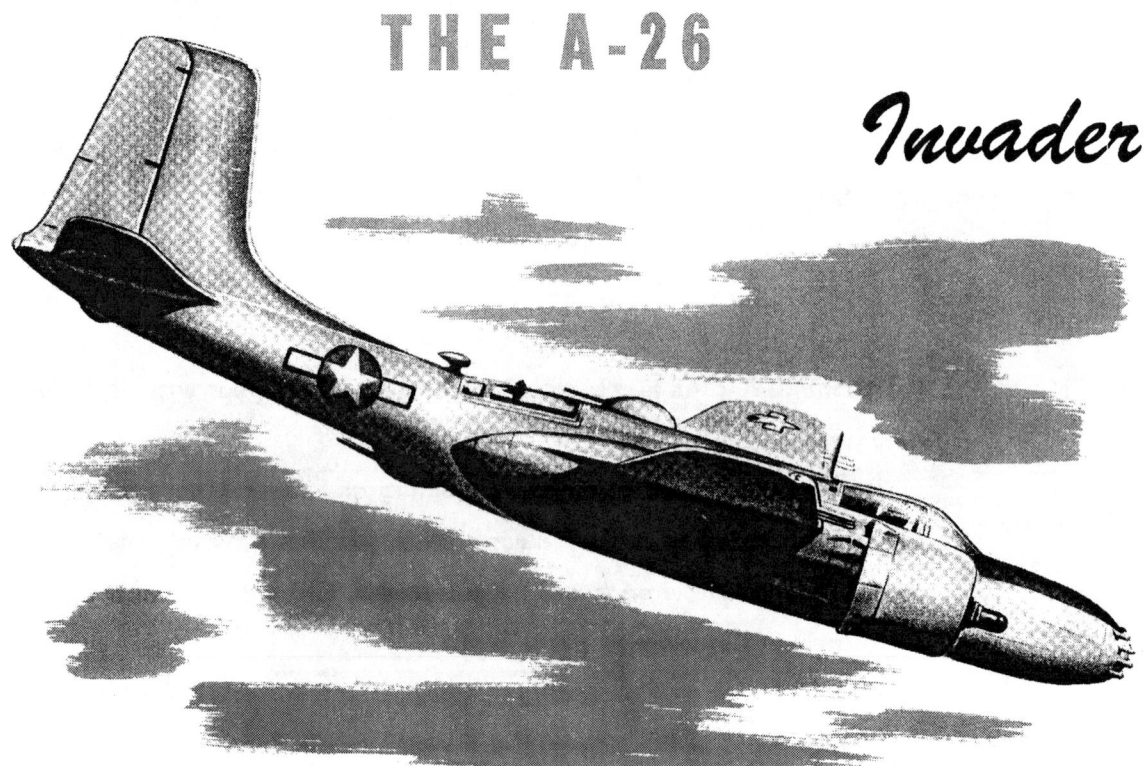

The Douglas A-26 Invader has been described as a glorified A-20, a new fighter-bomber, and a cross between a B-26 and a B-25. Actually the Invader is a new airplane modified and changed late in its design to meet the pinpoint requirements of the theater commanders. No other medium bomber has the versatility, the speed or the tremendous combination striking power the A-26 has. At its altitude it's as fast as a fighter, carries more bombs farther and faster than any other medium bomber and packs a nosefull of strafing fire power and two turrets of protective fire power at the same time.

Combat

The combat history of the A-26 is short but brilliant. It has lived up to and surpassed the results that the designers and the AAF theater commanders expected of it. The new A-26 groups had the first opportunity to show their stuff in the fall of 1945 when the German Western Army under Von Runstedt made its powerful counter-offensive in the Ardennes and forced the historic Belgian Bulge in the allied lines. The sorties flown and the withering damage done by the A-26 in support of our ground forces was eloquently stated by Von Runstedt when he was taken prisoner. He said: "But for the savage Allied strafing attacks our counter-offensive would have driven on to Paris."

As this book is being written A-26 groups are leaving for the Pacific. You as a new A-26 pilot will soon be a member of one of these groups and it is up to you to write the A-26 history against the Japanese.

Make no mistake about it, the Invader is not a small boy's flying machine. It is a high-speed airplane with a high wing loading. It requires exact procedures, top flying technique, and headwork to exploit its striking power. So use this manual, study it, learn it! It represents the combined experience to date of the factory engineering test pilots, AAF test pilots, and your instructors, who have many hundreds of hours of A-26 know-how upon which to draw.

RESTRICTED

GENERAL DESCRIPTION

The A-26 is a 2-engine mid-wing attack bomber of all-metal construction.

Engines

There are three series of Pratt & Whitney Double Row Wasp engines developing from 2000 to 2370 brake Hp on takeoff. The R-2800-27 engine develops 2000 brake Hp. The R-2800-71 engine develops the same Hp and is identical to the -27 with the exception of an improved GE ignition harness. The R-2800-79 engine is the water injection engine and develops 2370 brake Hp on takeoff.

Propellers

Three-bladed (12 feet, 7 inches in diameter), constant-speed, full-feathering hydromatic Hamilton Standard.

Landing Gear

Full retractable, hydraulic tricycle gear.

Wings

Two-spar, full cantilever, laminar flow. (Span, 70 feet; maximum width, 10 feet; maximum depth, 18⅓ inches.)

Fuselage

All-metal structure of alclad skin shaped and reinforced by aluminum alloy ribs, bulkheads, and longitudinal members. (Length with bombardier nose, 51 feet 3 inches; length with all-purpose nose, 50 feet 9 inches; maximum width, 5 feet 2 inches; height, 5 feet 10 inches.)

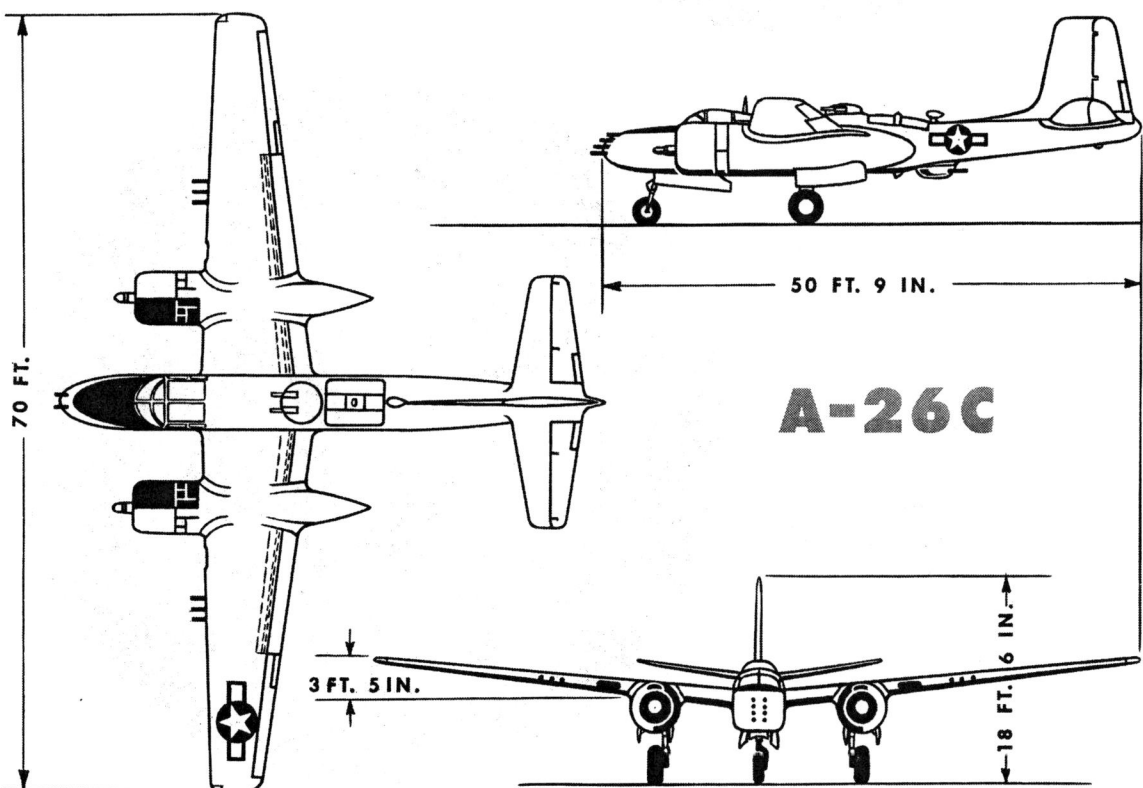

RESTRICTED

The A-26 is an extremely versatile airplane. It is designed with two interchangeable nose sections to meet exact tactical requirements.

1. ALL-PURPOSE NOSE.

There are six combinations of armament, as follows:

a. Six .50-cal. machine guns.
   Crew 2
b. Eight .50-cal. machine guns.
   Crew 2
c. One 37-mm. cannon and four .50-cal. machine guns.
   Crew 2
d. One 37-mm. cannon and two .50-cal. machine guns.
   Crew 2
e. Two 37-mm. cannon.
   Crew 2
f. One 75-mm. cannon and one 37-mm. cannon.
   Crew 3
g. One 75-mm. cannon and two .50-cal. machine guns.
   Crew 3

2. BOMBARDIER NOSE.
Crew 3
Plexiglas nose.
Fitted with bombsight and controls,
and two fixed .50-cal. machine guns.

RESTRICTED

OUTSTANDING FEATURES OF THE A-26

DOUGLAS HIGH-SPEED WING

The high-speed wing is a laminar flow airfoil which differs from the conventional airfoil in that the thickest dimension is nearer the center of the wing. The laminar flow airfoil is the most efficient high-speed wing developed thus far by aero-dynamists.

NEW HIGHLY EFFICIENT FLAP

The designers of the A-26 having produced the most aero-dynamically efficient high-speed wing, loaded to about 60 psi, found it necessary to develop a radically new and more efficient flap. This new double-slotted flap extends outward and downward producing as it extends (up to 40°) a much greater lift. As it continues to extend the last 12° of travel, it creates nearly all drag. This new flap is responsible for the comparatively slow approach speed and good landing characteristics of the airplane.

So What?

A good understanding of the wing and flap is important to you because the A-26 takes off and lands differently from any other airplane. Get that straight!

The A-26 takes off and lands differently from any other airplane. Unlike the B-25, the B-26 or the A-20, or any other airplane—the A-26 lands in an almost level attitude with the nose-wheel just off the runway. (See page 75).

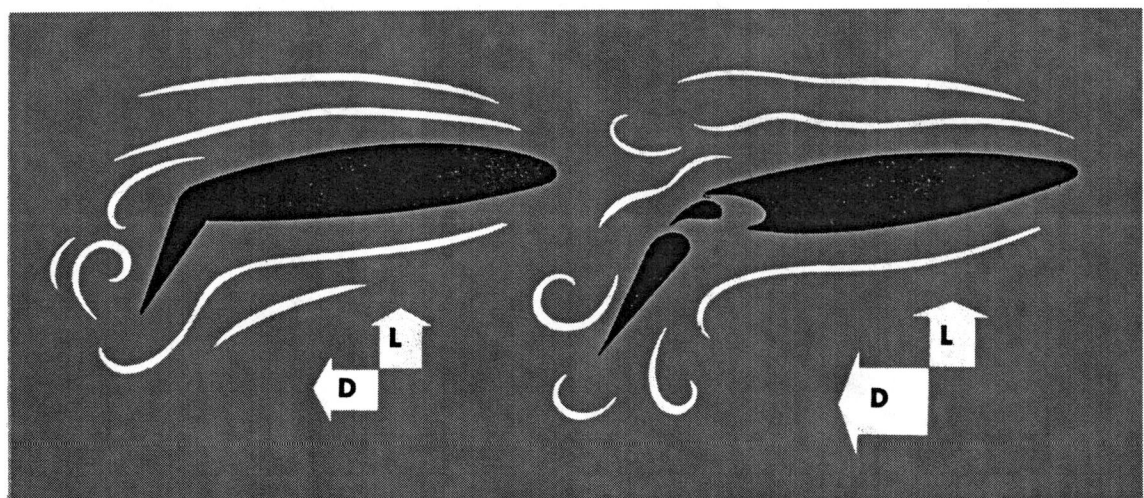

RESTRICTED

BUILT-IN ARMOR PLATE

In addition to the standard-gage armor plate for protection from direct machine gun fire, large areas of the fuselage, wing, and nacelle skin are protected with ⅜-inch or 5/16-inch Dural built as an integral part of the airplane for deflection protection from angular machine gun fire.

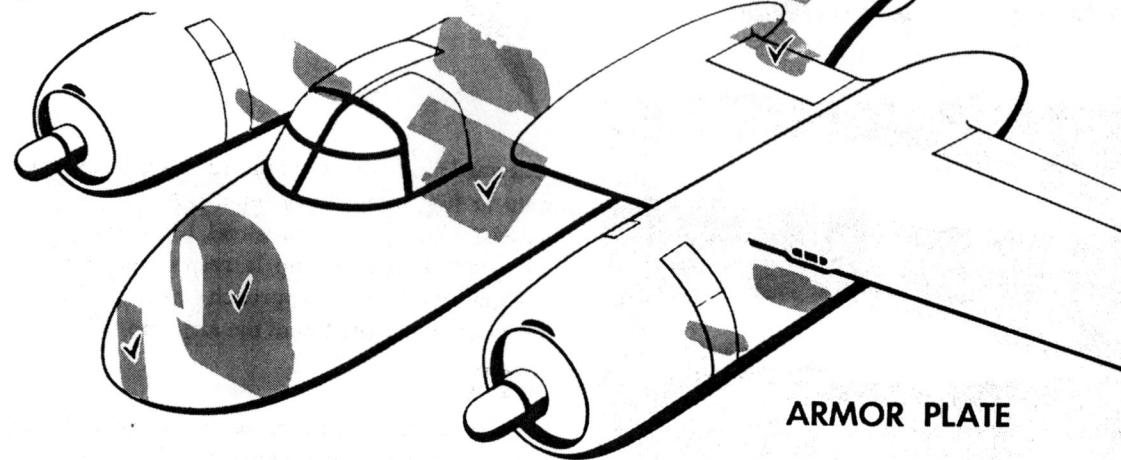

ARMOR PLATE

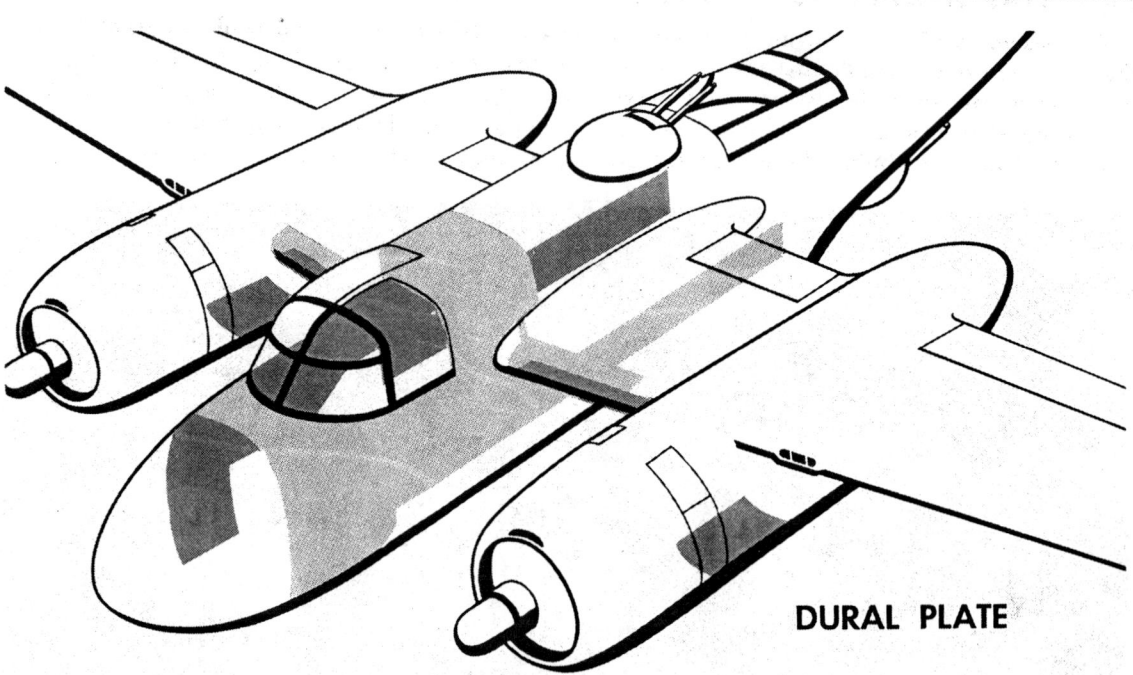

DURAL PLATE

RESTRICTED

A-26 Capacities and Limitations

1. **NOSEWHEEL SWING** . . . . 36° either direction

2. **DIVING SPEEDS** . . . .
   - 26,000 lbs. Gross . . . . 425 IAS
   - 32,000 lbs. . . . . 400 IAS
   - 35,500 lbs. . . . . 360 IAS

3. **LEVEL-FLIGHT SPEED** . . . . No limitation

4. **OPEN BOMB BAY DOORS**
   - WITH SPOILERS . . . . 425 IAS
   - WITHOUT SPOILERS . . . . 240 IAS

5. **FLAPS DOWN** . . . . 208 IAS

6. **WHEELS DOWN** . . . . 160 IAS

7. **TAKEOFF MANIFOLD PRESSURE** . . . . . 52" Hg.
   - —79 ENGINE WITH WATER INJECTION . . . Full throttle up to 60" Hg.

8. **RPM**
   - a. TAKEOFF AT FULL INCREASE RPM . . . 2700
   - b. GROUND RUN-UP APPROX. 25" . . . 2000
   - c. MAGNETO CHECK LOSS 100
   - d. FULL DECREASE RPM . . . . . . 1200 + or − 50
   - e. IDLING 550–700

9. **OIL CAPACITY (each tank) FULL** . . . . . 30 gals.
   4.5 gals. FOR EXPANSION

10. **OIL TEMPERATURES**
    - a. MIN. FOR TAKEOFF . . . . 40°C
    - b. DESIRED OPERATING . . . . . . 60–75°C
    - c. MAX. ALLOWABLE . . . . 100°C

11. **OIL CONSUMPTION—NORMAL OPERATING** . . 10 qts./hr/engine
    RATED POWER . . . . 27 qts./hr/engine

12. **OIL PRESSURE**
    - a. NORMAL IDLE . . . . 25 psi
    - b. MIN. OPERATING . . . . 50 psi
    - c. DESIRED OPERATING . . . . . . 70-80 psi
    - d. MAX. ALLOWABLE . . . . 100 psi

13. **FUEL CAPACITY**
    a. MAIN TANKS . . . . (each) 300 gals.
    b. AUX. TANKS . . . . (each) 100 gals.
    c. BOMB BAY TANK . . . . 125 gals.
       TOTAL NORMAL . . . . 925 gals.
    d. FERRY TANK (OPTIONAL) . . . . . 675 gals.
       TOTAL FERRY . . . . 1600 gals.
    e. TWO DROPPABLE WING TANKS (OPTIONAL)
       . . . . (each) 155 gals.
    f. AFT FUSELAGE TANKS (OPTIONAL) . . . 125 gals.

14. **FUEL PRESSURE**
    a. MIN. ALLOWABLE . . . . 13 psi
    b. DESIRED OPERATING . . . . 16-18 psi
    c. FUEL BOOSTER PUMP . . . . 22-24 psi
       WITH −79 WATER INJECTION—MAX.
          ALLOWABLE . . . . 25 psi
       ENGINE NOT RUNNING . . . . . . LOW 6-9 psi
       ENGINE NOT RUNNING . . . . . . HIGH 15-18 psi

15. **FUEL CONSUMPTION—NORMAL CRUISE** . . . approx. 150 GPH

16. **CYLINDER-HEAD TEMPERATURE**
    a. MIN. BEFORE RUN-UP . . . . 120°C
    b. MIN. BEFORE MAG CHECK AND TAKEOFF . 160°C
    c. MAX. BEFORE TAKEOFF . . . . . . 205°C
    d. MAX. ALLOWABLE (AUTO RICH) . . . . 260°C (1 hr. only)
       (AUTO LEAN) . . . . 232°C
    e. MAX. BEFORE STOPPING ENGINES . . . 150°C

17. **HYDRAULIC**
    a. CAPACITY OF SYSTEM . . . . approx. 8 gals.
    b. SYSTEM PRESSURE . . . . 850-1000 psi
    c. ACCUMULATOR . . . . 650 psi
    d. EMERGENCY AIR PRESSURE . . . . . 450-575 psi
    e. GEAR EXTEND OR RETRACT 160 IAS . . 12 sec.

18. **ELECTRIC**
    a. FLAPS EXTEND OR RETRACT 160 IAS . . 18 sec.
    b. COWL FLAPS . . . . 5-10 sec.
    c. OIL COOLER DOORS . . . . 15-20 sec.
    d. VOLTMETER (EARLY MODELS ONLY) 1700 RPM 26-28.5 volts
    e. AMMETERS (200 MAX. EACH) . . . . max. 20 amp. diff.

19. **INSTRUMENT SUCTION** . . . . 4.2" Hg. + or − .5"

20. **WEIGHT AND BALANCE**
    MAC . . . . 97.5 inches
    CG—LIMITS % OF MAC 18-32

Engines

The A-26 has two Pratt & Whitney R-2800 series engines. They are twin-row, 18 cylinder, (nine cylinders in each bank) air-cooled radials, each containing an internal single-stage, 2-speed, gear-driven blower. The earlier airplanes have the -27 engine; slightly later airplanes the -71 engine (which is the same engine with the exception of an improved GE ignition harness).

Water Injection

The -79 is the water injection engine. Operating with water at war emergency power the engines develop 2370 Hp each at sea level.

The purpose of the water injection system is to safeguard the engine against detonation while operating at war emergency power. Operating with water at war emergency power over and above prescribed rated power is for combat operation where greatest speeds for attack and evasive action are necessary. **Don't forget that operation with water on war emergency power creates additional strains upon the engine. Water injection should be used with discretion and only as needed.**

It is well known that engines operating at military power in rich mixture do not put out as much power as they would if the mixture could be leaned down to the best power mixture. Merely leaning down would cause severe detonation but with water injection to suppress detonation it is possible to operate the engine in its best power mixture which results in a 370 Hp additional output for each engine. The amount of power gained by leaning to the best power mixture will not alone give you full war emergency power rating. It will be also necessary to increase manifold pressures as indicated in the table below:

	RPM	MP	BRAKE HP	ALTITUDE
LOW BLOWER	2700 RPM	58" HG	2370 BHP	SEA LEVEL
HIGH BLOWER	2700 RPM	54" HG	2000 BHP	10,000 FT.

These war emergency power settings are the maximum available for full throttle. Do not use

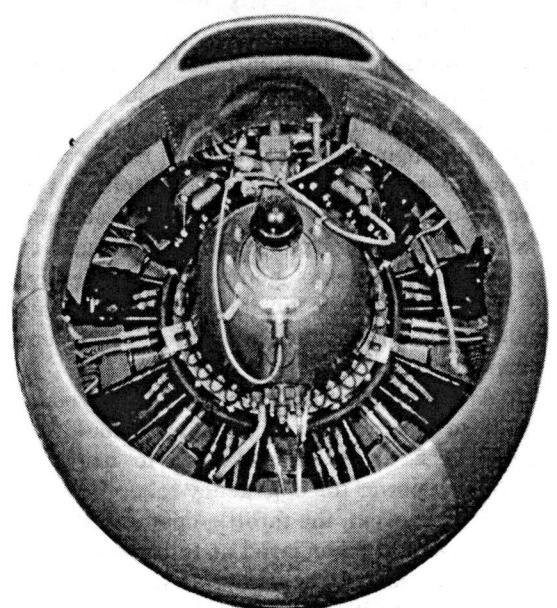

high blower below 10,000 feet; it will result in detonation.

The System

There are two identical water injection systems, one for each engine. Each system consists of a 21½-gallon water supply tank located in the wingtip, a water pump installed on the bulkhead aft of the fire wall, a solenoid control valve and pressure warning switch located near the pump, and a water regulator located on the carburetor.

The water is metered from a water regulator unit and mixed with metered fuel from the carburetor as the two liquids enter the fuel intake pipe. This mixture is then discharged into the intake air stream through the fuel discharge nozzle. Each water tank has an immersion heater and maintains a water temperature of 50°F. These heaters are automatic and become operative as soon as the airplane's battery switches are turned on.

Ground Check

Make the following ground check to determine if the water injection system is working. The purpose for ground checking the water injection system is to determine if water is entering the engines. It is not a power check.

a. After normal engine run-up turn the water pump switches on.

b. Two warning lights installed on the panel may flash momentarily as the pressure builds in the lines and then should remain off.

c. With engines operating at 30″ Hg. or with an rpm slightly over 2000, manually actuate the throttle-operated power switch. (Operate one system at a time.) Upon immediate closing of the switch, the engine should hesitate slightly, or cut out momentarily, then pick up power again. This indicates the water injection system is functioning.

d. At this point, the ground check is completed so the water pump switch should be turned OFF unless it is desired to use war emergency power for emergency takeoff conditions. In this event, the throttle-operated power switches should be engaged at full throttle before the airplane wheels have left the ground during the takeoff run. This is to prevent the power hesitation from occurring at a critical flight condition endangering takeoff. **War emergency power with water should be used for takeoff under emergency conditions only.**

Combat Operation

Use war emergency power with water injection in the following manner:

1. Place water pump switches ON.
2. With 2700 rpm move throttles to:
    a. Full throttle in low blower.
    b. Full throttle or 54″ Hg. manifold pressure (whichever comes first) in high blower. **High blower operation is used only at pressure altitudes over 10,000 feet.**
3. As water injection operation begins, a momentary roughness or cut of the engine will usually be noted. This is caused by the reduction in fuel flow as a result of the closure of the derichment valve. As the engine smooths out, cylinder head temperatures will decrease.
4. When water supply has been depleted, the pressure warning light will come on, signifying that power should be reduced immediately.

The A-26 engine is one of the most dependable engines built. To maintain them and use them properly, you must not deviate from the power settings indicated on your new color marker instruments and on your **Cruise Control Chart.**

WATER INJECTION SYSTEM

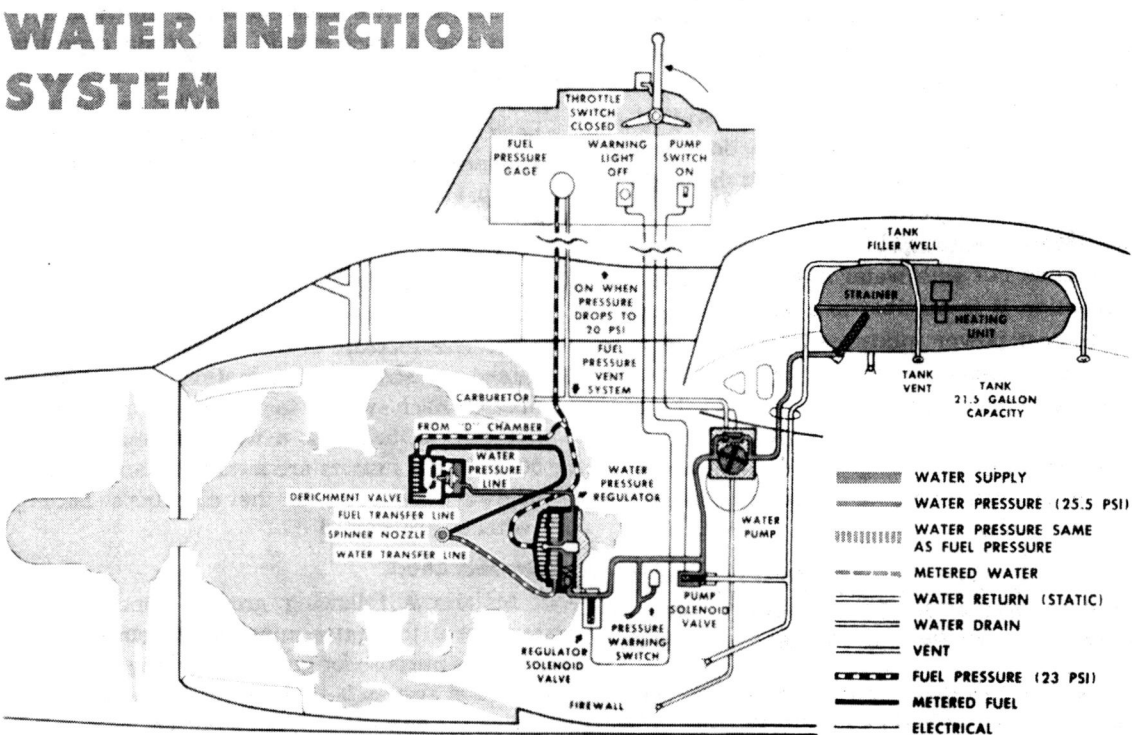

OBSERVE THESE LIMITS

		SEA LEVEL to	ALTITUDE
1.	Takeoff	52" Hg. and 2700 rpm	Full throttle
2.	Rated Power Unless using water injection Note: Do not exceed rated power settings except for takeoff and in case of emergency, and then never for more than 5 minutes.	42" Hg. and 2400 rpm	See Cruise Control Chart. Note that manifold pressure drops with increase in altitude.
3.	Continuous Cruising	33" Hg. and 2100 rpm	See Cruise Control Chart. Note that manifold pressure drops with increase in altitude.
	With —79 Engine using water injection	58" Hg. and 2700 rpm (LOW blower)	At 10,000 Ft. 54" Hg. and 2700 rpm (HIGH Blower)
4.	Mixture Control	Above 33" and 2100 rpm operate in AUTO RICH	Below 33" and 2100 rpm Operate in AUTO LEAN
	Do not attempt to lean your mixture further by pulling the mixture control back beyond the AUTO LEAN position. AUTO LEAN is the only position which gives you a proper lean mixture.		
5.	Cylinder-head Temperature	AUTO LEAN Do not exceed 232°C.	AUTO RICH Do not exceed 260° C.
6.	Engine Dive Limits	Always use a minimum of 15" to 20" Hg. in dives. Never dive the airplane with power off. Rapid cooling, followed by application of power, damages the engines.	
7.	Oil Temperature Limits	40°C ....to............100°C	
8.	Oil Pressure Limits	50 psi............to............100 psi	

Factors AFFECTING OPERATION

Pre-ignition

Pre-ignition is the burning of the fuel gases within a cylinder before the spark plug fires. It is caused by a hot spot within the cylinder, such as an overheated sparkplug, overheated exhaust valve, or a carbon deposit that continues to burn as the fresh gases are compressed.

Once pre-ignition starts it becomes progressively worse. The timing of the engine is uncontrolled; roughness and detonation follow, with resultant overheating, rapid loss of power, and possible engine failure.

Detonation

Under normal conditions the fuel charge in a cylinder burns relatively slowly. When detonation occurs, the top part of the fuel within the cylinder burns normally. This compresses the unburned part of the charge until the pressure and temperature in the cylinder rise so high that the unburned charge explodes, or detonates.

Detonation literally hammers the walls of the cylinders and causes the knock with which you are familiar in an automobile. Because of the outside noise in an airplane you can't hear the engine knock. That's why you must be on guard against detonation. You can avoid it by understanding it and following correct engine procedures.

Don't forget that detonation can cause complete engine failure during the short time that it takes you to make a takeoff run.

The indications of detonation are roughness and overheating of the engine.

These factors cause detonation—**avoid them**:

1. Low Grade Fuel

Do not use fuel lower than specification AN-F-27 Grade 98/130 or AN-F-28 Grade 100/130. Don't experiment. A lower grade fuel causes detonation, and engine failure results.

2. High Inlet Carburetor Air Temperatures

Use carburetor heat when known icing conditions exist. Use only enough heat to prevent icing. Check your carburetor air temperature gage frequently to be sure that the hot air door has not opened. The yellow marking on the dial indicates caution area.

3. High Blower at Low Altitudes

Never take off in HIGH blower. Do not use HIGH blower below 9000 feet except when shifting blowers to remove sludge from clutches. The HIGH blower impeller speed greatly increases the mixture temperature as it raises the manifold pressure. The increased mixture temperature at low altitudes causes detonation.

4. Mixtures Too Lean

A too lean fuel/air ratio, particularly when aromatic fuel is used, causes detonation. Always use AUTO RICH at any power setting above 33" and 2100 rpm and for all ground operation.

5. Abnormally High Manifold Pressure

Do not use excessively high manifold pressures except when necessary, and then only with the proper rpm. Increase rpm first and manifold pressure second, in proportion. Detonation depends not only on high temperatures and pressures but also on the length of time the mixture is exposed to these temperatures and pressures.

6. High Cylinder-head Temperatures

Excessively high cylinder-head temperatures lead directly to detonation by overheating the fuel mixture as it enters the cylinder.

Normal Combustion

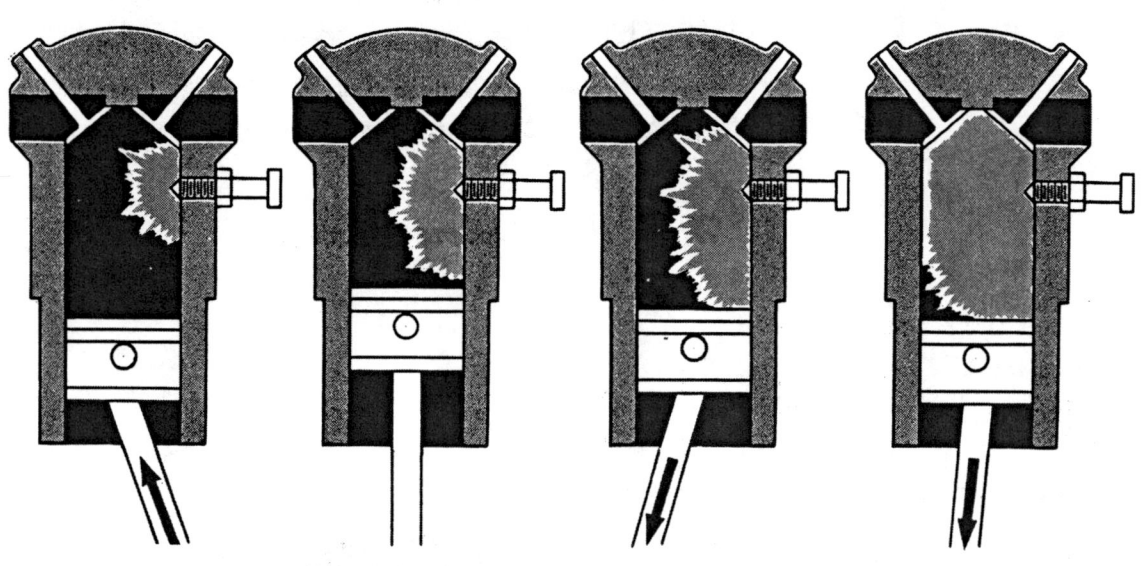

Detonation

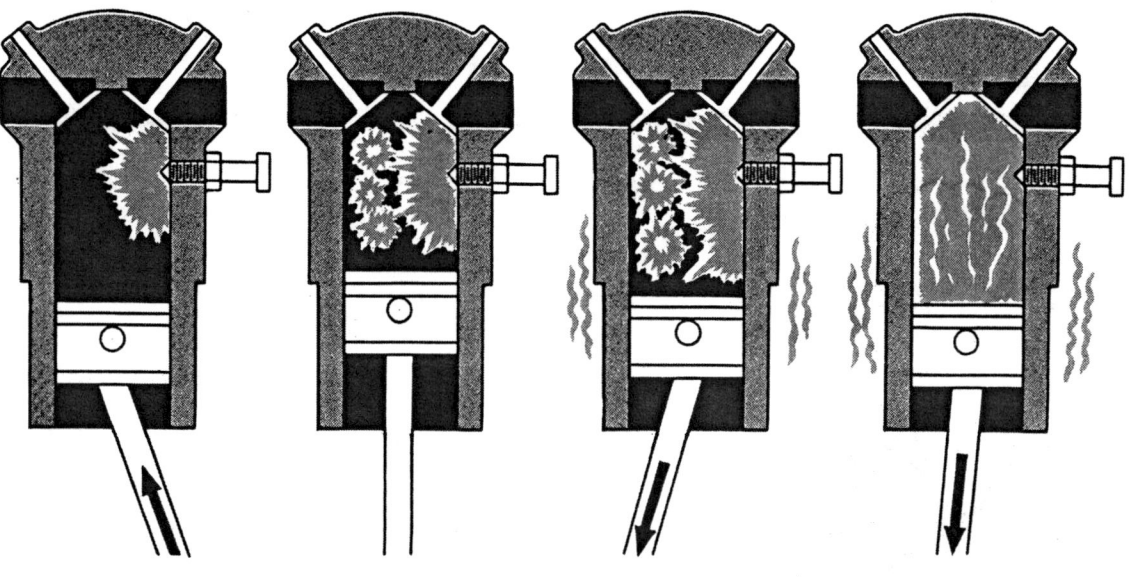

RESTRICTED

BLOWER OPERATION

Your engine blowers are virtually trouble-free. Blower difficulties are caused by incorrect procedure. Observe the accompanying procedures exactly, and the important tips that follow, and you and blower trouble will remain absolute strangers.

Move both blowers together

To Change to HIGH Blower

1. Reduce manifold pressure at least 3".
2. Move blower controls quickly, without hesitation, to HIGH blower.
3. Check to see that the oil pressure fluctuates, returns to normal and that manifold pressure increases.
4. Make sure that the control handles are locked firmly in the HIGH position.
5. Adjust manifold pressures to proper settings.

To Change to LOW Blower

1. Move control handles quickly, without hesitation, to LOW blower.
2. Make sure that the oil pressure fluctuates, returns to normal and that the manifold pressure decreases.
3. Check to make sure that control handles are firmly locked in the LOW position.
4. Adjust manifold pressures to proper settings.

RESTRICTED

IMPORTANT BLOWER TIPS

Shift the blowers from one stage to the other every 2 hours during flight to remove the sludge which forms in the blower clutches. Allow at least 5 minutes between shifts so the clutches have time to cool.

It is important to check the fluctuation of oil pressure as well as manifold pressure when you shift blowers. The oil pressure should drop and then return to normal.

Make sure that your blowers are always locked either in HIGH or LOW blower. Never leave the control lever in intermediate position.

Use a quick, definite motion to shift blowers.

When you shift from LOW to HIGH blower remember that the increased impeller speed absorbs from 100 to 300 additional Hp from your engine and increases fuel consumption. At lower power settings it is more advantageous for you to increase your rpm up to 2100 than it is to change into HIGH blower.

Do not change to HIGH blower until you reach critical altitude. This varies according to power setting. Critical altitude is the highest altitude at which you can maintain a given manifold pressure and rpm setting with full throttle. (See Cruise Control Chart, page 71.)

Use of Cowl Flaps

There are only a few simple rules to follow:
1. Ground Operation....Full open
2. Takeoff.............One-half to full open
3. AUTO RICH.........Adjust to keep cylinder-head temperatures below 260°C.
4. AUTO LEAN.........Adjust to keep cylinder-head temperatures below 232° C.
5. Normal Cruise.......Adjust to keep cylinder-head temperatures approximately 200° C.
6. After Landing........Always leave cowl flaps full open.

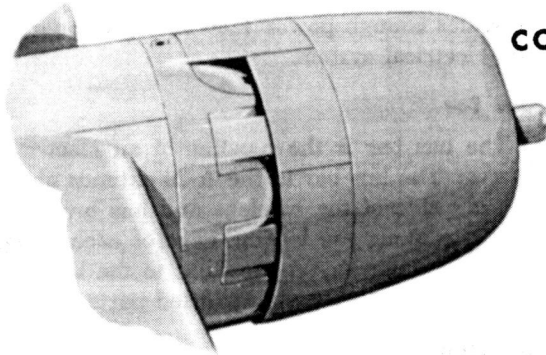

COWL FLAPS OPEN

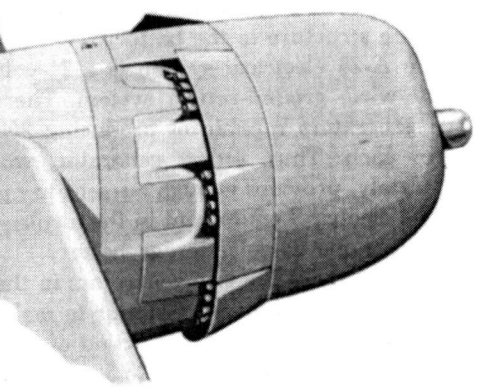

COWL FLAPS CLOSED

RESTRICTED

ELECTRICAL SYSTEM

The electrical system on the A-26 is efficient, reliable, and easy to understand. It's like a water pumping system. There are only three main things to consider. Source, distribution, and storage.

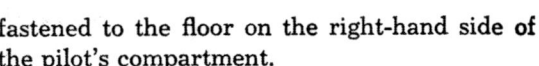

	ELECTRICAL SYSTEM	WATER SYSTEM
1. Source	Generator	Water pump
2. Distribution	Wire	Pipe
3. Storage	Battery	Storage tank

Different terms are used in an electrical system, although it functions exactly like a water system.

Pressure = Voltage

Quantity = Amperes

Resistance = Resistance (in ohms)

Water is resisted as it flows through the pipe according to the roughness or smoothness of the inside of the pipe. Electricity is resisted according to the size of the wire and the material of which it is made.

A water system has a drain-off pipe to return water to the reservoir. In an electrical system the return line consists of a ground through the airplane structure to the battery.

The A-26 electrical system is a 24-volt DC, single-wire, ground-return system. There are two generators capable of producing 200 amperes each. Thus, either generator, working separately, provides enough current to operate all the electrical equipment in the airplane and to charge the 24-volt storage battery.

Because there are two generators in the system, each has a voltage regulator to make certain that it is absorbing its portion of the load. These regulators are set at 28.5 volts and are fastened to the floor on the right-hand side of the pilot's compartment.

There is another automatic device in this system. It is called a reverse-current relay and is simply an electric counterpart of a check valve in a fluid system. It allows the current to flow from the generator to the main bus bar (where the current is distributed) but does not allow it to flow backward toward the generator. Thus, if one generator quits, it is automatically cut out of the system and the other generator provides enough power (200 amps) to operate the electrical system.

Bus Bar

The bus bar is the pipeline of an electrical system. The bus bar in the A-26 extends along the left side of the fuselage and has branches that run along the leading edge of each wing. There are as many connections to the bus bar as there are electrically operated parts.

Batteries

The batteries are the storage tanks, or reserve sources of power, used for starting the engines and operating the system when the generators are not functioning. They receive their current from the generators and maintain a full charge.

RESTRICTED

ELECTRICAL SYSTEM

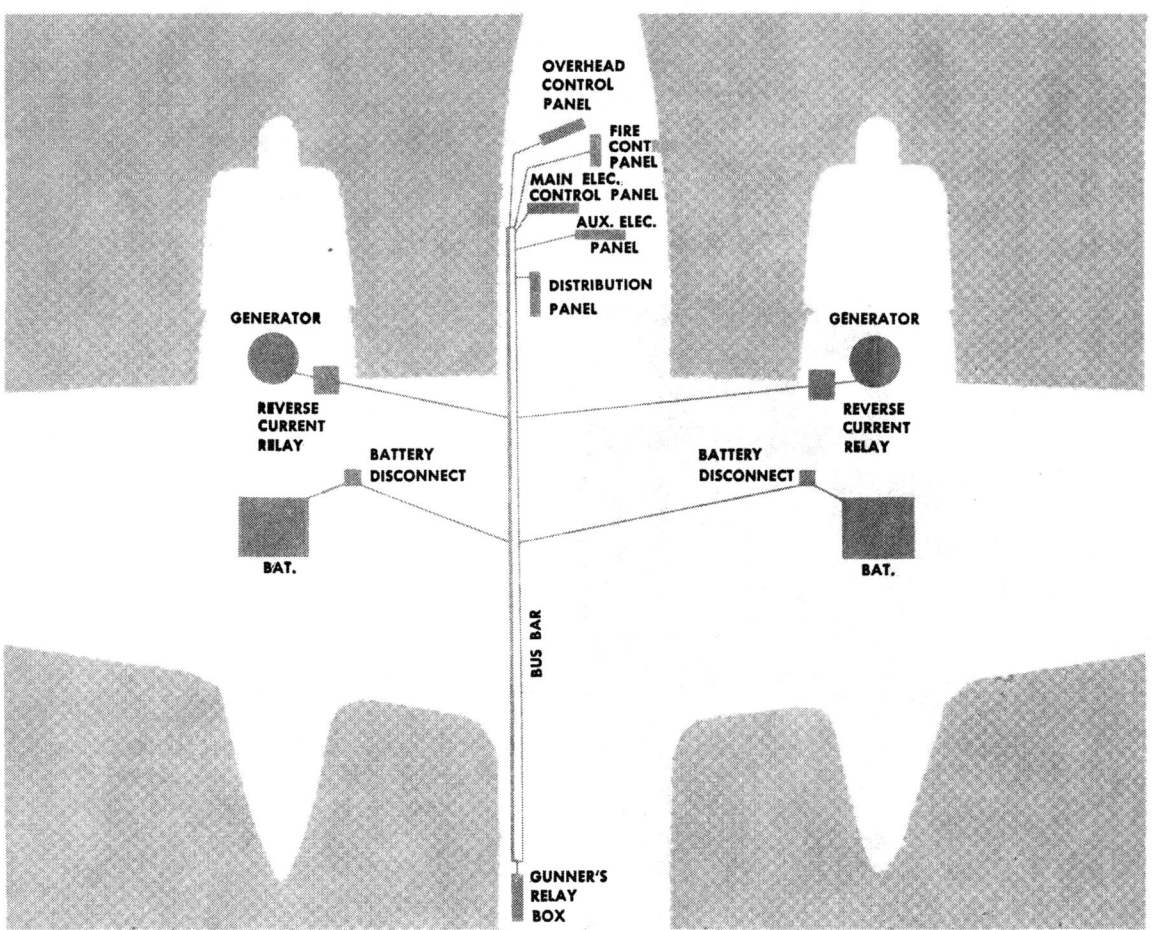

AMPERAGE LOADS ON ELECTRICAL SYSTEM

STARTER (ENERG.)	90.0	FUEL BOOST. (MAIN)	16.0
STARTER (MESH)	240.0	FUEL BOOST. (BOMB BAY)	8.0
PROP FEATHER	160.0	COWL FLAP MOTOR	17.0
TURRET SYSTEM (SCAN)	160.0	CARB. AIR FILTER	3.5
TURRET SYSTEM (IDLE)	100.0	CARB. AIR HEAT	3.5
WING FLAP MOTOR	60.0	PITOT TUBE HEAT	3.5
.50 CAL. FIRING SOL.	84.0	INSTRUMENTS	.5
.50 CAL. GUN HEATER	70.0	INTERIOR LIGHTS	3.0
LANDING LIGHT	43.0	PNEU. GUN CHARGER	2.3
ALL RADIO EQUIPMENT	MAX. 60.0	BOMB CONTROL	5.0
HEATED SUITS	30.0	OIL DILUTION	4.0
PNEU. COMPRESSOR	20.0	ENGINE PRIMER	2.0
WATER INJECTION	24.0	PROP ANTI-ICER	2.0
INVERTER	20.0	OIL COOLER CONT.	.8
EXTERNAL LIGHTS	MAX. 15.0	WING DE-ICER VALVE	2.0

RESTRICTED

ELECTRICAL CONTROL PANELS

There are a number of different combinations of electrical control panels on the A-26. The latest are illustrated here. **Study your own airplane. Your instructor will insist on a blindfold check.**

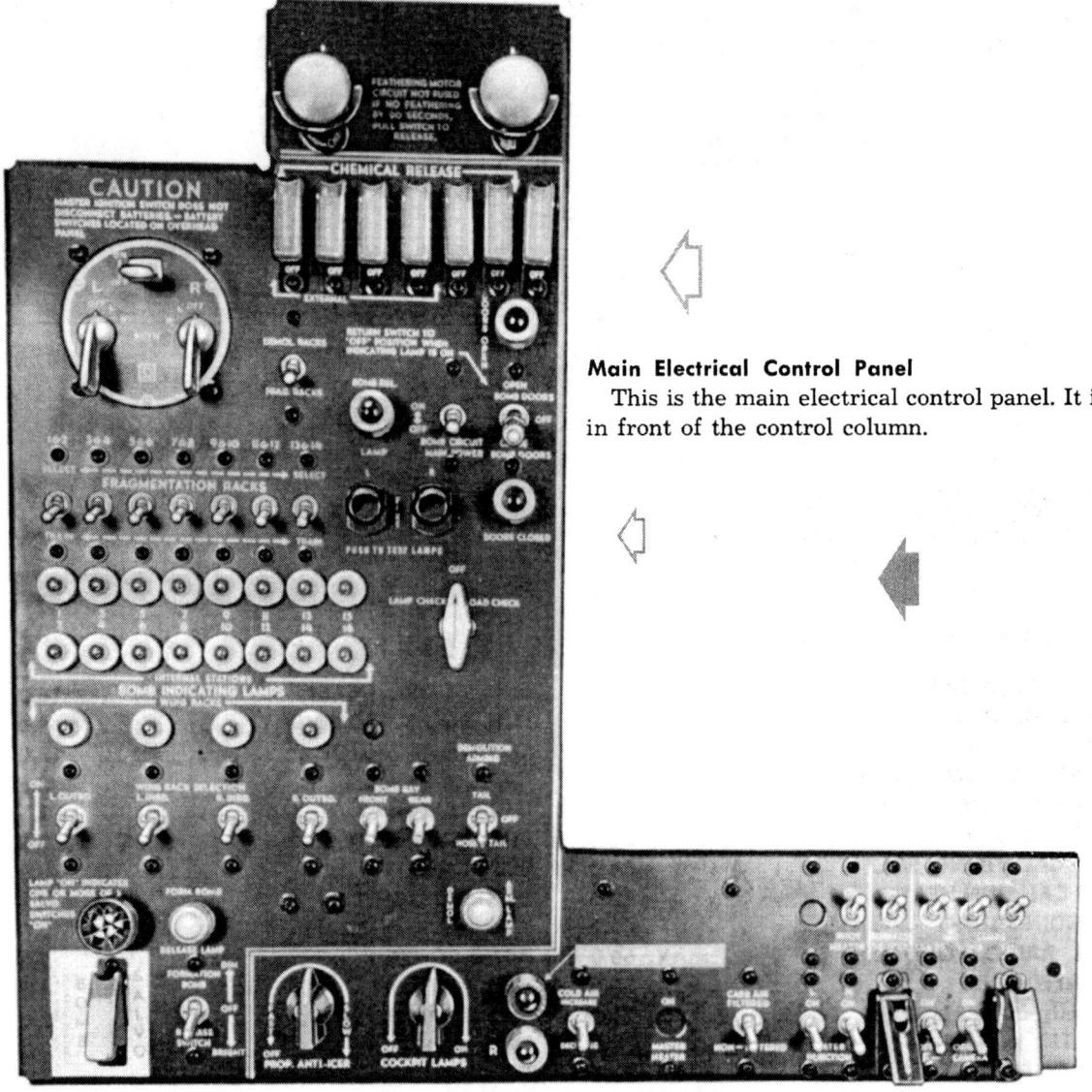

Main Electrical Control Panel
This is the main electrical control panel. It is in front of the control column.

RESTRICTED

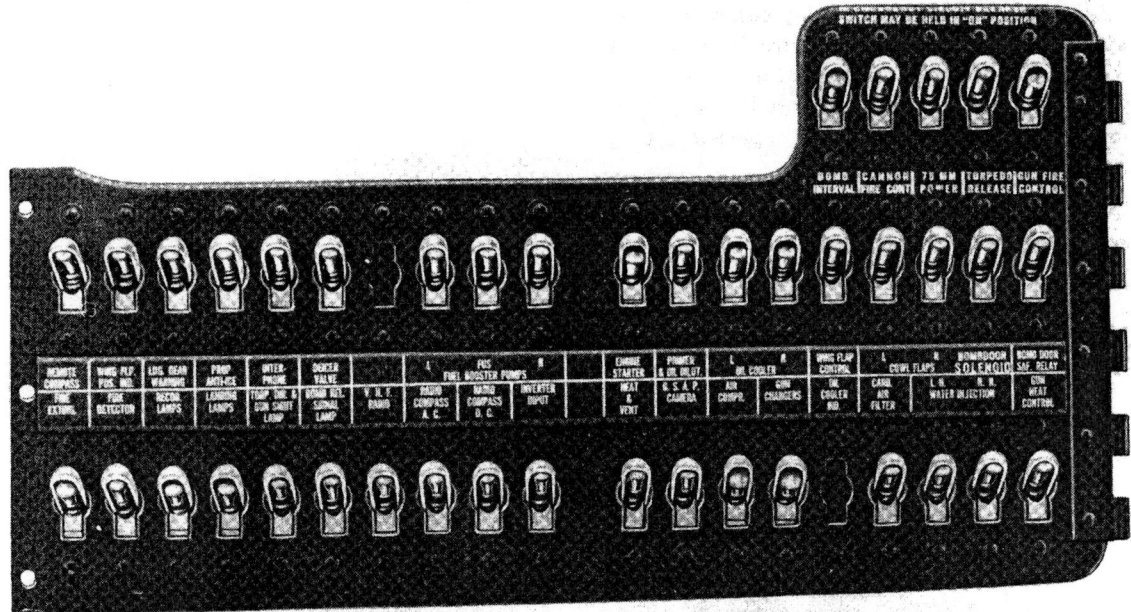

Distribution Panel

This panel has a series of circuit breaker switches, or electrical pop-off valves, designed to protect the circuit when the current load exceeds the capacity of the wires. These circuit breakers may be re-set, but they pop open or remain open until the circuit is repaired.

Two ammeters located in the lower right-hand corner of the instrument panel indicate the load on the system and must be checked with both engines running at 1700 rpm.

When you check the two generators to make sure they are carrying an equal amount of load, they should not differ more than 20 amperes. The voltage must be within .5 volts of being equal.

Besides the re-set switches you can reach in flight, there are two more places where you can locate electrical trouble on the ground. The forward electrical junction box is forward of the instrument panel and contains manual re-set circuit protectors.

Overhead Control Panel

This is the overhead electrical control panel. It is directly over the pilot's head.

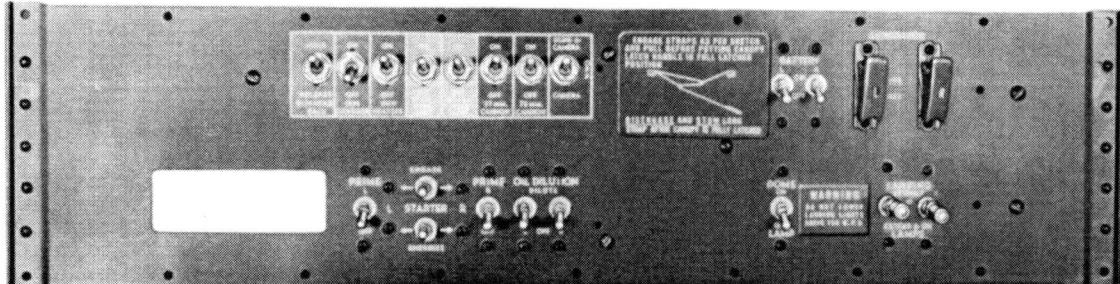

RESTRICTED

Gunner's Relay Box

Also, there is a gunner's relay box which contains nine more manual re-set circuit protectors.

Manual re-set circuit protectors differ from circuit breakers because they are literally fuses and burn out and have to be replaced if they are held in the ON position.

CAUTION: Turn the electrical system off before setting the re-set circuit protectors.

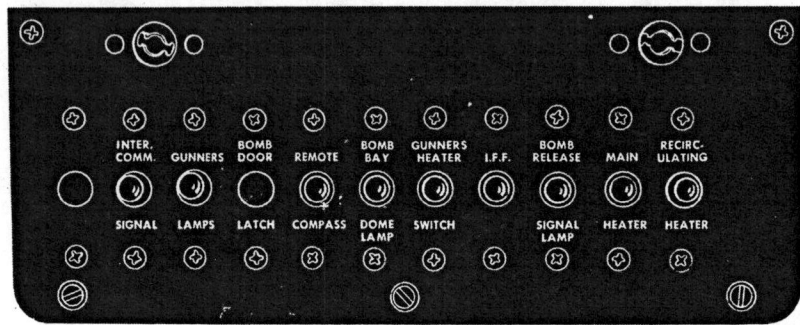

BE SURE YOUR GUNNER THOROUGHLY UNDERSTANDS THIS

HYDRAULIC SYSTEM

The A-26 hydraulic system performs three functions:

1. It extends and retracts the wheels.
2. It opens and closes the bomb bay doors.
3. It operates the brakes.

Pumps

There are two engine-driven pumps, one in the accessory section of each engine. They are gear-type, positive pumps of simple design and are virtually trouble-free. One pump alone produces sufficient power to operate the hydraulic system. Thus, single engine flight does not mean hydraulic emergency. However, one pump alone requires more time to operate the hydraulic system.

Pressure Accumulator

The pressure accumulator carries continual pressure of 1000 psi (+ or —20). It is a spherical, welded steel container divided by a synthetic rubber diaphragm, carrying air pressure on one side and hydraulic pressure on the other. On the air pressure side there is an initial pressure of between 600 and 750 psi. This air section functions as a cushion to absorb fluid surges in the hydraulic system and to aid in maintaining constant pressure in the system.

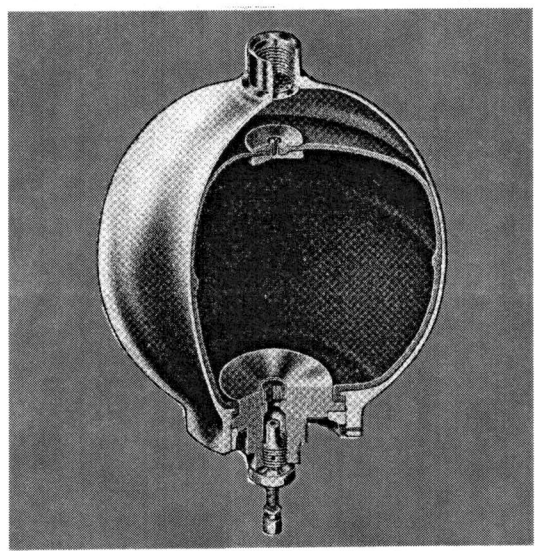

To check a faulty accumulator diaphragm:
1. With hydraulic pressure 800 psi or above, operate the brake.
2. As the pressure **hesitates** just before it drops to zero, that momentary reading should be 650 psi or normal air pre-load in the accumulator.

Pressure Regulator

The pressure regulator is an automatic device controlling the amount of pressure maintained in the accumulator. When the pressure reaches 1000 (+ or —20) the regulator bypasses the fluid to the hydraulic reservoir. As the system operates, the pressure in the accumulator is expended and when it reaches 850 (+ or —20) the bypass valve closes and the pumps again build up accumulator pressure to 1000 psi.

Main Hydraulic Reservoir

This welded aluminum container is in the rear of the pilot's compartment just behind the gun loader's seat. Its capacity is 1¾ U.S. gallons. It supplies fluid to the main system and also to the auxiliary reservoir. A glass sight gage showing fluid level is built into the main reservoir.

Filter

A Purolator unit, to filter the hydraulic fluid in the main system, is at the right of the main hydraulic reservoir on the pressure line between the pumps and the pressure regulator.

Study the simple diagrams on the following pages. Know them thoroughly. Most hydraulic emergencies are not emergencies at all, but merely the result of the pilot's insufficient knowledge of the hydraulic system.

RESTRICTED

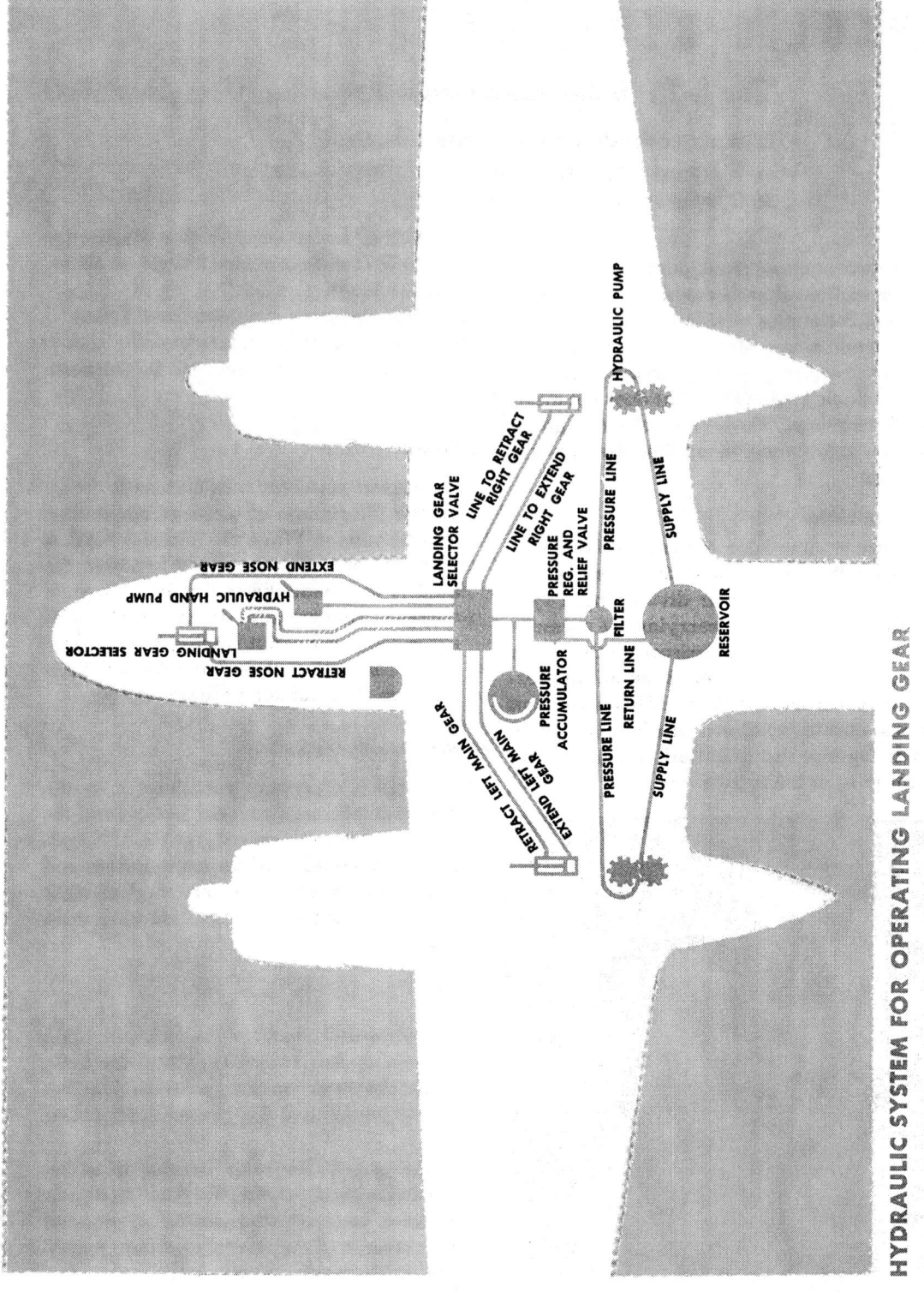

24

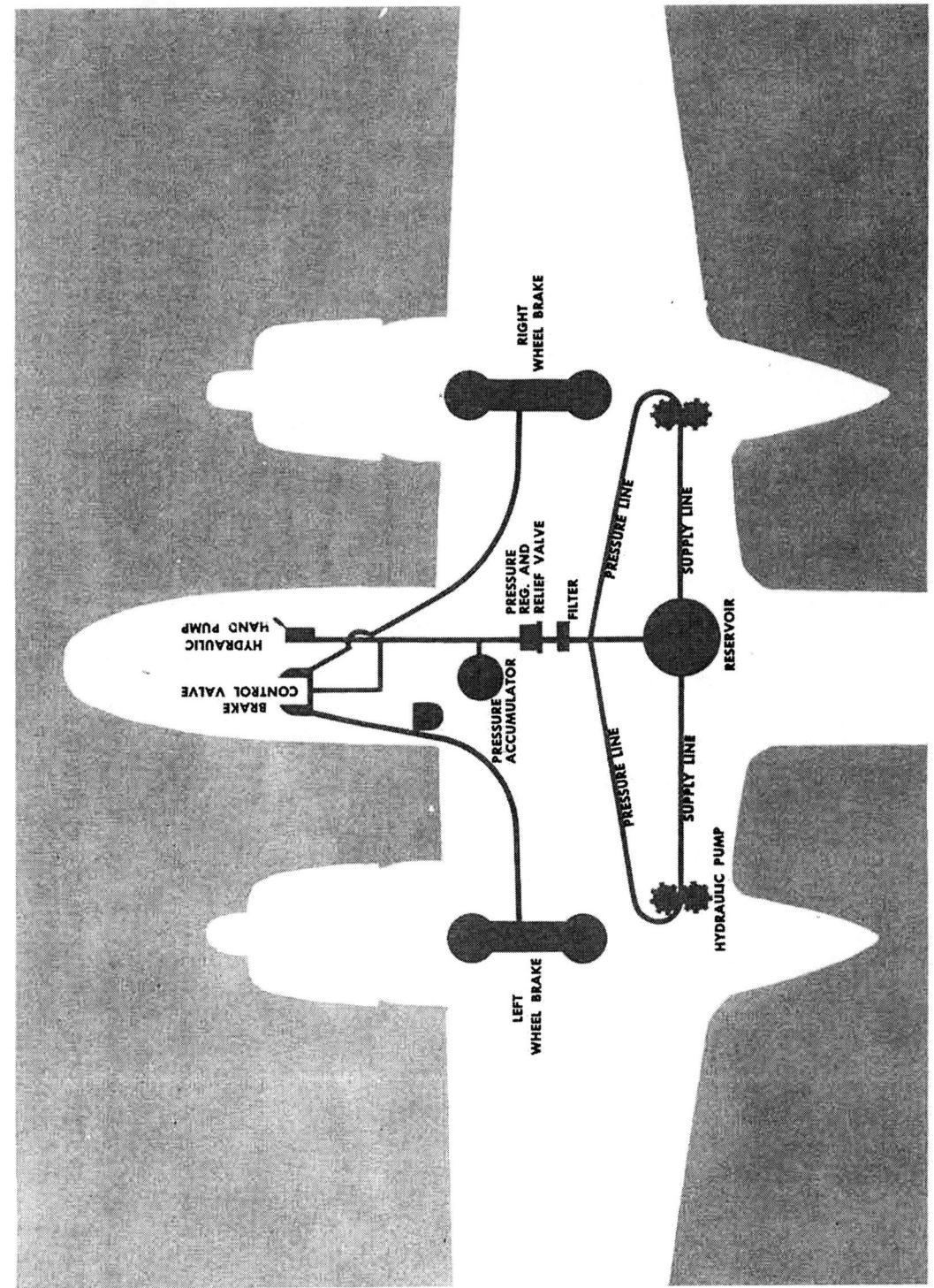

HYDRAULIC SYSTEM FOR BRAKES

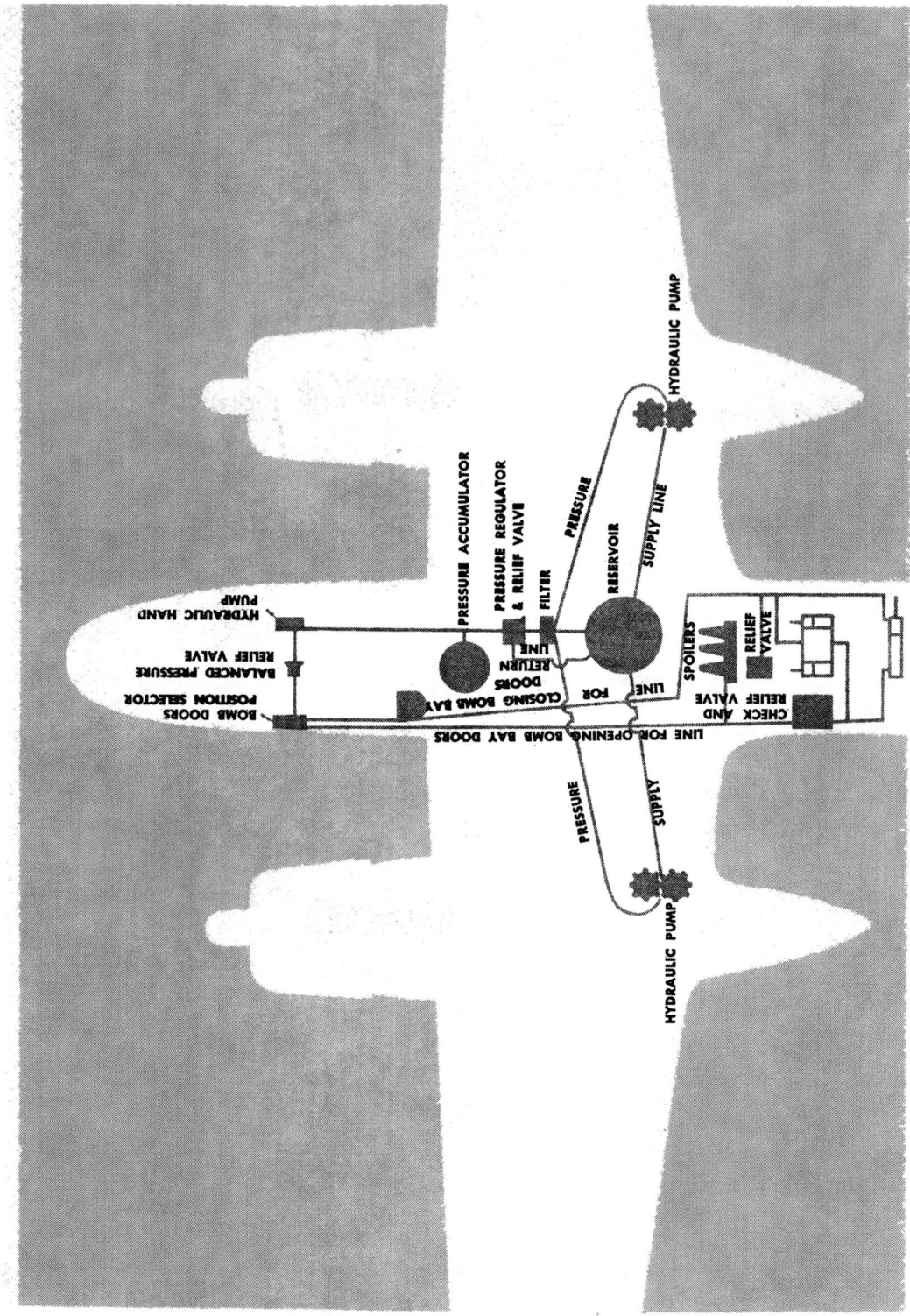

HYDRAULIC SYSTEM FOR OPERATING BOMB BAY DOORS

Check Valves

Three check valves operate as traffic cops of the hydraulic system and permit the flow of fluid in one direction only. Two of these valves are in the pressure lines (one in each line) where the two lines connect at the Purolator filter. The other check valve is in the brake pressure line near the left-hand power brake valve.

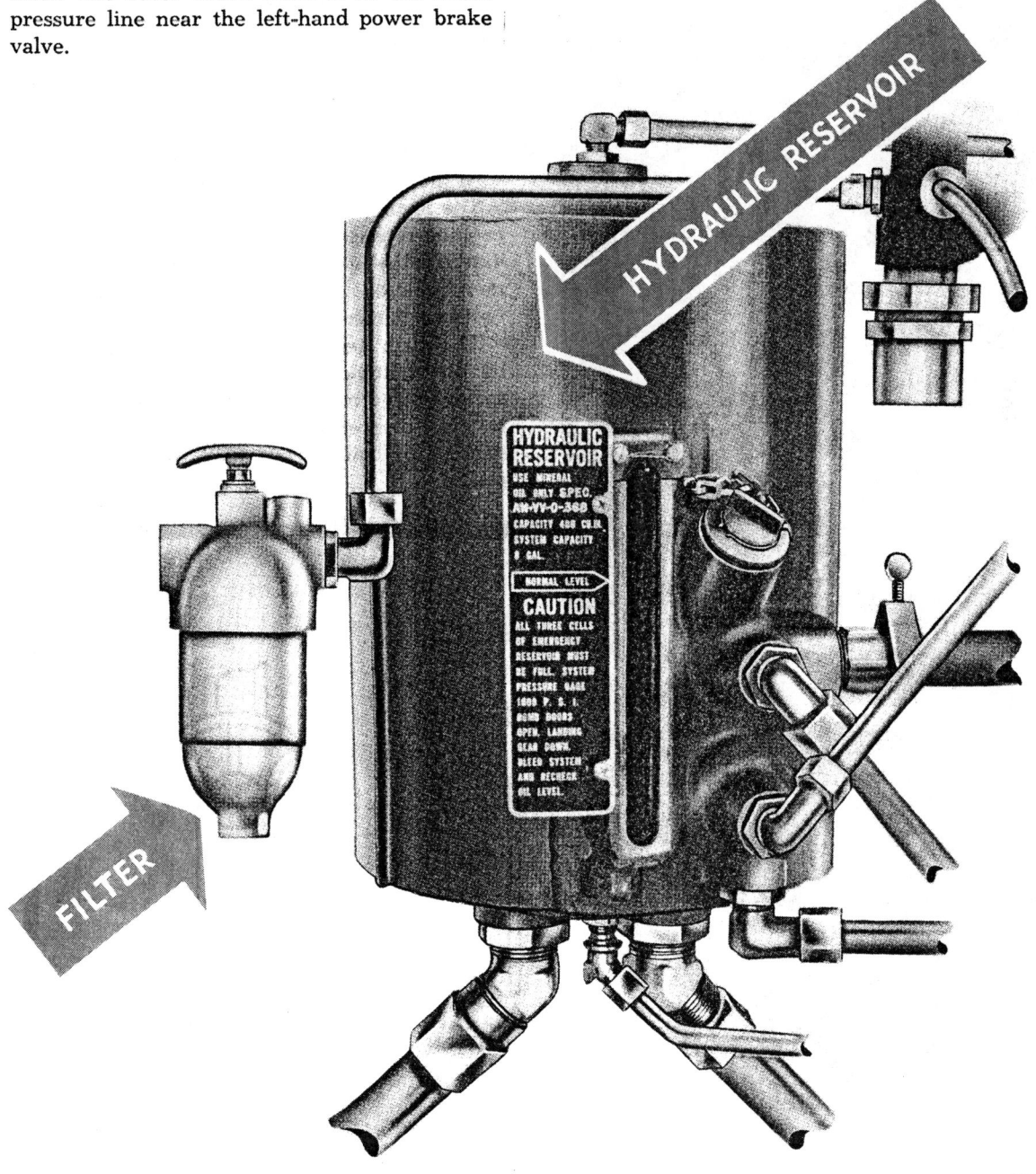

RESTRICTED

MAIN LANDING GEAR

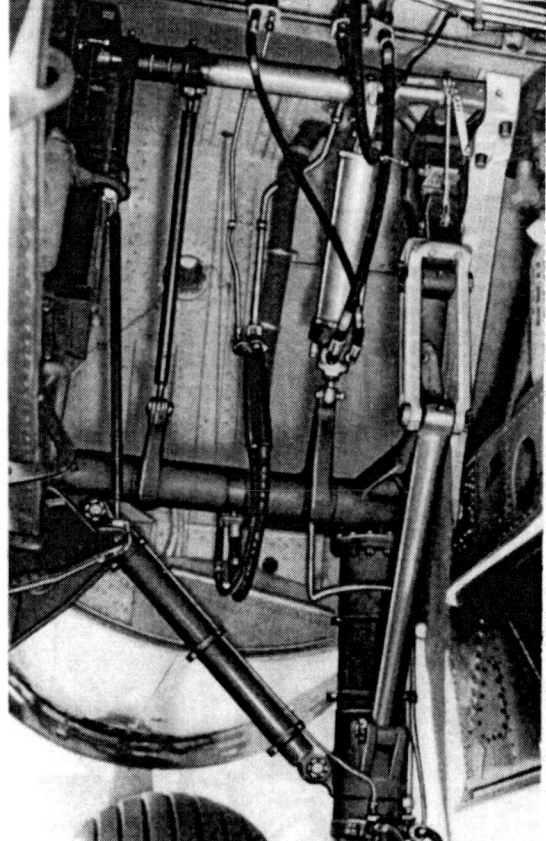

The wheels of the main landing gear of the A-26 **extend against** and **retract** with the slipstream. This is why you must pay strict attention to the airspeed limitations for lowering the gear.

Select the position of your gear with the lever mounted on the pedestal. The lever controls a selector valve that has four openings: one for the pressure supply line to the valve, one for the line that goes to the side of the actuating cylinder that retracts your gear, one for the line that goes to the side of the actuating cylinder that extends the gear, and one to return the fluid to the reservoir.

The lever has only three positions. The UP position retracts the gear, the DOWN position extends the gear, and the neutral position merely closes all four ports of the valve, thus reducing the amount of line under pressure.

The main gear doors operate mechanically by direct linkage to the main gear strut. A spring-loaded mechanical latch locks against a stop on the retracting link. This same latch secures the landing gear in the UP or DOWN position.

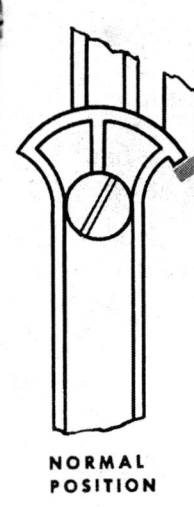

NORMAL POSITION

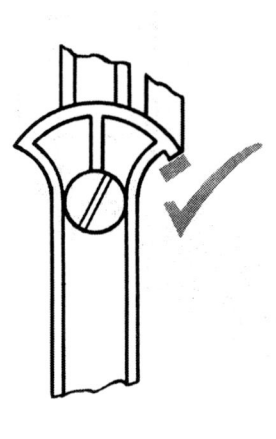

INCORRECT ADJUSTMENT, DOWN LOCK OVERTRAVELED

28

RESTRICTED

NOSE GEAR

On the earlier model airplanes when pilot experience level on the A-26 was necessarily low, a number of nose gear failures were reported. Since that time Tech Order compliances have been issued and on later airplanes certain points of the nose gear assembly have been beefed up. Unquestionably a large contributing factor was the pilot's inability to land the airplane accurately. The A-26 is a rugged, heavy, high-speed airplane but **it lands differently from any other airplane. It lands and takes off in an almost level attitude.** A nose-high landing attitude quickly stalls out and pounds the nose gear on the runway causing failure. (See landing section, page 75.)

How It Operates

One motion of the gear lever operates both the nose and main gear. The nosewheel doors operate hydraulically by a separate actuating cylinder. A mechanical latch prevents the nose gear from extending until the doors are open. It also prevents the doors from closing until the gear is completely retracted. A plunger type latch locks the nose gear in place when it is fully extended.

Solenoid Safety Device

There is a release switch on the left main shock strut. While there is weight on this strut, depressing it, a steel pin prevents the gear handle from being moved to the UP position. On takeoff, when the weight is removed from the wheels, a solenoid retracts the pin, allowing the gear handle to be moved to the UP position. **Always keep the gear handle in the DOWN position while the airplane is on the ground.**

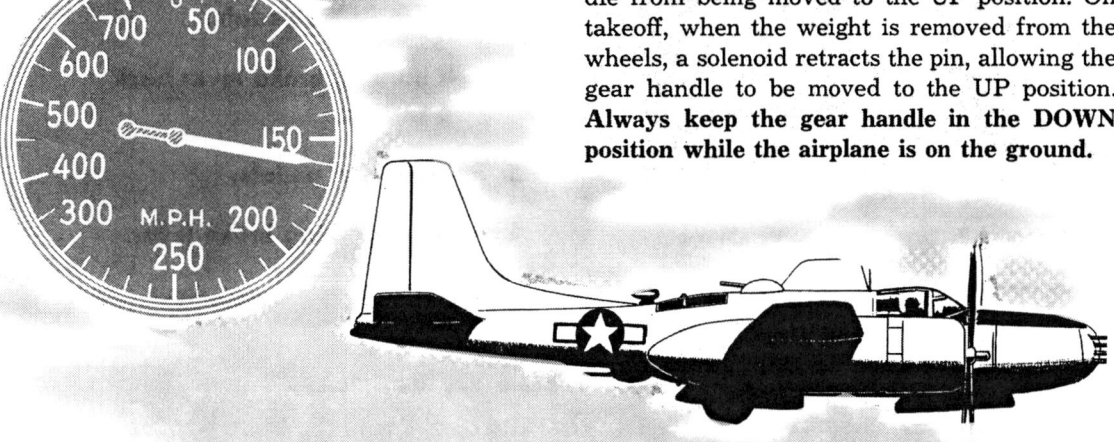

DON'T LOWER LANDING GEAR UNTIL AIRSPEED HAS DROPPED TO 160 MPH OR LESS

RESTRICTED

Solenoid Failure

If this solenoid fails, the pin stays in place, preventing the gear handle from being moved to the UP position. If this happens, depress the solenoid pin, and at the same time move the landing gear lever to the UP position.

Wheel Indicators

There are several different types of wheel position indicators located on the instrument panels of various airplanes.

On earlier airplanes there is a wheel position indicator on the instrument panel which shows the position of the gear at all times. In addition to the Mickey Mouse indicator on some models there are two warning lights, red and green. The red light indicates that the gear is in unsafe position for landing. The green light indicates that the gear is down and locked.

Check the operation of this warning light

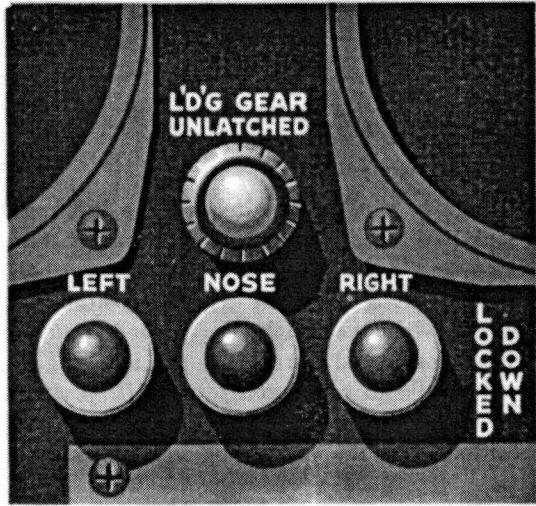

WHEEL POSITION INDICATORS

before every landing with a test switch on the left side of the instrument panel. Your red warning light burns when the throttles are retarded if the gear is up and locked.

On later airplanes there are three green lights, one for each gear, which indicate that the wheels are down and locked and one red light which indicates that the wheels are unsafe for landing.

Important Landing Gear Tips

Do not attempt to lower your gear until your airspeed has dropped to 160 mph or less. Your nose gear will not extend at higher speeds. You may cause damage by attempting it.

Hydraulic Brake System

The A-26 power brake system consists of a separate braking action for each wheel with two brake units of the multiple-disc type in each main landing wheel. Although they are power brakes, the amount of braking action is directly proportional to the force you apply to the brake pedals. Use your brakes carefully. Your brakes are like money in the bank. Be thrifty, so that when you need all you've got, you'll have all you need.

Faulty Brake Action

Air trapped in the lines of the hydraulic brake is the most common cause of faulty brake action. Generally, several applications of brakes will remove the trapped air. If this fails, turn the airplane back to the crew chief and have him bleed the brake system.

To operate Parking Brakes:

1. Depress brake pedals.
2. Pull parking brake lever back and hold.
3. Release foot pedals.
4. Release parking brake lever.

Bomb Bay Door System

The operation of the bomb bay doors is similar to that of the wheel system. There is a 4-way selector valve with two lines running to each of the two forward and one aft bomb bay actuating cylinders.

RESTRICTED

On later series, bomb bay door spoilers are used to allow doors to be opened at high speeds. These spoilers operate automatically by a separate actuating cylinder.

Bomb Bay Switch

The bomb bay control switch is located on the instrument panel directly in front of the pilot. Two warning lights are located near the switch. The red light (above) indicates bomb doors OPEN. The green light (below) indicates bomb doors CLOSED.

On earlier airplanes a control lever next to the pilot's left knee operates the bomb bay doors. The lever has five positions:
1. CLOSED
2. NEUTRAL
3. OPEN
4. SELECT (this is used when entering the bomb run and does not concern the hydraulic system).
5. SALVO

The bomb bay doors on earlier airplanes can be locked in the CLOSED position by two solenoid switches, one forward and one aft in the bomb bay. The doors cannot be opened when these switches are on, so crew members can walk safely through the bomb bay in flight.

The hydraulic bomb bay door system is trouble-free if you observe the proper procedure and airspeed limitations.

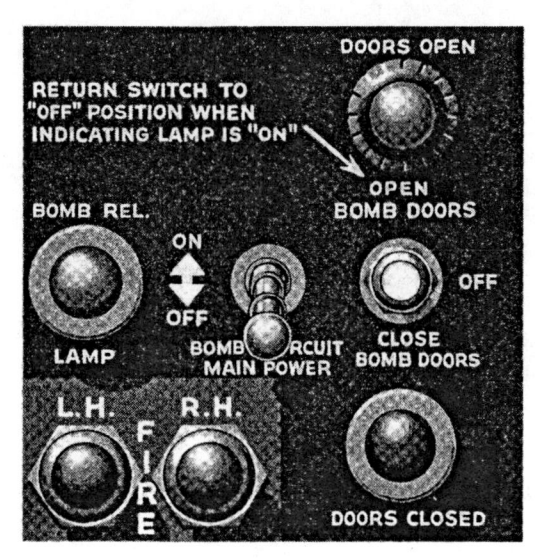

BOMB BAY DOOR SWITCH

BOMB BAY DOOR SPOILERS EXTENDED

RESTRICTED

EMERGENCY HYDRAULIC SYSTEM

The A-26 has an emergency hydraulic system to use in case of failure of the main hydraulic system. This emergency system operates only the landing gear and the bomb bay doors. Although auxiliary braking action can be had by putting the selector on SYSTEM and using the hand pump, there is no emergency hydraulic system for braking action. There is an air bottle installed for emergency brake action. (See page 88.)

Emergency Fluid Reservoir

Your emergency reservoir is divided into three separate cells, each with a bull's-eye inspection window. All three cells are filled by gravity from the main reservoir, and although you may lose the fluid in your main reservoir, you still have ample hydraulic fluid in the three emergency cells for at least one emergency operation of each unit. One cell is to extend the landing gear, one to open the bomb bay doors, and one to close the bomb bay doors. In this system there is a double-acting, piston-type hand pump which you use to supply fluid either to the main system (when the engine-driven hydraulic pumps fail), or to the emergency hydraulic system. The emergency selector valve directs the fluid from the hand pump through the emergency lines to the equipment to be operated.

Although there are separate emergency pressure lines, the fluid returns from each operation through the main return lines. Therefore, you must set the corresponding main hydraulic selector control for the desired operation, as well as the emergency selector valve. When you complete the operation, always return the emergency selector handle to SYSTEM.

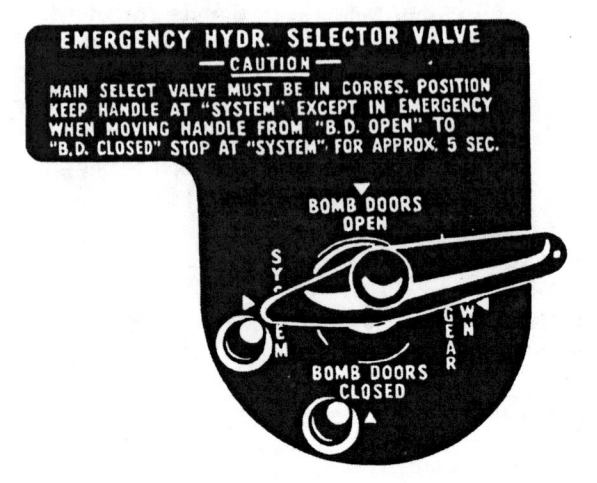

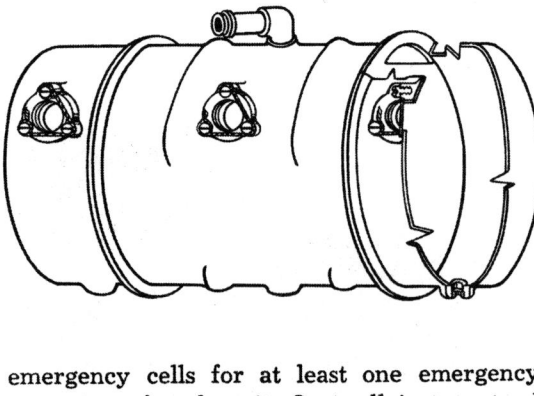

BOMB DOOR MANUAL CONTROL

RESTRICTED

FUEL SYSTEM

On the following page is a simplified drawing of the A-26 fuel system. It includes five self-sealing tanks: two main tanks, two auxiliary tanks, and a bomb bay tank. The main tanks hold 300 gallons each and are in the nacelles about 3½ feet behind the engines.

Two auxiliary tanks, of 100 gallons each, are in the wings between the nacelle and the fuselage. The bomb bay tank, holding 125 gallons, is installed in the forward bomb bay. The bomb bay tank is removable but cannot be salvoed. Fully fueled, you have a total of 925 gallons. At 62.5% power, this gives you 6+ hours in the air.

Optional Fuel Tanks

In addition to the five standard fuel tanks a choice of three optional tanks can be installed depending on the mission. They are:
  a. Ferry tank .... 675 gals.
  b. Two droppable wing tanks (each) 155 gals.
  c. Aft fuselage tank (installed in place of lower turret. Used for low-level strafing missions) .... 125 gals.

Fuel Gages

These gages are on the right side of the instrument panel. A float arm in each tank registers, through an electrical transmitter, the quantity on the fuel gage.

Fuel Pressure Gage

A fuel pressure gage on the instrument panel indicates the fuel pressure to the carburetor.

Booster Pumps

A 2-speed electric booster pump is installed in each tank. Use low boost for starting the engine, use high boost for:
  a. Takeoff
  b. Landing
  c. High-altitude flight
  d. When engine pump fails to supply fuel to the carburetor.

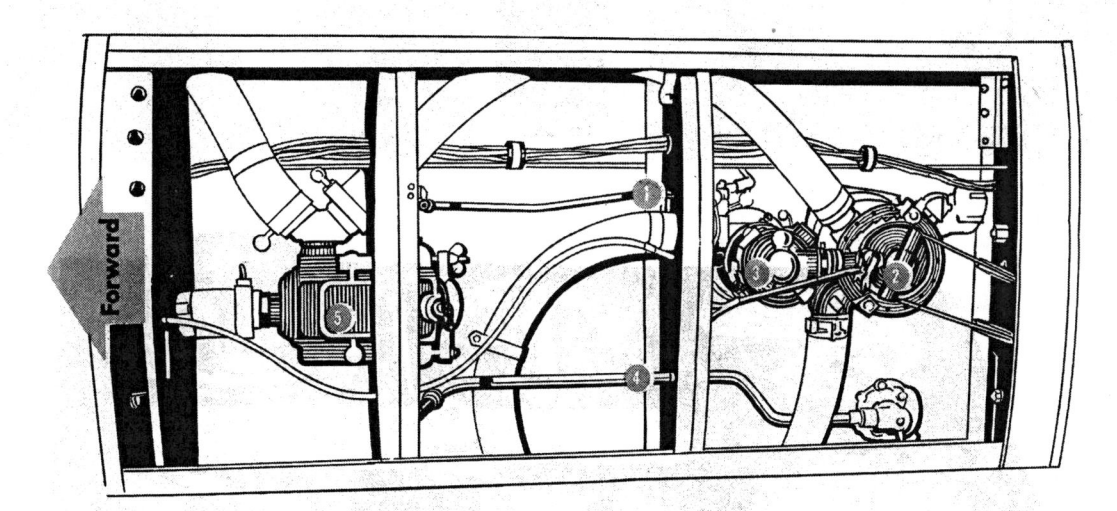

RIGHT HAND NACELLE FUEL TANK LOOKING UP

1 Booster Pump Drain Line
2 Fuel Container Selector Valve
3 Booster Pump
4 Drain Line (Residual Fuel)
5 Fuel Strainer

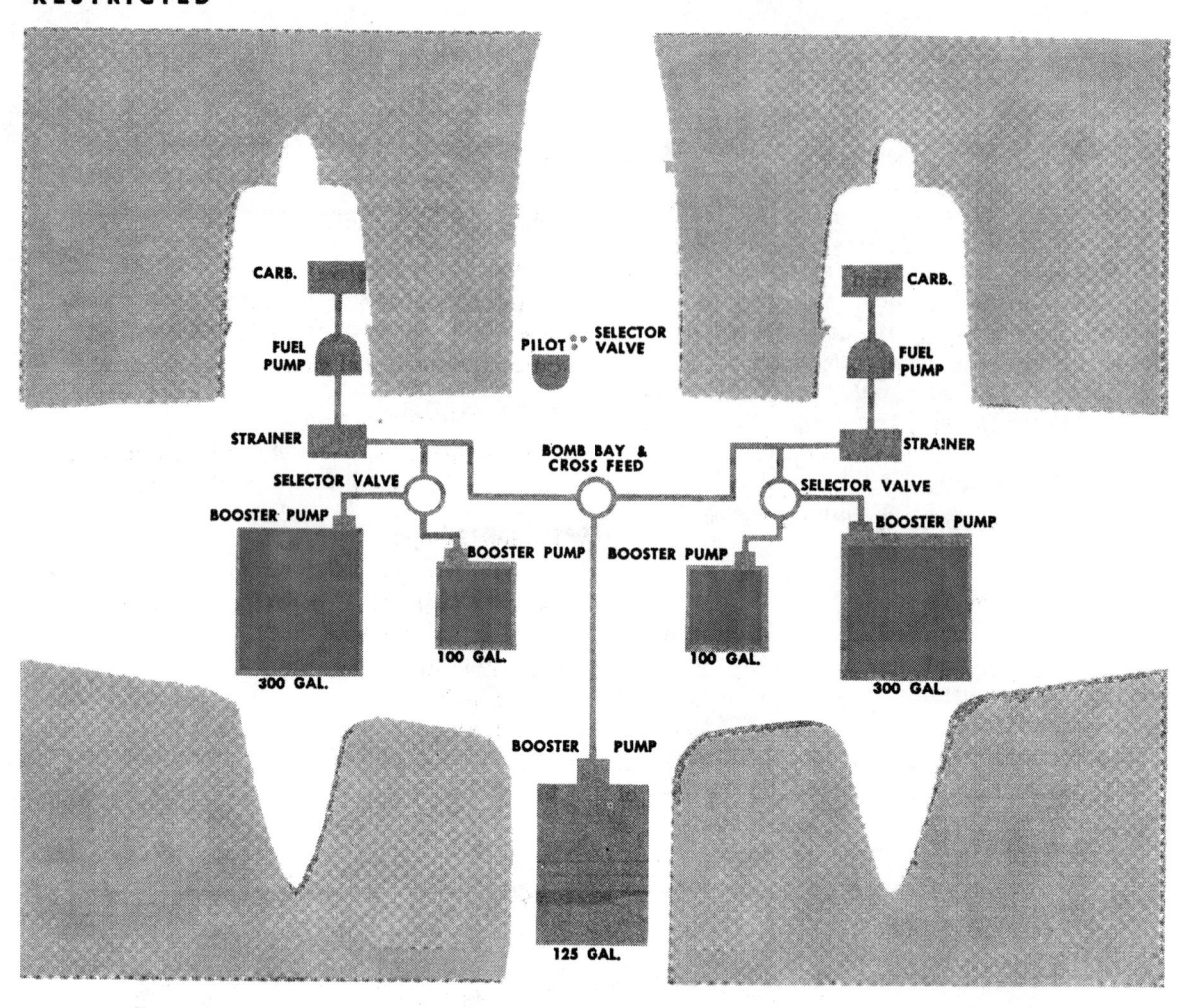

RESTRICTED

CARB.			CARB.
FUEL PUMP	PILOT ⦿⦿ SELECTOR VALVE		FUEL PUMP
STRAINER	BOMB BAY & CROSS FEED		STRAINER
SELECTOR VALVE			SELECTOR VALVE
BOOSTER PUMP	BOOSTER PUMP BOOSTER PUMP		BOOSTER PUMP
300 GAL.	100 GAL. 100 GAL.		300 GAL.

BOOSTER PUMP

125 GAL.

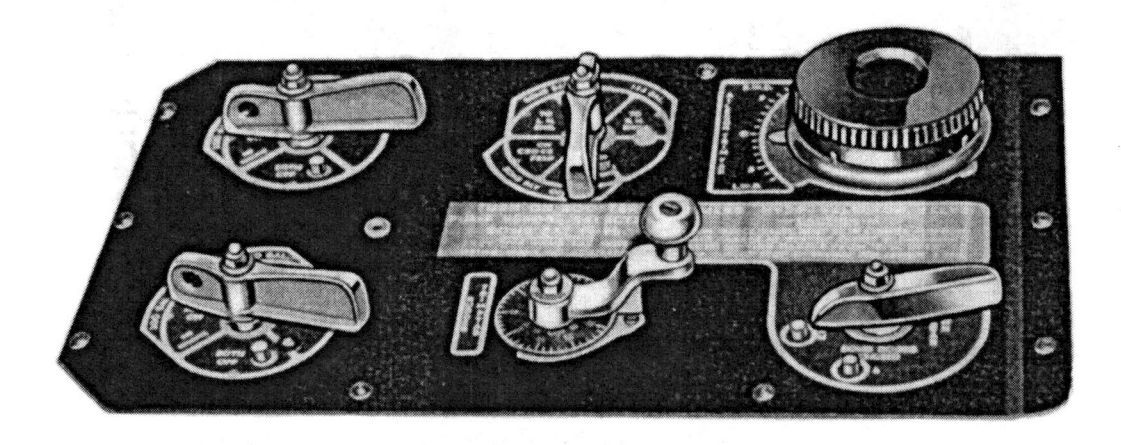

FUEL SELECTOR VALVES

RESTRICTED

Booster Pump Switches

Three switches on the pilot's control pedestal just forward of the prop controls operate the five booster pumps. The switch on the right operates the booster pump or either the right main or the right auxiliary tank, depending on the selector valve setting. The middle switch operates the bomb bay booster pump but unlike the other booster pump it is independent of the bomb bay selector valve and must be turned off when the bomb bay tank is not being used. Some airplanes have a switch for each booster pump.

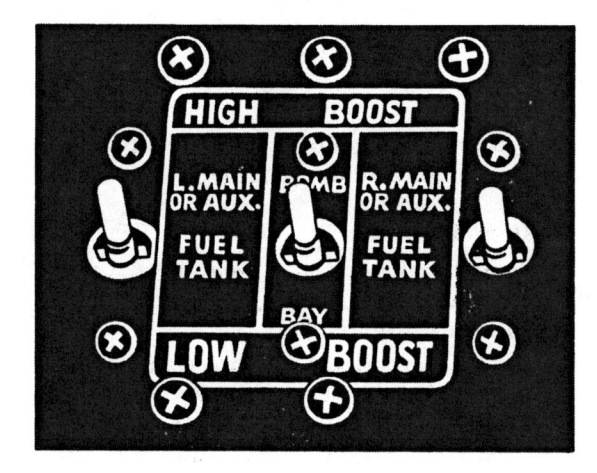

BOOSTER PUMP SWITCHES

For example: When you use fuel from the right main tank, turn on the right booster pump. When you change to right auxiliary, merely change your fuel selector valve and it automatically turns off the right main booster and turns on the right auxiliary booster. The switch on the left operates booster pumps on left main and auxiliary tanks in the same way.

Fuel Flow

From the five booster pumps the fuel passes to the selector valves, which are at the bottom of the nacelles. The selector controls which actuate these valves by means of cable linkage are at the right of the pilot's seat.

There are three positions on each of the two selector controls: one for main, one for auxiliary tanks, and a third position for OFF, which you use when not taking fuel from these tanks.

From the selector valve the fuel flows into a fuel strainer, and from there into the carburetor.

Bomb Bay Selector Valve and Crossfeed

The lines from the bomb bay selector valve and crossfeed also join the fuel system at the inlet side of the strainer. This valve is aft of the main selector controls.

The bomb bay selector valve and crossfeed can be set in eight positions, but only four of these allow fuel flow through the unit. The other four are merely OFF positions.

Keep in mind that the source from which the fuel is coming is the bomb bay tank, and the selection of R.H. ENG. means the fuel is being directed to the right-hand engine, L.H. ENG. to the left-hand engine, and BOTH ENGS. to both engines. The ON CROSSFEED position of this valve is an entirely different operation that cuts out any fuel flow from the bomb bay tank and acts only as a connecting line for transfer of fuel from the tanks on one side of the airplane to the engine on the opposite side.

Fuel should not be directed from any main tank into another because of the danger of vapor lock and possible loss of pressure to the operating engine.

Transfer System for Aft Fuselage Tanks and Droppable Wing Tanks

When the optional 125 gal. aft fuselage tank is installed, fuel is fed into the bomb bay auxiliary tank by operating a fuel transfer switch. **When transferring fuel be certain the bomb bay auxiliary tank can hold all the fuel being transferred.**

When droppable wing tanks (155 gals. each) are installed the fuel is transferred to the main tanks by operating transfer switches located on the step above the control pedestal. **Be certain there is ample room in the main tanks to hold all the fuel being transferred.**

To drop droppable wing tanks:
1. Turn wing bomb rack switches on.
2. Press bomb release button on control wheel.

RESTRICTED

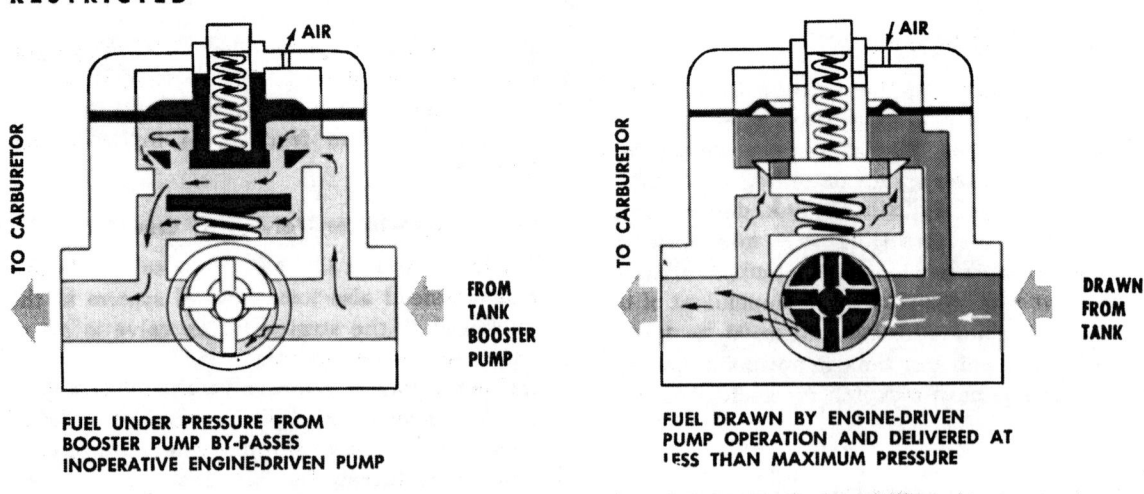

FUEL UNDER PRESSURE FROM
BOOSTER PUMP BY-PASSES
INOPERATIVE ENGINE-DRIVEN PUMP

FUEL DRAWN BY ENGINE-DRIVEN
PUMP OPERATION AND DELIVERED AT
LESS THAN MAXIMUM PRESSURE

ENGINE-DRIVEN FUEL PUMP OPERATION

Strainer Unit

The fuel flow from all tanks passes through a strainer unit to the engine-driven pumps. The strainer is a simple screen type, with a removable screen for cleaning. It includes a draincock for draining the lines to the carburetor or from the selector valves. This must be done on preflight to eliminate water.

Engine-driven Fuel Pumps

The engine-driven fuel pumps are rotary positive-displacement types. Each contains a relief valve in the top of the pump housing which regulates the pressure to the carburetor.

There is also a bypass valve in the top of the pump housing which permits the fuel to be bypassed around the pump to the carburetor in case of fuel pump failure.

The booster pumps provide the pressure to supply fuel to the carburetor if the engine-driven pumps are not operating.

Carburetor

The carburetor is a diaphragm, pressure-injection type. The fuel flows to the carburetor and is there metered to the impeller section by metering jets. These metering jets are controlled by air pressure, regulated by the throttle unit.

A fuel head enrichment jet gives you a rich mixture at high power for the purpose of cooling the engines. An idling metering jet provides proper mixture at idling speeds.

Mixture Control

An automatic mixture control in the carburetor gives constant mixture at any altitude within operating limits.

FULL RICH on the mixture control handle cuts out automatic mixture control. It is safetied so that you cannot use it except in emergency. Use AUTO RICH when operating above 62.5% power and AUTO LEAN at 62.5% power or less. These mixture controls are at the right side of the pilot's pedestal.

Do not pull mixture controls back farther than AUTO LEAN in an attempt to obtain a leaner mixture.

Priming

There is a priming solenoid on each carburetor. The spring-loaded switches operating these primers are directly over the pilot's seat and should be used only when boosters are on. Depressing these switches allows the fuel to flow through small primer lines to the top eight cylinders.

There is also an overflow line from the carburetor back to the main tanks which permits the fuel that cannot be consumed by the carburetor to return to the system.

RESTRICTED

OIL SYSTEM

The A-26 has identical independent oil systems to lubricate and cool the engines. The accompanying illustration shows the cycle completed by the oil in the system. It is pumped from the hopper tank (1) in the oil container through the engine (2). From there it flows back to the oil temperature regulator (3), which adjusts the temperature, returning to the hopper tank (1) in the oil container.

Oil Tank

A self-sealing oil tank, incased in an aluminum alloy shell, is in each of the nacelles just behind the firewall. Each oil tank has a capacity of 30 gallons at the FULL mark. Maximum capacity is 34.5 gallons. Even though engine oil pressure drops to zero 1.5 gallons still are retained by a standpipe within the tank for emergency feathering of the propeller. There is expansion space of 4.5 gallons in each tank to allow for normal expansion or oil dilution in cold weather operation. The oil level of the tanks is measured with the dip sticks.

Hopper Tank

The hopper tank is a tube 6 inches in diameter that stands in each oil tank. It is perforated at the top and bottom.

The hopper tank is designed to:

1. Furnish the engine with warm oil.

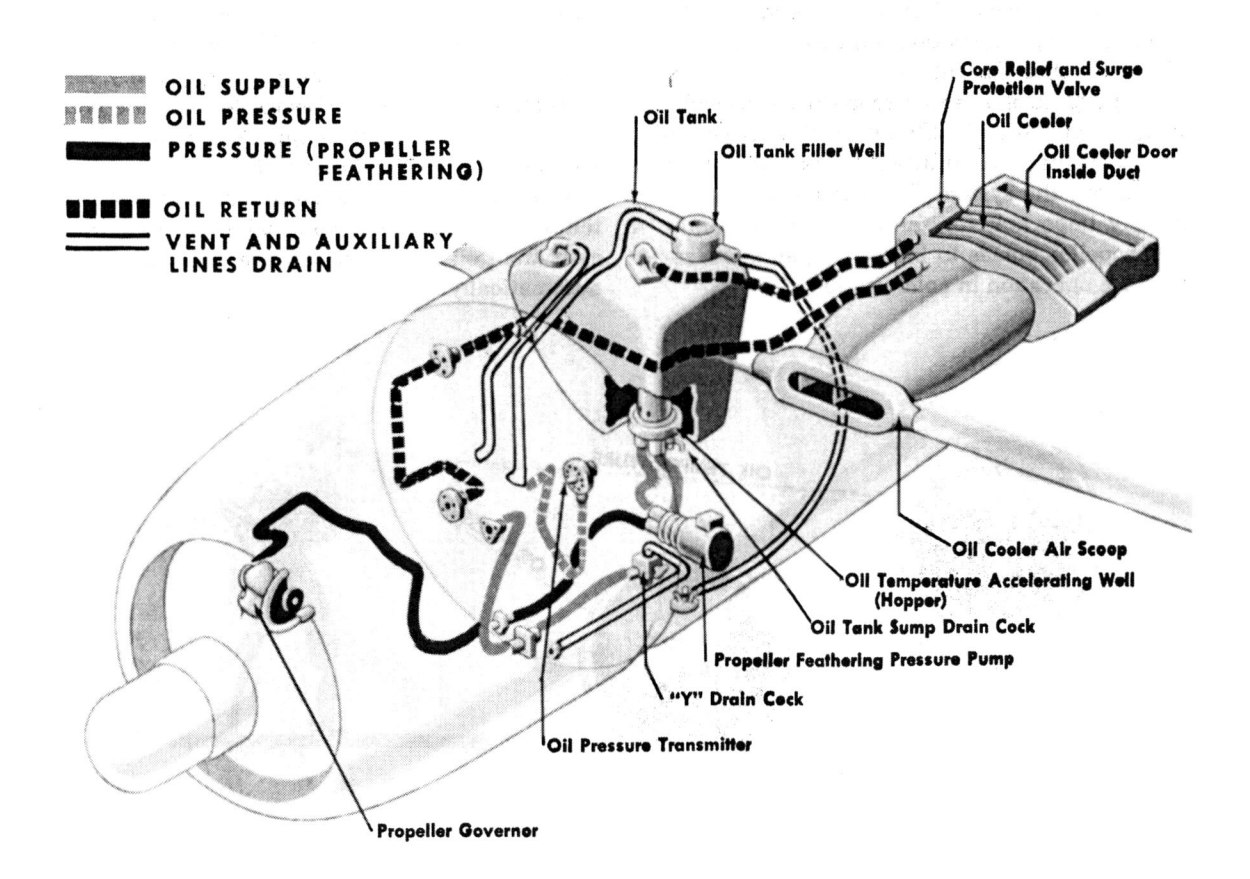

2. Warm the surrounding bulk oil.

3. Limit the amount of oil diluted during cold weather operation.

Oil Cooler Doors

Oil temperature is regulated by oil cooler doors. In earlier airplanes the doors are controlled manually by cockpit switches. In later airplanes the oil cooler doors are operated automatically by a thermostat control. On these automatic models there is an OPEN-CLOSE override switch for manual control in case the thermostat control fails to work properly.

Oil Dilution Solenoid Valve

For cold weather starting there is an oil dilution system. Fuel drawn directly from the fuel pressure line enters the system at the Y oil drain valve. The only purpose of oil dilution is to thin the oil for cold weather operation.

Step-by-step instructions on this are given in "Cold Weather Operations."

The purpose of an exact procedure is to make certain that the oil is diluted as little as necessary and that the diluted oil is distributed throughout the system. For example: It is extremely important for the diluted oil to enter the propeller domes to insure proper increase-decrease operation in cold weather.

Oil Temperature and Pressure Gages

The oil temperature and pressure gages are highly important, as they may be your only warning before you lose an engine.

The oil temperature bulb is connected to the bottom of the sump, and records the temperature of the oil just before it enters the engine. The oil pressure reading is taken where the oil enters the engine under greatest pressure.

Engine Pump

An engine-driven, gear-type pump supplies oil to the engine. The oil passes through a screen before it enters the pump.

Important Tips About the Oil System

1. Always check your pressure and temperature gages in relation to each other.

2. Listen to your props. If one tends to overspeed, it may be your first indication of oil system failure, quickly followed by engine failure.

3. Check your pressure gage frequently for oscillation. If the needle begins to fluctuate you may be close to engine failure. In any case, land and determine the trouble.

4. Watch your oil temperature carefully. Oil temperatures exceeding normal limits may indicate that oil cooler doors are not operating automatically.

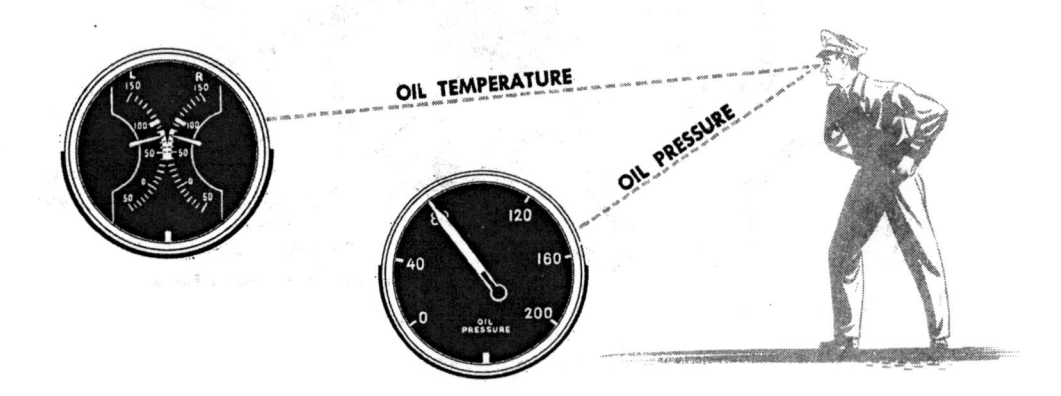

Watch these instruments

PROPELLERS

The A-26 has Hamilton Standard hydromatic propellers. They are 3-bladed, constant-speed, full-feathering propellers with a diameter of 12 feet 7 inches. There are three fundamental forces affecting the operation of these propellers. If you understand these forces and the mechanism that controls them, you know all you need to know about your propellers.

First Force is a twisting movement that takes place when the rotating blades turn toward the least wind resisting angle. This is high rpm and causes the piston in the propeller dome to be pushed to the back side of the dome. The blade angle depends entirely upon the position of the piston in the dome.

Second Force is the engine oil pressure that is conducted from the engine to the forward side of the piston through the hollow piston shaft. This force aids the first force in pushing the piston toward the back of the dome. The piston turns the blades toward high rpm by a cam and gear assembly.

Third Force is supplied by a special engine-driven pump. You regulate the pressure from this pump in the cockpit by the prop controls. Therefore, the prop is held at a constant speed by balancing the first two forces from the forward side of the piston by an equal amount of force on the back side of the piston.

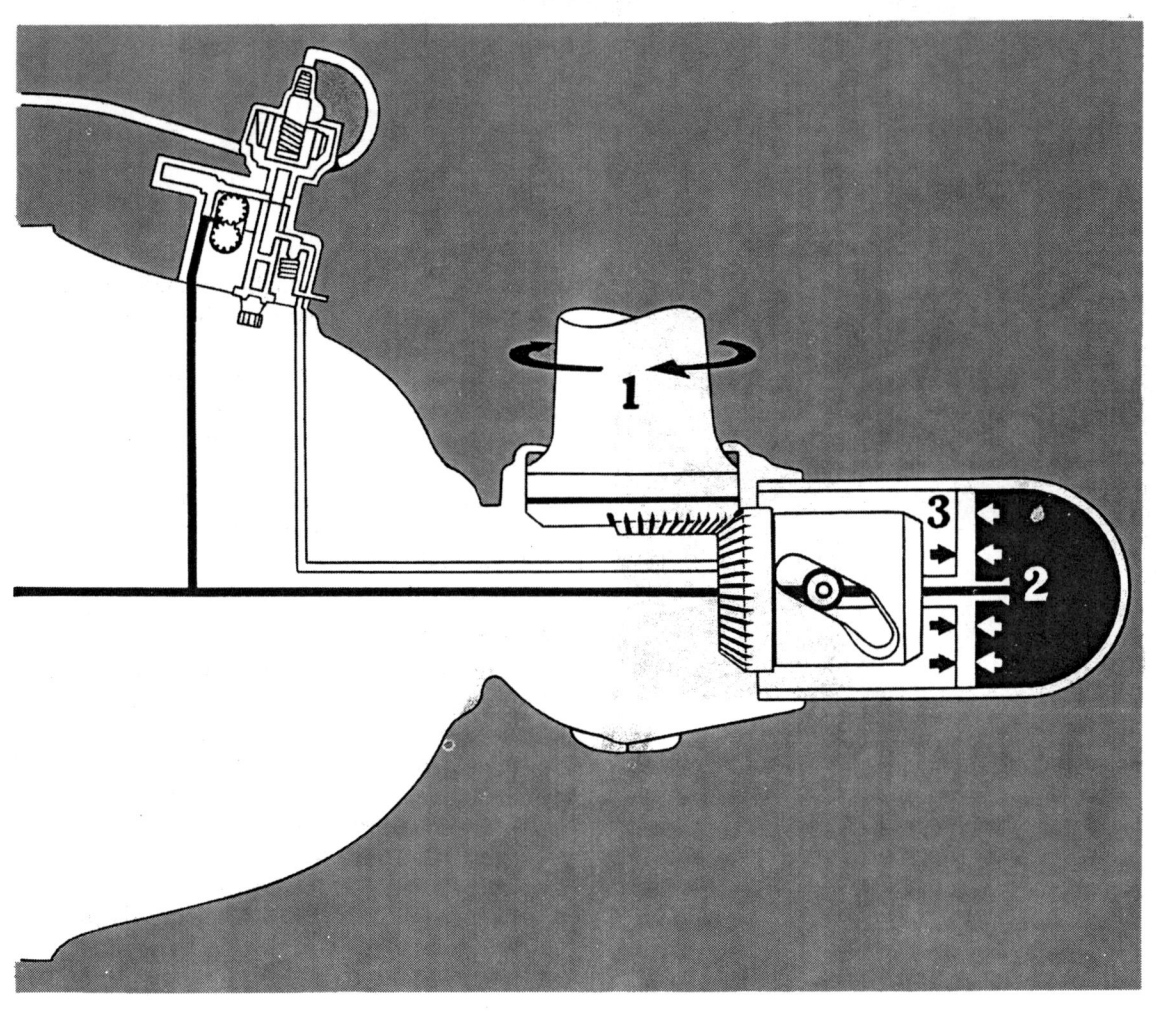

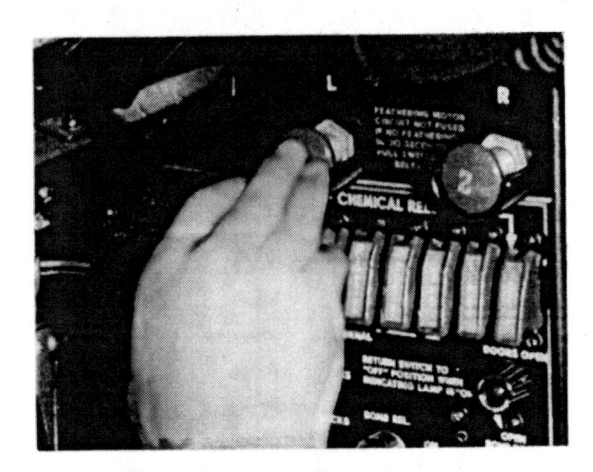

The feathering device on this propeller has an electric pump which you start by pressing the red feathering button on the instrument panel. It takes oil from the engine oil tank and forces it, under extremely high pressure, to the prop governor housing. This high pressure in the housing actuates a transfer valve which disconnects the prop governor from the system and allows the high-pressure oil to be forced to the back side of the piston in the propeller dome.

The high-pressure oil supplied by the feathering pump overrides the two forces at the front of the piston and forces the piston to the front of the dome, which puts the prop blades in a full-feathered position. Since there is no outlet, the pressure builds up to approximately 500 psi and actuates an electric cut-off switch, turning off the feathering pump.

Feather Button Failure

If the feather button fails to pop out when the prop reaches the full feathered position, quickly pull the button out by hand. Otherwise the blades will continue in the feathering cycle and start to unfeather which will cause engine overspeeding and possible damage.

WARNING: There is no fuse on the feathering circuit. When you feather propellers, if you get no action within 90 seconds quickly pull the feather button out so as not to burn out the feathering motor.

Unfeathering Propeller

To unfeather the propeller, depress the feathering button until the prop is turning over at approximately 800 rpm. Then release the feathering button. By holding the feathering button down you override the electric cut-off switch and allow the feathering pump to continue to build up pressure. When the pressure has increased to approximately 600 psi a distributor valve redirects the high-pressure oil through the hollow piston shaft to the front side of the piston. This forces the blades toward the high rpm angle and the prop governor is automatically back at work.

See "Single Engine Flight" P. 83-84 for complete feathering and unfeathering procedures.

RADIO EQUIPMENT

Radio serves as the voice and ears of your airplane. Knowing radio equipment is especially important to the A-26 pilot because in most airplanes the pilot is also the navigator. Detailed radio procedure is given in the section entitled "Navigation." For additional information, ask your communications officer. He can give you tips about your radio that will help you avoid navigation errors.

Command Set (SCR-274-N)

This command set is essentially the same as you have used all through flying school. It consists of three independent receivers which you control on your radio panel. These three receivers cover the following bands:

1. 3.0 to 6.0 Mc.
2. 190 to 550 Kc.
3. 6.0 to 9.1 Mc.

Your three transmitting sets cover the following ranges:

1. 4.0 to 5.3 Mc.
2. 5.3 to 7.0 Mc.
3. 3.0 to 4.0 Mc.

The transmitter selector switch is to the left of your seat. Your transmitting mike button is on the throttle. The transmitters and receivers are mounted behind the pilot's seat.

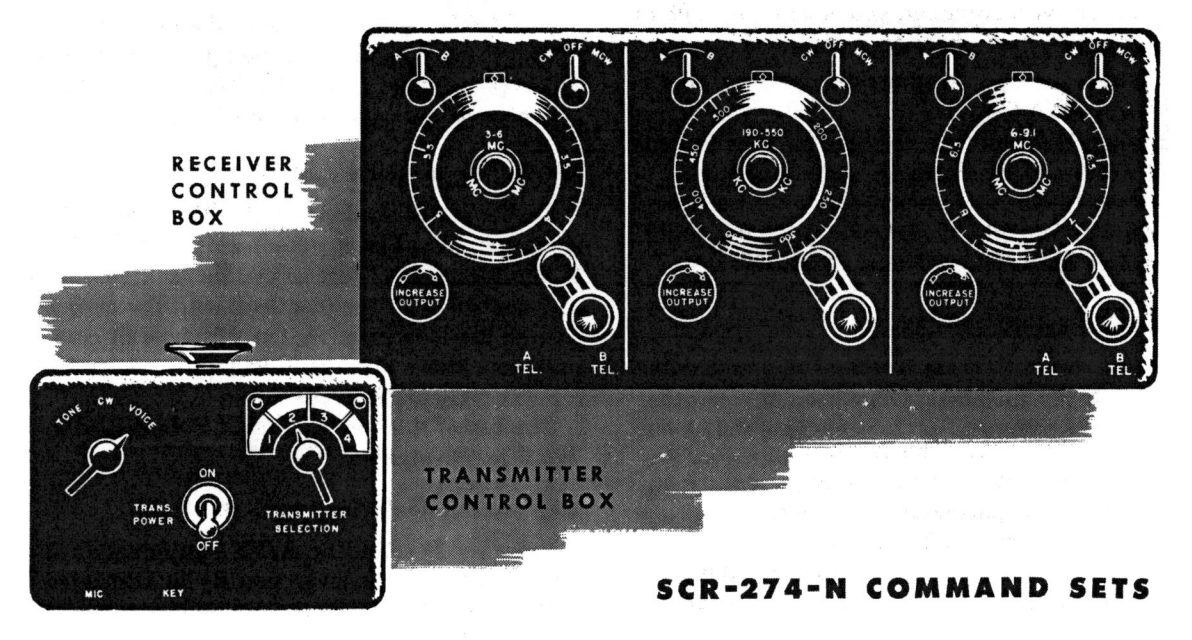

RECEIVER CONTROL BOX

TRANSMITTER CONTROL BOX

SCR-274-N COMMAND SETS

RESTRICTED

Radio Reception

The CW-OFF-MCW switch on the pilot's control box belongs on MCW during any normal operation.

Use MCW to receive:
1. Radio range signals and voice transmissions.
2. Tower transmissions.
3. Interplane transmissions.

Use CW **only** to receive code messages.

You don't use the A Tel and B Tel switch if there is VHF (very high frequency) equipment in the plane. With VHF equipment, always leave the switch in the A Tel position.

If the airplane does not carry VHF, and you want one of your crew members to guard another wave length, plug his headset in the B Tel position and turn his jackbox to the LIAISON position.

For normal use keep the switch in the A Tel position.

Radio Tips

Tune your receivers accurately. Don't sit and strain to hear the tower when it's easy to tune them clearly.

Don't hesitate to ask any communications man to show you how to tune your transmitter and receiver. Although you can't do it in flight, you must know how to do it on the ground.

When receiving, keep the switch on the pilot's control box on MCW.

When transmitting, keep the selector switch on VOICE. (Unless you are sending code.)

If you smell gasoline vapors, air out the cockpit first. Then turn off the radio equipment until gasoline fumes are no longer detected.

Radio Compass AN-ARN-7

Your radio compass is a receiving unit only, used chiefly for navigation although it supplements the command set for receiving the tower and radio ranges. The receiver unit is on the right-hand side of the fuselage just behind the gunner's compartment. The frequency ranges covered by its four bands are:

Band I	100 to 200 Kc.
Band II	200 to 410 Kc.
Band III	410 to 850 Kc.
Band IV	850 to 1750 Kc.

Select your bands on the radio compass control box.

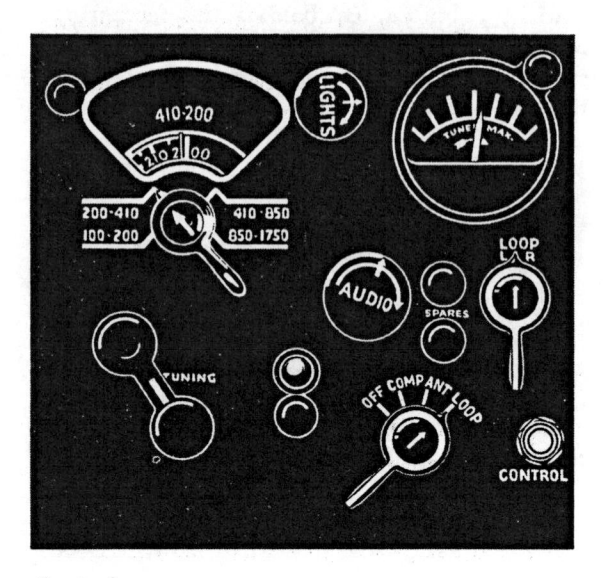

Control

Volume by audio knob.

Turn your operation selector switch to:
  COMP for directional operation.
  ANT for receiving with vertical sense antenna.
  LOOP for receiving with the loop antenna.

Rotate the loop by depressing the LOOP L-R knob toward either R or L. Make finer adjustments with the small tuning knob.

NM-26V Type Radio Compass

Earlier series airplanes use the NM-26V type radio compass. Select your bands on this type of compass control just as you do on the other. The control steps are identical, with the exception of the loop rotation. On this type of compass you rotate the loop manually by use of a crank on the azimuth control.

The use of this navigation aid is described in detail in "Navigation."

IFF (Identification, Friend or Foe)

Your highly confidential IFF equipment must always be ON whenever you fly in restricted areas. The receiver is just behind the gunner's

RESTRICTED

compartment. It has a built-in destructor unit and is connected to the destructor circuit by a plug. **Never insert this plug except in flight.** The destructor unit, designed to destroy your IFF, can be set off by two buttons in the pilot's compartment or by a pendulum-set impact switch which automatically sets off the destroying charge during a very rough or crash landing.

Interphone

The interphone is the airplane's local phone system for crew members to communicate with each other. It is controlled by the interphone jackbox. Each crew member has his own jackbox. By switching his lever to the CALL position, he can talk to any other crew members, regardless of the setting of their jackboxes.

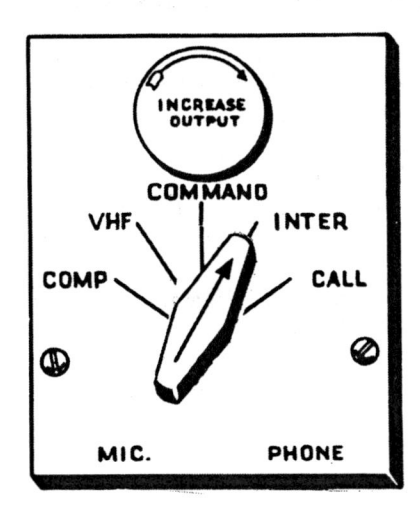

VHF Equipment

Your VHF (very high frequency) radio supplements the command set and can be used for many command set functions. Static and electrical weather disturbances do not affect VHF reception and as soon as practical VHF radio ranges will be as numerous as low frequency radio ranges are today. Discuss VHF with your Communications Officer who will advise you of its use in your area.

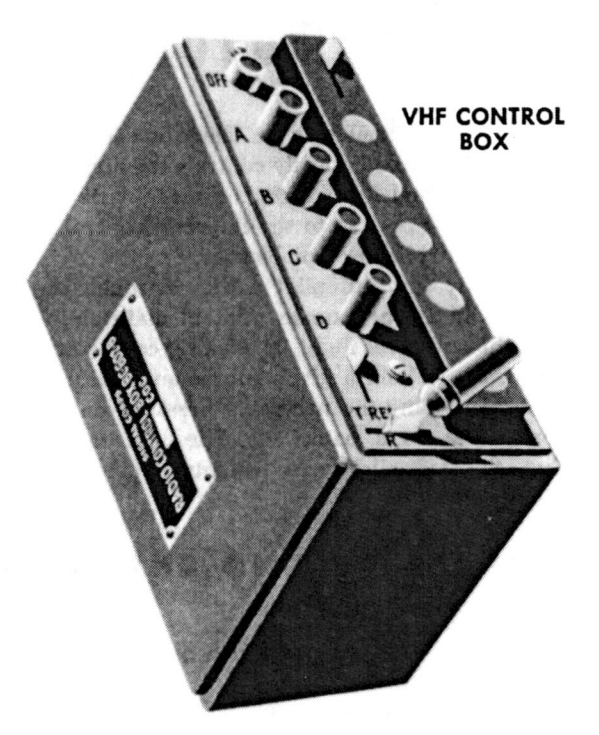

You have four channels on the push button operated VHF. Switch your interphone jackbox to VHF (marked LIAISON on earlier airplanes), turn on your VHF switch selector channel and you are ready to transmit or receive.

VHF Range

The distance range available with VHF is limited to line-of-sight transmission. Any obstacle between you and the station jams your transmission and reception.

THE C-1 AUTOPILOT

The C-1 autopilot is an electromechanical robot which automatically controls the airplane in straight and level flight, or maneuvers the airplane in response to the fingertip control of the human pilot or bombardier.

Actually, the autopilot works in much the same way as the human pilot in maintaining straight and level flight, in making corrections necessary to hold a given course and altitude, and in applying the necessary pressure on the controls to turns, banks, etc. The difference is that the autopilot acts instantaneously and with a precision that is not humanly possible.

The autopilot detects flight deviations the instant they occur, and just as instantaneously operates the controls to correct the deviation. Properly adjusted, the autopilot will neither overcontrol nor undercontrol the airplane, but will keep it flying straight and level with all 3 control surfaces operating in full coordination.

The C-1 autopilot consists of various separate units electrically interconnected to operate as a system. The operation of these units is explained in detail in AN-11-60AA-1.

PILOT'S GROUND CHECKLIST FOR THE C-1 AUTOPILOT

1. Center turn control.
2. Turn on C-1 master switch bar.
3. Set control transfer knob at "PILOT."
4. Set tell-tale shutter switch "ON."
5. Set all adjustment knobs to pointers-up position, making sure pointers are not loose.
6. Tell bombardier to center PDI.
7. Turn on Servo PDI switch.
8. Operate controls through extreme range several times, observing that tell-tale lights flicker and go out as streamline position is reached from either direction.
9. Turn on aileron, rudder, and elevator switches.
10. Turn aileron centering knob clockwise, then counter-clockwise, observing that wheel turns to the right and then to the left.
11. Repeat Item 10 for rudder and elevator, observing action.
12. Have bombardier move directional arm for full right turn, then to left, observing to see if aileron and rudder move in proper direction.
13. Have bombardier center PDI and engage secondary clutch.
14. Rotate turn control knob for right and left turns, observing aileron and rudder controls for proper movement.
15. If all checks are satisfactory, turn the C-1 master switch bar "OFF."

HOW TO OPERATE THE C-1 AUTOPILOT

Before Takeoff

1. Set all pointer on the control panel in the up position.
2. Make sure that all switches on the control panel are in the "OFF" position.

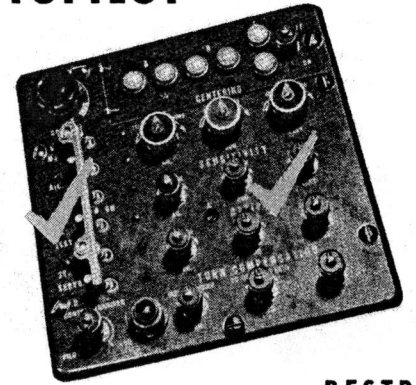

After Takeoff

1. Turn on the master switch.

2. Five minutes later, turn on PDI switch (and Servo switch, if separate).

3. Ten minutes after turning on the master switch, trim the plane for level flight at cruising speed by reference to flight instruments.

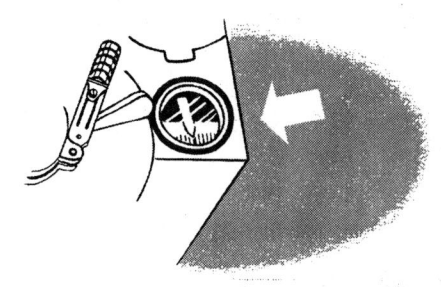

4. Have the bombardier disengage the autopilot clutch, center PDI and lock it in place by depressing the directional control lock. The PDI is held centered until the pilot has completed the engaging procedure. Then the autopilot clutch is re-engaged, and the directional arm lock released.

Alternate Method: The pilot centers PDI by turning the airplane in direction of the PDI needle. Then resume straight and level flight.

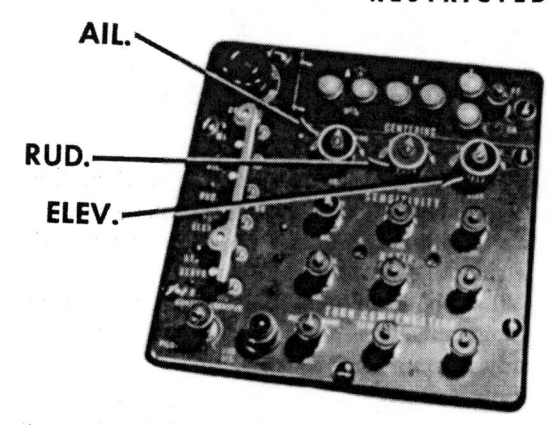

5. Engage the autopilot. Put out aileron telltale lights with the aileron centering knob, then throw on the aileron engaging switch. Repeat the operation for rudder, then for elevator.

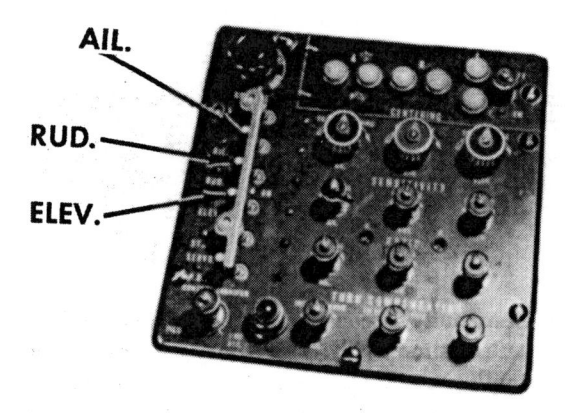

6. Make final autopilot trim corrections. If necessary, use centering knobs to level wings and center PDI.

Caution:

NEVER ADJUST MECHANICAL TRIM TABS WHILE THE AUTOPILOT IS ENGAGED

RESTRICTED

FLIGHT ADJUSTMENTS AND OPERATION

After the C-1 autopilot is in operation, carefully analyze the action of the airplane to make sure all adjustments have been properly made for smooth, accurate flight control.

When both **tell-tale** lights in any axis are extinguished, it is an indication the autopilot is ready for engaging in that axis.

Before engaging, each **centering knob** is used to adjust the autopilot control reference point to the straight and level flight position of the corresponding control surface. After engaging, centering knobs are used to make small attitude adjustments.

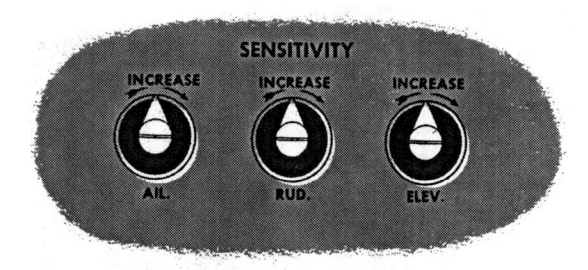

Sensitivity is comparable to a human pilot's reaction time. With sensitivity set high, the autopilot responds quickly to apply a correction for even the slightest deviation. If sensitivity is set low, flight deviation must be relatively large before the autopilot will apply its corrective action.

Ratio is the amount of control surface movement applied by the autopilot in correcting a given deviation. It governs the speed of the airplane's response to corrective autopilot actions. Proper ratio adjustment depends on airspeed.

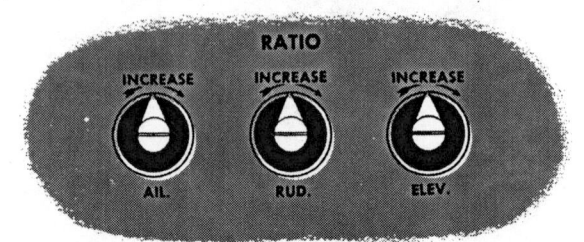

If ratio is too high, the autopilot will overcontrol the airplane and produce a ship hunt; if ratio is too low, the autopilot will undercontrol and flight corrections will be too slow. After ratio adjustments have been made, centering may require readjustment.

To adjust **turn compensation**, have bombardier disengage autopilot clutch and move engaging knob to extreme right or extreme left. Airplane should bank 18° as indicated by artificial horizon. If it does not, adjust aileron compensation (bank trimmer) to attain 18° bank. Then, if turn is not coordinated, adjust rudder compensation (skid trimmer) to center inclinometer ball. Do not use aileron or rudder compensation knobs to adjust coordination of turn control turns.

Emergency Use of Autopilot

REMEMBER THE ROLE THAT THE AUTOPILOT CAN PLAY IN EMERGENCIES

1. If the control cables are damaged or severed between the pilot's compartment and the Servo units in the tail, the autopilot can bridge the gap. There have been many instances where the autopilot has been used thus to fly an airplane with damaged controls.

2. If the autopilot has been set up for level flight, it can be used to hold the airplane straight and level while abandoning ship.

46

RESTRICTED

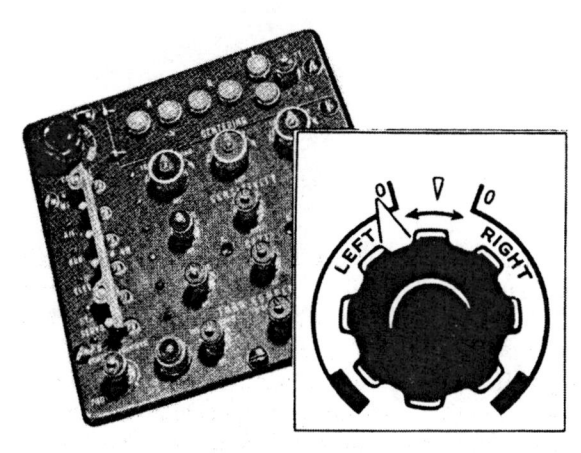

The **turn control** is used by the pilot to turn the airplane while flying under automatic control. To adjust turn control, first make sure turn compensation adjustments have been properly made, then set turn control pointer at beginning of trip-lined area on dial. Airplane should bank 30°, as indicated by artificial horizon. If it doesn't, remove cap from aileron trimmer and adjust trimmer until a 30° bank is attained. Then, if turn is not coordinated (inclinometer ball not centered), adjust rudder trimmer to center ball. Make final adjustments with both trimmers and replace caps. Set turn control at zero to resume straight and level flight; then re-center.

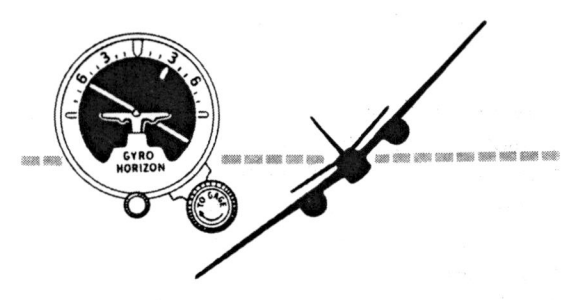

Never operate the Turn Control without first making sure the PDI is centered

The **turn control transfer** has no effect unless the installation includes a remote turn control.

The **dashpot** on the stabilizer regulates the amount of rudder kick applied by the autopilot to correct rapid deviations in the turn axis. If a rudder hunt develops which cannot be eliminated by adjustment of rudder ratio or sensitivity, the dashpot may require adjustment.

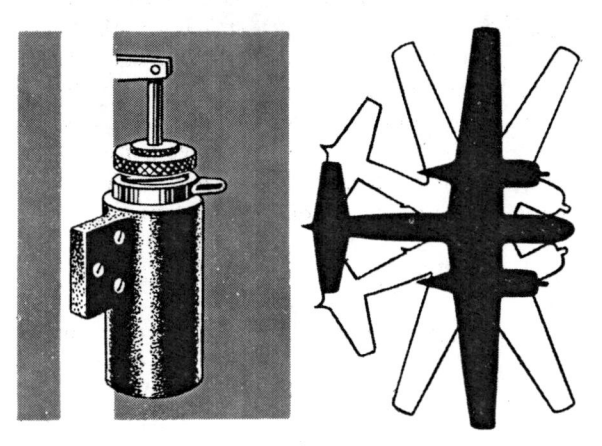

This is accomplished by loosening the locknut on the dashpot, turning the knurled ring up or down until hunting ceases, then tightening the locknut.

Cold Weather Operation—When temperatures are between —12° and 0°C (10° and 32°F) autopilot units must be run for 30 minutes before engaging. If accurate flight control is desired immediately after takeoff, perform the autopilot warm-up before takeoff by turning on the master switch during the engine run-up—but make sure autopilot is off during takeoff. If warm-up is performed during flight, allow 30 minutes after turning on master switch before engaging. When temperatures are below —12°C (10°F) units must be preheated for one hour before takeoff. Use special heating covers or blankets with heating tubes.

EMERGENCY AND MISCELLANEOUS EQUIPMENT

Emergency and miscellaneous equipment is an easy thing to kiss off as unimportant. The chances are that you may get away with it. If you don't, it may cost you your life. Too many good pilots have been lost at sea without their emergency equipment and never been heard from again. Too many aircraft have gone down in flames that the pilot or his crew could easily have extinguished inside the airplane.

1. LIFE RAFT

A life raft becomes the most important thing in the world to you and your crew when you are over water and find you must ditch your airplane.

There are only two important factors to insure your safety before each possible overwater flight:

a. **Check your equipment. Know that it's all there and in good order.**

b. Know how to use your equipment.

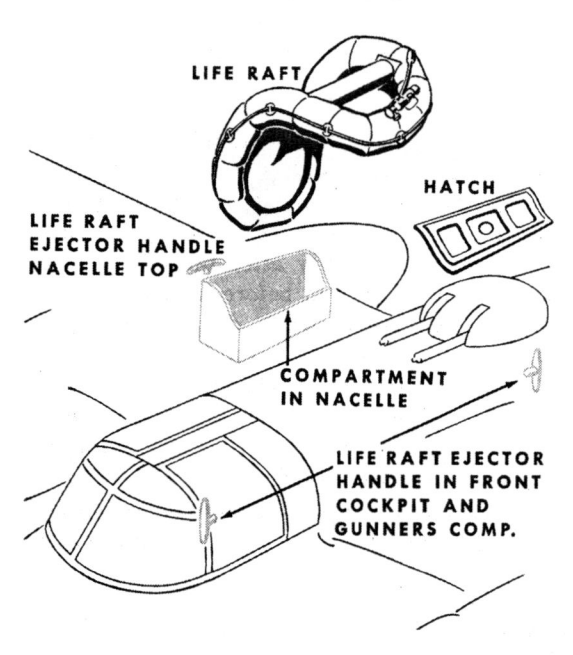

On later airplanes a self-expelling life raft is stowed in the right-hand nacelle aft of the wing. The raft is expelled by pulling one of the three release cables; one is in the pilot's compartment, one in the gunner's compartment, and another located on the nacelle by the life raft door. Both the pilot's and the gunner's release cable expel the raft and inflate it. The release handle on the nacelle itself, however, merely pulls the pins from the life raft door. The raft must be pulled out by hand which action will automatically inflate it at the same time. The raft is a pneumatic self-inflating type and contains the following accessories:

3 seamarker dyes
1 floating type flashlight
1 compass and match container
1 shade and camouflage cloth
1 sail and water catching cloth
1 assembly fishing kit
9 units emergency subsistence rations
1 scout knife
7 cans drinking water
1 police whistle
1 first-aid kit
1 pyrotechnic pistol (5 signals)
1 sea anchor
3 oars
1 hand pump
1 raft repair kit
1 bailing bucket
4 repair plugs
1 container assembly
40 feet of cord
1 signaling mirror
1 set religious pamphlets
4 tubes sunburn ointment
4 water containers
1 cellulose sponge

On earlier airplanes a 5-man pneumatic life raft is stowed in the forward bulkhead of the gunner's compartment. It is the gunner's duty to push the raft through the escape hatch and to inflate it by breaking the CO_2 seal as soon as the raft is free of the airplane.

To Use

A. Release your life raft from its position by pulling the emergency release cord. You can do this either from outside the airplane or from the inside through the top escape hatch.

B. Make sure the entire raft is outside the airplane before you inflate it with the CO_2 bottle attached to the raft.

C. Inflate it by twisting the handle on the CO_2 bottle neck before you launch the raft.

D. Get your crew members in and paddle away from the sinking airplane.

2. FIRE EXTINGUISHERS

You have two emergency fire extinguishers in the A-26. One is located behind the pilot's seat and the other is in either the aft bulkhead of the nosewheel well or in the gunner's compartment.

The fire extinguisher in the nosewheel well should be used only in the open because of the dangerous fumes and gases produced by the carbon tetrachloride charge in this fire extinguisher. You can use the other inside the airplane. Check both these fire extinguishers and be sure that they are always charged and in place.

Late model A-26's are equipped with engine fire extinguishers. (See Fires, page 100.)

3. EMERGENCY REPAIR KIT

Your emergency repair kit is stowed in the left nacelle and includes:

Screwdrivers	Wire
Pliers	Bolts
Hammer	Nuts
Wrench	Fuses
Tape	Sparkplugs

Check these emergency supplies. Be sure they're all there.

4. FLARES

To the right of the pilot's seat is a canvas bag containing a Very pistol and various colored flares. Check it. Make sure it's there.

5. OTHER EQUIPMENT

Stowed in the right nacelle is a starter hand crank and gear box. You may need this at a strange airport.

Stowed in other positions in the airplane are such important items of equipment as your first-aid kit, fire ax, map cases. Check them with your crew chief. Be sure your airplane is fully equipped for every emergency.

PLAY IT SAFE

CHECK EMERGENCY AND MISCELLANEOUS EQUIPMENT BEFORE EACH FLIGHT, AND KNOW HOW TO USE IT

WEIGHT AND BALANCE

Your airplane is designed to fly at gross weights up to 37,000 lbs., **provided the airplane is loaded properly.** However, the recommended gross weight is 35,500. It is not so much the **amount of weight** that counts, but **where it is loaded.**

Many airplanes that are lost for no apparent reason have cracked up because of improper loading. Two of the reasons why a nose or tail-heavy airplane is dangerous are:

1. Difficulty in control. It stalls more quickly and is difficult to land.

2. Dangerously high structural strains when flying in turbulent air.

Expendable Load

Don't forget that your center of gravity (CG) can change materially during flight. The consumption of fuel, expending of ammunition, and dropping of bombs must be considered before the flight begins.

Your airplane may be loaded within safe limits for takeoff and, after your mission, be unsafe to land. Keep your **expendable load** in mind, so that your CG stays within safe limits during the entire flight.

Under normal operating conditions, the A-26 is well within safe mean areodynamic chord (MAC) limits.

ARMAMENT EQUIPMENT

The A-26 is literally a flying gun platform. No other tactical airplane has so much pilot-operated armament.

Two Noses

Your airplane can have one of two different nose assemblies, which are interchangeable.

Nose No. 1

This all-purpose nose may be used in any of the following combinations:
1. Six .50-cal. machine guns.
2. Eight .50-cal. machine guns.
3. One 37-mm. cannon and four .50-cal. machine guns.
4. One 37-mm. cannon and two .50-cal. machine guns.
5. Two 37-mm. cannon.
6. One 75-mm. and one 37-mm. cannon.
7. One 75-mm. cannon and two .50-cal. machine guns.

Nose No. 2

This is the bombardier nose. It includes bombsight brackets and bombing controls, as well as two fixed .50-cal. machine guns.

Gun Turrets

The A-26 has an upper and a lower turret. Each mounts two .50-cal. machine guns and ammunition boxes for 500 rounds per gun. Both these turrets are fired remotely by the rear gunner, who has a 70° field of vision through either the upper or lower periscope head. Both turrets are moved and fired electrically by the gunner at his sighting station. A self-replenishing air bottle charges the guns automatically if they jam.

Upper Turret

The guns in the upper turret have unlimited azimuth rotation and operate between straight up and as low as 5° below horizontal.

Lower Turret

The guns in the lower turret have unlimited azimuth rotation and operate from straight down to as high as 5° above horizontal. This permits 10° crossfire between the guns in the upper turret and the guns in the lower turret.

Contour Followers

Both turrets have contour followers which limit the zone of fire. The upper turret is prevented from firing lower than 5° broadside or lower than horizontal while the turret is in the forward and aft positions.

The lower turret guns are forced to point 25° below horizontal when the turret is swung directly forward. The guns are limited to 5° above horizontal in the broadside position.

Automatic Fire Interrupters

Automatic fire interrupters shut off gun fire when either turret is aimed at wingtips, propeller arcs, or tail surfaces.

The upper turret may be locked forward and fired by the pilot with the fixed-gun group.

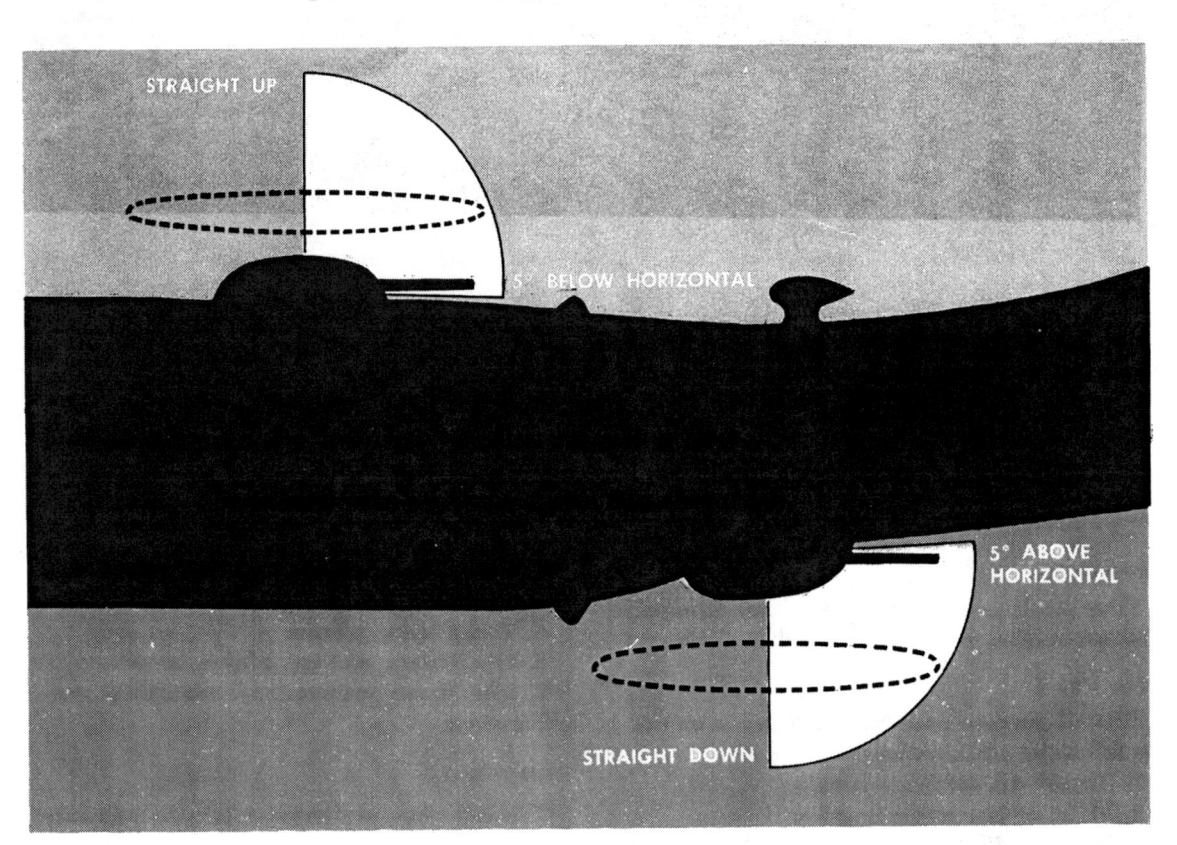

Nose Guns

Regardless of what combination of armament is used in the all-purpose nose of the airplane, you operate all the guns with one set of switches. On earlier airplanes the nose guns, like the external wing guns, must be charged before takeoff. On later airplanes you can charge them from the pilot's compartment at any time. The trigger on the left-hand side of your control wheel operates the nose and wing guns simultaneously.

External Wing Guns

On earlier airplanes eight .50-cal. machine guns are mounted on hangers suspended from the wings (four on each side) outboard of the engine nacelles. Ammunition boxes are carried in the wing. Only one charging handle is needed for each set of four guns. They must be charged before takeoff.

Internal Wing Guns

Later airplanes have six .50-cal. internal wing guns installed (3 on each side) outboard of the engine nacelles. The guns and their armament boxes are carried inside the wings and, like the nose guns, can be charged pneumatically by the pilot. The guns are selected by switches on the overhead fire control panel.

Rockets

Fourteen zero rail rocket launchers carrying seven 5-inch rockets under each wing are installed as optional tactical equipment on some later A-26's. The rockets are launched from the rails electrically by the punch button on the left side of your control wheel.

Bombing Equipment

The A-26 is an extremely versatile offensive weapon. It has tremendous strafing firepower. It can bomb from various altitudes down to skip bombing, and it can launch torpedoes.

Your airplane has wing and fuselage bomb racks adapted for carrying variable bomb loads up to 6000 lbs.

There are four bomb rack panels in the bomb bay, two forward and two aft. The right and left forward bomb rack panels have seven bomb stations each, but only five of them may be used at any one time. The right and left aft bomb rack panels have five bomb stations each, but only three of them can be used at any one time. Each station is plainly marked for the size bomb to be carried.

Bombs of 500 or 1000 lbs. are carried in a single station installed farther forward.

Although there are 24 bomb stations in the airplane, making it extremely versatile in the types and numbers of bombs carried, only 16 of those stations can be used at any one time.

Torpedoes

A second single-station panel is provided between the forward and aft bomb bays to carry two torpedoes.

Pilot's Bomb and Rocket Release Control

Release your bombs or launch your rockets by pushing the bomb release button on the left side of your control wheel.

Bomb Circuit Selector

With your circuit selector you select either FUSELAGE or WING AND FUSELAGE bomb racks.

Armament Selector Switch

Use your armament selector switch to fuse the bombs for the type of bombing to be done. For impact bombing and to salvo your bombs armed, select NOSE and TAIL. For delayed action bombing, set your arming switch on TAIL. To salvo bombs safe, set it on OFF.

Rack Selection

Select your demolition racks or fragmentation racks with the switch selector marked DEMOL and FRAG.

Intervalometer

Your intervalometer gives you a choice of single release or automatic train release of fuselage and wing bomb loads. The purpose of this automatic interval release is to provide release of one or all of your bombs at regular intervals measured in feet between impacts.

Wing Bomb Racks

The 4 wing bomb racks each hold a 100, 300, or 500-lb bomb. The bombs are released by turning the desired selector switch and pushing the bomb release button. To salvo your wing bombs (without salvoing your fuselage bombs), put bomb selector switch in the WING and FUSELAGE position, then move the wing rack salvo switch to SALVO. On some models there is just one salvo switch which salvos both wing and fuselage bombs together.

Wing Chemical Tanks

Four chemical tanks may be carried on your wing bomb racks. You fire them by electrical switches on your auxiliary electric control panel. The tanks may be dropped in the same manner in which you drop your wing bombs.

Torpedo Stations

Two torpedoes may be loaded in the bomb bay as alternate armament. When torpedoes are carried, the bomb rack panels and the removable portion of the front bomb bay rail are removed. The bomb bay doors must be left open. Release your torpedoes electrically by the bomb release button with your torpedo circuit switch ON. Salvo your torpedoes manually with the bomb control salvo switch (or lever in some early model airplanes).

Torpedo Director

You can pull the torpedo director, on a rack over your windshield, into your line of vision when you are ready to make your launching run. You can make adjustments easily with one hand, in flight.

75-mm. Cannon

A 75-mm. cannon, installed in one of the alternate noses, extends back into the pilot's compartment. A gun loader sits on a bicycle seat behind the gun. He has racks for twenty rounds of 75-mm. shells. The empty shells are ejected through a chute into a canvas bag container in the bomb bay. You fire the gun electrically with the button on the right side of the control wheel.

GUN, BOMB, TORPEDO, AND ROCKET CONTROLS

OVERHEAD—FIRE CONTROL PANEL

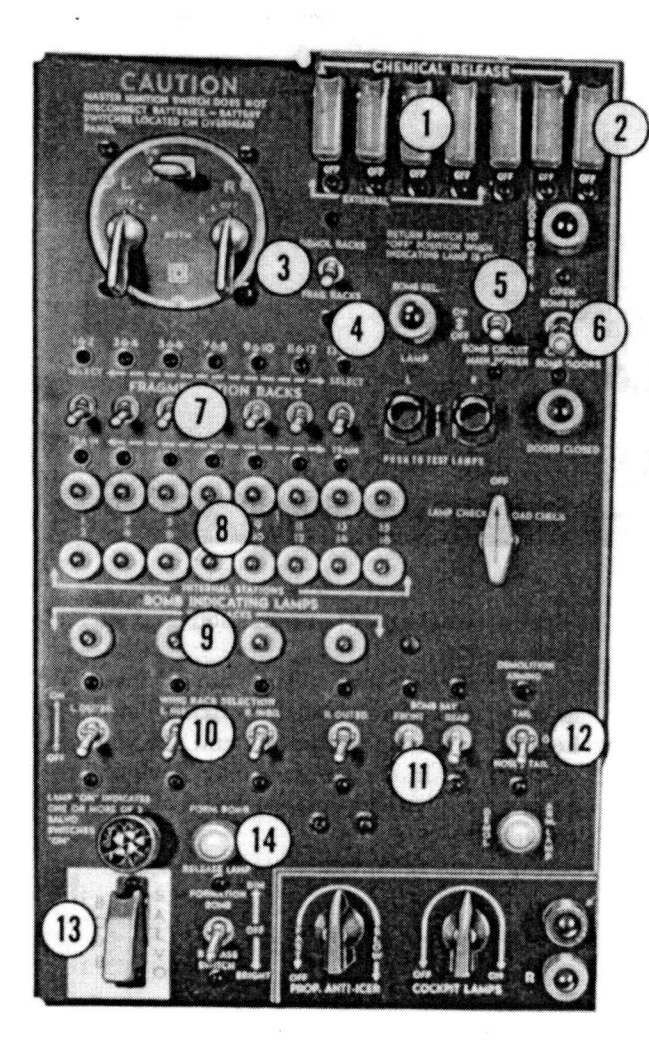

SIDE—ROCKET CONTROLS

FRONT—BOMB CONTROLS

1. CHEMICAL RELEASE SWITCHES.
2. TORPEDO SWITCH.
3. DEMO-FRAG SELECTOR SWITCH.
4. BOMB RELEASE LAMP.
5. BOMB CIRCUIT MAIN POWER SWITCH.
6. BOMB BAY DOOR OPERATING SWITCH AND INDICATOR LAMPS.
7. FRAG RACK SELECTOR SWITCHES.
8. INTERNAL BOMB STATION INDICATOR LAMPS.
9. WING RACK INDICATOR LAMPS.
10. WING RACK SELECTOR SWITCHES.
11. BOMB BAY RACK SELECTOR SWITCHES.
12. BOMB ARMING SWITCH AND LAMP.
13. BOMB SALVO SWITCH.
14. FORMATION BOMB RELEASE SWITCH AND LAMP.

PILOT'S INSPECTION AND CHECKS

If you had a choice, which would you take: a beautiful girl, a million dollars, or a good crew chief? Not so fast! What good would the beautiful girl and the million dollars do you if you weren't around to enjoy them? That's right; better put the good crew chief at the top of the list. Most crew chiefs are capable men who are as proud of your airplane as you are, and just as eagerly sweating out the mission as you and your crew.

The following checklist assumes that you have a good crew chief. The items listed are kept to an absolute minimum and are your responsibility. In combat you may have to preflight your own airplane, so learn all you can about it. Be fussy!

Don't neglect a single item on the following pilot inspection check!

OUTSIDE VISUAL CHECK

Inspect your A-26 carefully for skin cracks, wrinkles, loose rivets, fabric tears, and propeller nicks. Don't fail to observe every detail of your airplane's general appearance.

BEFORE BEGINNING YOUR CHECK, MAKE CERTAIN THAT ALL COCKPIT SWITCHES ARE OFF AND THAT YOU HAVE 650 PSI MINIMUM HYDRAULIC PRESSURE.

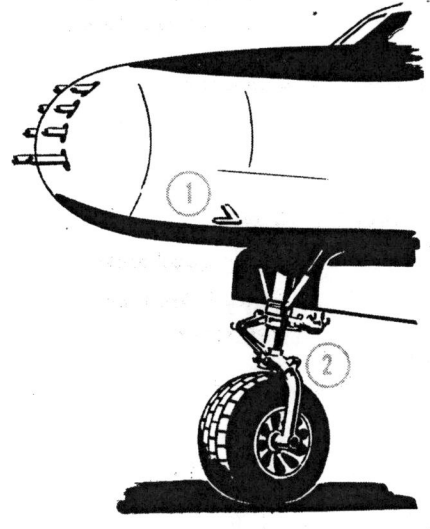

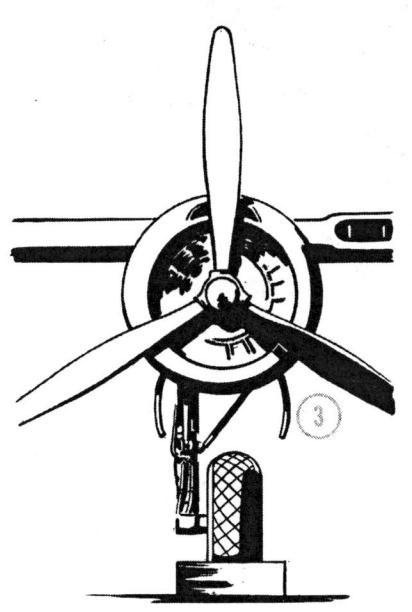

Check	Must Be
1. PITOT COVERS	Off
2. NOSEWHEEL	
a. NOSEWHEEL SNUBBING PINS	Engaged, with cap secure.
b. OLEO STRUT	Properly extended. No leaks. No cracks.
c. TIRE	Good condition. Properly inflated. No slippage evident. (Ring deflection markers touch the ground when your tires are properly inflated.)
d. DOWN-LOCK SAFETY PIN	Removed.
e. HYDRAULIC LINES	No leaks.
f. UP-LATCH ASSEMBLY	Clearance.
g. INSPECTION WINDOW	Clear.
3. LEFT ENGINE NACELLE	
a. PROPELLER PULLED THROUGH	Nine blades if engine has not been turned over within 2 hours. Checked for nicks.
b. COWLING LOCKS AND DZUS FASTENERS	Locked.
c. WHEEL CHOCKS	In place.
d. HYDRAULIC LINES	No leaks.
e. TIRE	Good condition. Properly inflated. No slippage.
f. OLEO STRUT	Properly extended. No leaks. No cracks.
g. DOWN-LOCK PIN	Removed.
h. DOWN-LOCK	Proper overlap.
i. CANVAS CURTAIN	Zipped shut.

RESTRICTED

Check	Must Be
4. LOWER TURRET	Guns locked in aft position. Dome cover secure.
5. BOMB BAY	No fuel or hydraulic leaks. Bomb bay door locks off.
6. GUNNER'S COMPARTMENT	Seat locked. All gun switches off and circuit breakers closed.
7. RIGHT ENGINE NACELLE	

a. Repeat left engine checks in the same order.

ON TOP OF AIRPLANE

1. GAS, OIL, AND WATER COVERS	Secure.
2. ANTENNA	Under good tension.
3. TOP OF WING AND NACELLES	Free of skin tears and wrinkles.
4. TOP TURRET GUNS AND DOME COVERS	Locked.

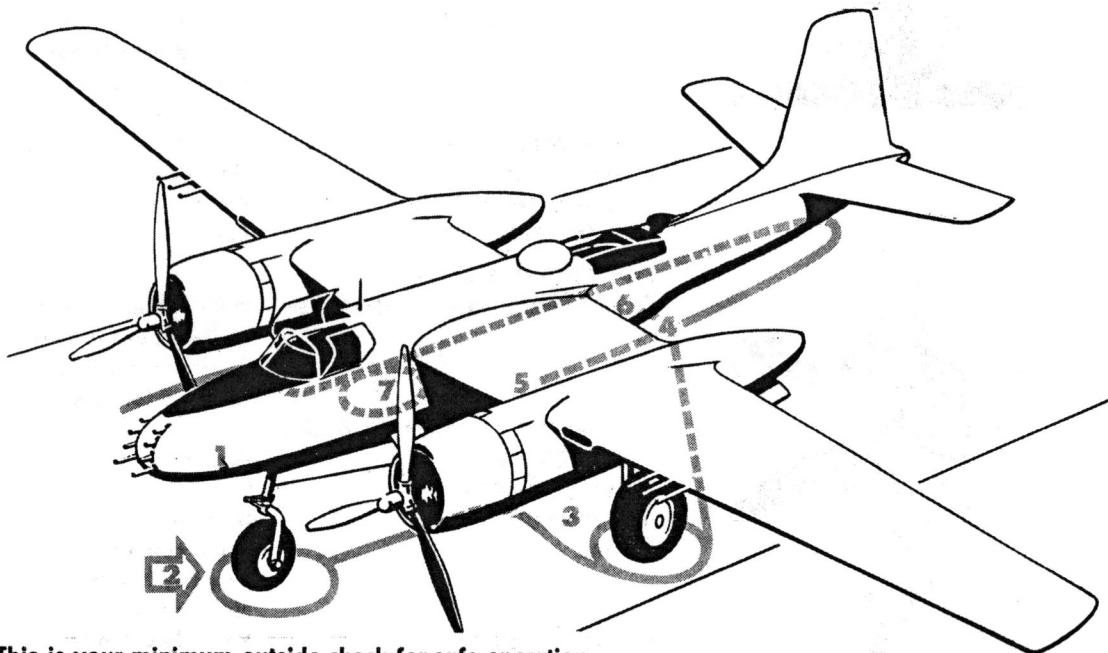

This is your minimum outside check for safe operation. Either everything is right and passes inspection, or you turn the airplane back to your crew chief for correction.
Be thorough. You make this check for the safety of yourself and your crew.

RESTRICTED

VISUAL INSIDE INSPECTION

Always proceed in this orderly fashion in the cockpit. Do not deviate from it.

Check   *Must Be*

1. FORM 1, WEIGHT AND BALANCE PREFLIGHT FORMS . . . . Checked and signed
2. LADDER (if installed) . . . . Pulled up
3. HATCH . . . . Closed and locked Pins checked
4. SEAT AND RUDDER PEDALS . . Adjusted for full travel and comfort
5. PARACHUTE—SAFETY HARNESS On and adjusted
6. HYDRAULIC RESERVOIR . . . Normal level— hydraulic pressure 0
7. AIR BRAKE BOTTLE . . . . 450 psi. minimum
8. BOMB INTERVALOMETER . . Off
9. HYDRAULIC SELECTOR VALVE . On SYSTEM
10. CROSSFEED—BOMB BAY . . OFF
11. TANK SELECTORS . . . . . Both on MAIN
12. CARBURETOR HEAT . . . . COLD
13. CARBURETOR FILTER . . . . Direct
14. WING FLAP CONTROL . . . Neutral
15. FLIGHT CONTROLS . . . . Unlocked and checked for movement and travel
16. MIXTURE CONTROLS . . . . IDLE CUT-OFF
17. PROP CONTROLS . . . . . Full INC RPM
18. THROTTLES . . . . ¼ open
19. LANDING GEAR LEVER . . . DOWN
20. BLOWERS . . . . LOW
21. AIR BRAKE LEVER . . . . Safetied on RELEASE
22. MANIFOLD PRESSURE DRAIN . OFF
23. PARKING BRAKES . . . . On, hydraulic pressure up
24. BOMB BAY DOOR CONTROL . NEUTRAL
25. CIRCUIT BREAKERS . . . . All up
26. BOMB PANEL . . . . . . All switches OFF or NEUTRAL
27. GUN PANEL . . . . . . All switches OFF
28. BATTERY SWITCHES . . . . ON (unless external power is used)
29. COWL FLAPS . . . . . . Open
30. OIL COOLER DOORS . . . . As desired

RESTRICTED

STARTING ENGINES

Start the right engine first.

Check   *Must Be*

1. FIRE GUARD . . . . Stand clear
2. MASTER IGNITION . . . . ON
3. RIGHT BOOSTER PUMP . . . On LOW BOOST
4. ENERGIZE RIGHT ENGINE . . Approximately 10 seconds
5. PRIME RIGHT ENGINE . . . Approximately 3 seconds
6. ENGAGE RIGHT ENGINE . . . Continue to energize
7. MAGNETO SWITCH . . . . BOTH (after engine turns over)
8. MIXTURE CONTROL . . . . Move to AUTO RICH when engine fires
9. SET THROTTLE . . . . . . To 800 rpm
10. OIL PRESSURE . . . . . . Pressure within 30 seconds, otherwise shut engine off and investigate.
11. BOOSTER PUMPS . . . . . Right booster OFF Left booster on LOW BOOST
12. BOMB BAY DOORS . . . . Call gunner. Signal alert crew to clear bomb bay doors. Close when clear.

Start Left Engine.
Repeat steps 1-11 above to start the left engine.

60   RESTRICTED

Starting Tips

1. If engine does not fire, advance mixture control to AUTO RICH for not more than 3 seconds with engine still engaged. Return mixture control to IDLE CUT-OFF until engine fires regularly, then advance to AUTO RICH.

(**Caution:** Fire may result if blower section is flooded.)

2. If engine is flooded, open throttle to full forward position with mixture control in IDLE CUT-OFF and engine still engaged, then return throttle to ¼ open.

3. Do not continue to operate the starter for more than 60 seconds or it will burn out.

In cold weather prime the engines more than you do in warm weather. See "Cold Weather Operation."

AFTER STARTING ENGINES

Check	Must Be
1. RADIO	On
2. HYDRAULIC PRESSURE	1000 psi
3. TOWER	Call for taxi instructions
4. REMOVE CHOCKS	Give thumbs-up signal

TAXIING

The natural tracking characteristics of the tricycle landing gear make the A-26 especially easy to taxi. Because of this you may have a tendency to pick up too much speed when taxiing straight, necessitating either excessive use of the brakes or fast turns which put dangerous overloads on the gear.

Don't be a taxicab driver. Flashy, hot-pilot ground handling goes hand in hand with sloppy flying. Remember that all airplanes have their limitations on the ground as well as in the air. Develop a smooth, coordinated taxiing technique. There are only a few simple taxiing rules to observe:

1. Always roll straight ahead for a few feet before attempting a turn.
2. Baby your brakes. Good taxiing technique requires a minimum of braking action. Smooth coordination of the throttles and rudder will do the job.
3. Think ahead. Be alert. Be cautious. Avoid last-minute decisions that mean slamming on the brakes and making abrupt turns.
4. Know your terrain. Don't taxi into soft or rutted ground. Examine it first if you are taxiing on a strange airport.
5. Be prop-clearance cautious. Remember that the propeller tips clear a hard surface runway by only 15 inches.
6. Taxi slowly. Use your throttles and rudder, and where necessary, brakes, in one coordinated operation. You can maintain normal taxiing speed with throttles closed (500-600 rpm).
7. **When you park, slow the airplane down evenly, maintaining equal brake pressure so the nosewheel remains straight when the airplane stops.**

Baby Your Brakes

Taxiing Tips

Good coordination is the main thing to achieve. To make a smooth coordinated turn, avoid abrupt use of your brakes. Don't be a rocking-horse pilot. Rough braking control puts unnecessary strain on the nose gear.

Think ahead. On taxiing down the ramp for any stop or turn, slowly apply pressure on your brake pedals at least several hundred yards before you turn, thereby checking your brakes before you actually need them and insuring smooth braking action.

Always slow your airplane down to at least a fast walk before attempting a turn. Before you park, be sure there is nothing behind the airplane that will be damaged by prop wash.

INITIAL FLIGHT RUN-UP AND CHECK

Your engine run-up and check just before takeoff is your last opportunity to detect faulty engine operation.

Don't become mechanical. Think *what* you're doing and *why* you are doing it. The steps listed here are the minimum for safety. A short-cut in engine run-up is a short-cut to trouble.

Run-up both engines together

1. **IDLE YOUR ENGINES AT 1000 RPM UNTIL**
   a. Oil temperature is . . . . . 40°C.
   b. Oil pressure is . . . . . 50 psi min. and relatively steady.
   c. Cylinder-head temperature is . 120°C, min.

Important Even in coldest weather never attempt to hasten cylinder-head warm-up by closing engine cowl flaps.

2. **THROTTLES** . . . . 1700 rpm
3. **PROP CONTROLS** . . . . . Move full aft, then full forward (repeat and lock).

Note Allow full drops of rpm before returning controls to full forward position. This is to get full circulation of warm oil into the propeller dome to insure maximum efficient propeller governor control.

4. **GENERATOR SWITCHES** . . . Both ON
5. **AMMETERS** . . . . Operating
6. **BLOWERS** . . . . Checked

RESTRICTED

BEFORE TAKEOFF

1.	MAGNETOS (Both engines 2000 rpm)	Checked Allowable drop 100 rpm
2.	TRIM TABS	As desired
3.	FUEL SUPPLY	Sufficient
4.	FUEL SELECTORS	Main tanks, bomb bay off
5.	CARBURETOR AIR.	COLD
6.	WING FLAPS	As needed (minimum 15°)
7.	MIXTURE CONTROLS	AUTO RICH
8.	PROP CONTROLS	INC RPM
9.	BOOSTER PUMPS	HIGH BOOST
10.	ENGINE INSTRUMENTS . . .	WITHIN LIMITS
	a. Cylinder-head temperature. .	150° to 205°C
	b. Oil temperature	60° to 90°C
	c. Oil pressures	60 to 80 psi
	d. Fuel pressure	15 to 22 psi
11.	FLIGHT INSTRUMENTS . . .	NORMAL
	a. Turn Indicator	Set with magnetic compass and uncaged.
	b. Artificial Horizon	Uncaged and level.
	c. Altimeter.	Runway elevation
	d. Vacuum Selector Valve . .	Check operation both engines.
12.	COWL FLAPS	As desired
13.	OIL COOLER DOORS	As desired
14.	BATTERIES AND GENERATORS .	ON

TIPS FOR CHECKING MAGNETOS

a. Turn right engine mag switch from BOTH to RIGHT and back to BOTH; then LEFT and back to BOTH. Keep your eye on the right tachometer for a drop of 100 rpm, maximum. A drop of from 0 to 100 rpm is allowable. Allow your tachometer needle to drop and become steady before returning switch to BOTH, but do not run on one magneto for more than 5 seconds. Return mag switches to BOTH momentarily after each check to allow the engine to regain rpm before checking the other mag.

b. Look outside at your right engine cowling and repeat your magneto check. Rough or faulty operation that does not show up on your tachometer reveals itself by unusual shaking and trembling of the engine cowling.

Before Takeoff Check

This final check is in logical sequence. Do not deviate from it. **Any short cut you make is a short cut to trouble.** Remember, a smart pilot makes his final check not just because the book says so, but to determine for himself whether to accept the airplane for flight or taxi it back to the line.

Don't be too proud to return your airplane to the flying line if everything does not check within the allowable limits. **You can't have a better reputation in the Air Forces than that of being a fussy pilot.**

Make sure your gunner knows that it is his responsibility to have the top turret guns locked forward for all takeoffs and landings.

RESTRICTED

TAKEOFF

Because of its inherent stability, tricycle gear, and abundant power, A-26 takeoff is effortless and easy.

Takeoff logically starts with turning your plane so you have a clear view of the base leg, final approach, and runway. When the final approach is clear and you have received permission from the tower to take off, take the runway. **Never take the runway without permission from the tower.**

Turn easily onto the runway and line up. As soon as you are rolling straight, advance the throttles, using smooth accelerated movement to 52″ Hg. Make the throttles snug, but do not lock them. Do not use brakes on takeoff except in emergency. Coordinating throttle and rudder gives you adequate directional control.

As you start to accelerate down the runway, quickly check:

1. Rpm.
2. Cylinder-head temperature.
3. Oil pressure.
4. Oil temperature.
5. Fuel pressure.

You do not have time for exact readings. Just be certain that none of the instruments exceed the red-line limits.

It is not necessary to lift the nosewheel off the runway before takeoff. Lifting the nosewheel too high off the runway actually slows you down and gives you a longer takeoff run.

When you reach takeoff speed (125 mph normally loaded at 31,000 lbs. See Stalling Speed Chart, page 72), ease the airplane smoothly off the ground with one definite motion. It's good technique to feel the weight of the nosewheel as you go down the runway, but A-26 takeoff requires no tricks or special procedures. It is as simple as ABC.

A. Line up with runway and ease power on.
B. Maintain directional control with rudder and throttles.
C. At 125 mph, fly airplane off the ground.

Takeoff Tips

As soon as you are airborne, it may be necessary to carry considerable back pressure on the control column because of the drag of the wheels. Do not trim the airplane at this point; it merely magnifies the amount of opposite trim you need as soon as you retract the wheels. Concentrate on attaining single engine speed (135 mph) without losing altitude.

As soon as you're safely airborne and there is no danger of settling back down on the runway, retract your landing gear. **Never brake** your wheels before retracting them.

Important: You may have a tendency to ease the control column forward unconsciously as you reach for the landing gear handle. Be extremely careful to avoid this tendency, because at this time you have precious little altitude and cannot afford to lose any of it.

As the landing gear retracts, the center of gravity of the airplane shifts aft, causing the nose to rise sharply. After you are safely past 135 mph (single engine speed at normal gross weight), reduce throttle settings to rated power (see Cruise Control Chart) and climb the airplane at 170 mph. Place the flap handle in the UP position and trim for proper climb attitude. Return landing gear and flap handles to neutral.

Short-field Takeoff

Short-field takeoff is one of the most important maximum performance maneuvers you learn in the A-26. You may never need to squeeze the most out of your airplane on takeoff in the continental United States, but in the small operational fields in the war theaters, short-field takeoff becomes usual instead of unusual procedure.

The short-field takeoff in this airplane differs little from the normal takeoff.

For short-field takeoff:

1. Use every inch of available runway. **Line up with your nosewheel straight.**

2. Use ½ to ¾ flaps.

3. Hold your brakes and advance throttles to 40" Hg.

4. Release the brakes evenly, and as you start to roll, advance the throttles quickly to 52" Hg., maintaining directional control with the throttles and rudder.

5. Fly the airplane off the ground at minimum takeoff speed (see Stalling Speed Chart).

Crosswind Takeoff

Crosswind takeoff presents little or no problem in the A-26. With the tricycle gear there is little tendency for the airplane to weathercock on the takeoff run. When you are airborne, correct for the crossdrift.

CLIMB AND CRUISE

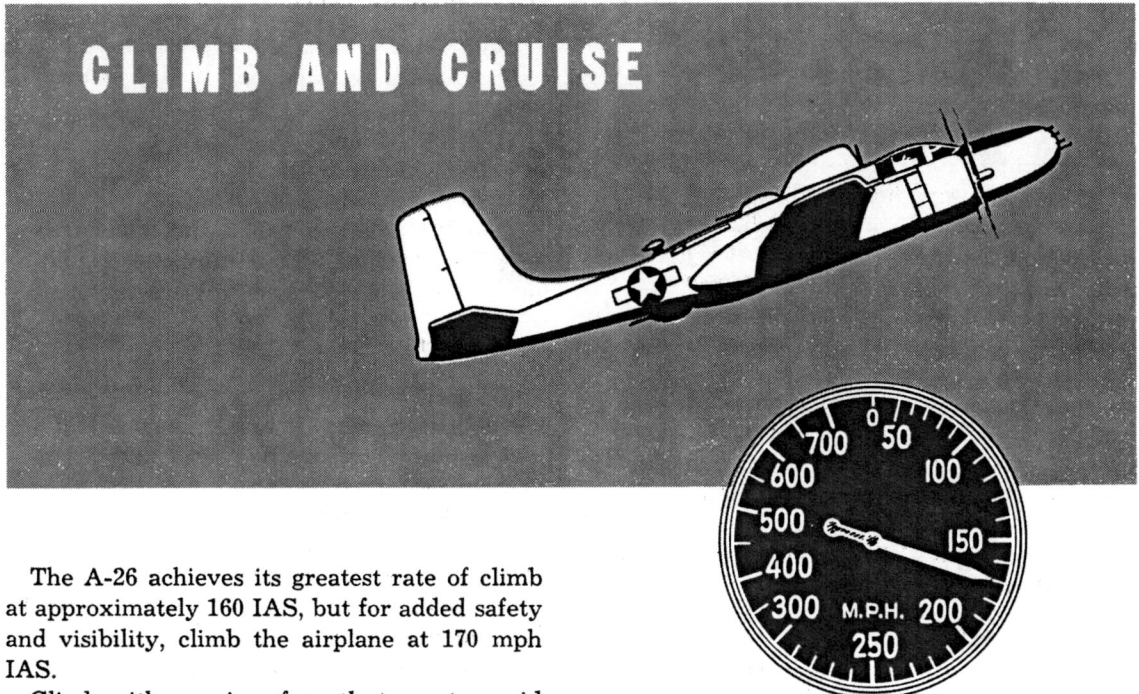

The A-26 achieves its greatest rate of climb at approximately 160 IAS, but for added safety and visibility, climb the airplane at 170 mph IAS.

Climb with a series of gentle turns to avoid blind spots in forward vision.

Check your oil and cylinder-head temperatures frequently and make certain they stay within operating limits during the climb.

Always climb with the mixture control in AUTO RICH.

Be comfortable. After you have established the proper airspeed and attitude, trim your airplane so it climbs hands-off.

Don't become a trim-cripple. Fly the airplane first—then trim for comfort.

Leveling Off

Climb to approximately 500 feet above desired cruising altitude before you begin to level off.

After leveling off, slowly reduce your power settings to normal cruise (see Cruise Control Chart), then lower the airplane's nose and descend to cruising altitude. This is an old airline pilot's trick to attain the proper **flight attitude**. It can mean added airspeeds of 5-10 mph at the same power settings.

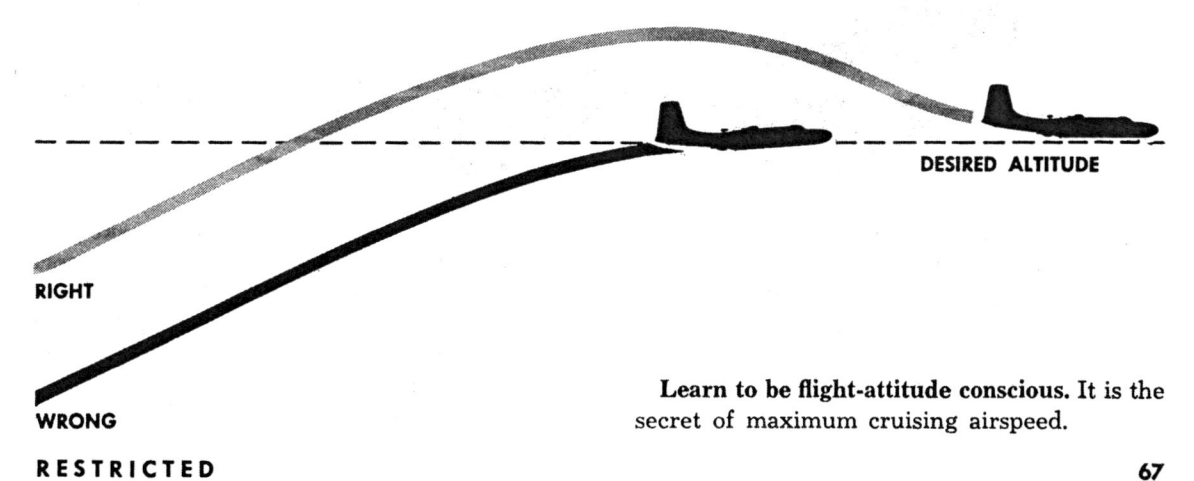

RIGHT

WRONG

DESIRED ALTITUDE

Learn to be flight-attitude conscious. It is the secret of maximum cruising airspeed.

RESTRICTED

Next turn your booster pumps off one at a time, and keep an eye peeled on your fuel pressure gage to make sure that your pressure stays within operating limits. The high power settings required for takeoff and climb draw a much larger amount of fuel to the carburetor. You need your booster pumps for this extra load until you have established your normal cruise.

Adjust your cowl flaps and oil cooler doors as soon as possible to maintain proper engine operating limits. Carrying them open more than is needed creates burbles that cut your airspeed as much as 10 mph.

Be alert. Check your instruments and make sure all your temperatures and current power settings are within proper limits before you move the mixture control to AUTO LEAN.

Here's an important mixture control tip: **Never use AUTO LEAN when you are operating above blue-line limits.**

Trimming Technique

Remember that careful trimming enables you to squeeze that extra 5 mph more out of the airplane at any power setting. Rough overtrimming is a sure mark of poor pilot technique.

Observe These Trimming Rules:

1. Hold airplane straight and level.
2. Trim to relieve manually held pressures:
   a. Trim elevators.
   b. Trim rudders.
   c. Trim ailerons.
3. Release controls to test trim.
4. Check needle and ball. Make minor corrections as needed. Your airplane is not trimmed unless needle and ball are centered.

Stay Alert—Don't Goof Off

Develop the habit of making a **complete cockpit check** at regular intervals during flight. Many an otherwise good pilot who knows and follows correct procedures and uses good technique, has goofed off in flight to wake up later highly embarrassed to find, for example, that he has run a tank dry and lost an engine.

And don't think it can't happen to you! On long flights engine noise, vibration, and concentration cause fatigue. And fatigue causes a good pilot to goof off **unless he forces himself to check his cockpit completely every 15 minutes.**

Remember, it only takes a few seconds—it may save a lifetime!

POWER CONTROL

A knowledge of cruise control will serve you in three important ways:
1. It will give you absolute and dependable fuel consumption estimates.
2. It will give you top operating efficiency for your airplane under any normal or abnormal conditions.
3. It will reduce engine wear and make your already dependable engine performance that much more dependable.

You may be flying over great stretches of water. It is imperative that you know cruise control to make certain that you have fuel enough to get to the target and back.

RESTRICTED

Your R-2800 series engines are designed for definite loads and have definite limits. The main limitations of your engines are:
(LOW BLOWER, AUTO LEAN, AN-F-28 grade 100/130 fuel)

BLOWER RATIO	BHP	RPM	BMEP
LOW	1100	2100	150
HIGH	975	2100	140

When any of these limits are exceeded, the engine is operating under stresses it was not designed for and continued operation may lead to engine failure. Remember, the engine is designed for certain pressures, called **designed BMEP** (brake mean effective pressure). Theoretically, peak engine efficiency means operating at this **designed BMEP**. Operating over this limit results in detonation, valve burning and engine strain which, if prolonged, will cause engine failure.

Look at it this way. Most engine wear is caused by friction, so the lower you keep your rpm and still keep within engine limits the less friction you will have. As rpm is reduced, fuel consumption is reduced proportionately because there are less explosions per minute. For example, at 5000 feet it is better to cruise with 1720 rpm and 34" manifold pressure than it would be to get the same power by pulling 30" and 2000 rpm.

MANIFOLD PRESSURE

DENSITY ALTITUDE	STANDARD TEMPERATURE °C						
10000	−5	31.9		F. T.			
9000	−3	32	32.2		F. T.		
8000	−1	32.5	32.8	32.5		F. T.	
7000	1	32.5	32.8	33	32.8		
6000	3	33.3	33	33.3	33.7	33	
5000	5	33.6	33.3	33.6	34.1	33.7	33
4000	7	34	33.7	34.2	34.1	34.1	33.7
3000	9	34.2	34.2	34.5	34.9	34.5	34.2
2000	11	34.4	34.5	34.8	35.2	35	34.6
1000	13	34.6	34.7	35.3	35.6	35.3	35
SEA LVL.	15	35	34.7	34.8	35	35.2	35.3
RPM		2080	2000	1900	1800	1700	1600
BHP		1070	1030	980	930	875	820
GALS/HR. (APPROX.)		168	158	149	140	131	123
IAS (APPROX.)		262	260	255	248	243	235

ENGINE CALIBRATION

P & W Double WASP
R-2800-27-71,-79
AN-F-28
GRADE 100/130
AUTO LEAN
LOW BLOWER
BMEP 145 ± 2½%—
STANDARD AIR

INSTRUCTIONS FOR USE

1. To find density altitude.
   A. Set altimeter at 29.92.
   B. For each 10° C. difference from standard temp. (Standard on chart and free air temp. gage), add 1000 ft. to altimeter reading if warmer, subtract 1000 ft. if colder.
   C. Result of "A" and "B," above, gives density altitude.
2. To make manifold pressure adjustments.
   A. Find density altitude (step 1, above).
   B. For each 10° C. difference between standard temp. *for the density altitude and the carburetor air temp. gage*, add 1" MP if warmer, subtract 1" MP if colder.
   C. Result of "A" and "B" will correct operating conditions to standard, as charted.
   Example: Altimeter reads 5000 ft. with 29.92 setting. Free air temp. 25° C., carb. air temp. 15° C. BHP of 930 is desired. By step 1 density altitude is found to be 7000 ft. By step 2 MP is increased from 32.8" to 34".

Study chart on page 69. It will give you fuel consumption for various power settings from sea level to 10,000 feet. At first glance the manifold pressure may seem unusually high for lower rpm settings, but remember that the engine benefits materially by maintaining power with reduced engine speed and high manifold pressure, rather than by reduced manifold pressure and high rpm.

You will notice that the manifold pressure is approximately 35" for all cruising rpm at sea level. As the altitude is increased manifold pressure should be gradually decreased until at 10,000 feet approximately 32" is given for 2080 rpm. This decrease in manifold pressure amounts to about ¼ inch per 1000 feet, so that when a chart is not at hand it should be easy to establish approximately the same settings by knowing this simple relationship between manifold pressure and rpm. Remember that all these figures on the chart are given for cruising flight —LOW BLOWER and AUTO LEAN—and if any one is exceeded the mixture control must be shifted to AUTO RICH immediately.

Use this chart. Get the most out of your fuel and have efficient safe engine operation.

LONG RANGE CRUISE

STUDY THIS CHART

Throughout transitional and tactical training you will receive instructions on how "to get the furthest with the leastest." You will be taught in ground school and in flight training to use the ATC Long Range Cruise Control Chart. ATC has, by flight test and analysis, developed a highly accurate plan of flying great distances on the smallest amount of fuel. The chart on the opposite page represents many hundreds of thousands of hours experience and is so accurate that if followed exactly it will give you dependable fuel consumption figures.

Maximum Endurance

Under unusual weather conditions you may be faced with the problem of waiting the weather out and staying in the air for the longest possible number of hours. To do this:

Fly at lowest safe altitude with airspeed of 150 to 160 mph with manifold pressure 35" and the rpm setting as low as possible to still maintain the airspeed. Theoretically the best airspeed for maximum endurance is one mile per hour above stalling speed. Since this is impracticable and unsafe the low airspeed of between 150 and 160 is recommended because it is possible at this speed to trim the airplane hands off and flub around in the air for a long period of time using as little fuel as 70 to 80 gallons per hour for both engines. This will give you **the greatest time in the air,** not the greatest distance.

Maximum Distance

To make the greatest distance fly with 35" manifold pressure and whatever rpm setting necessary to give you 210 to 215 mph.

Remember:

Longest time in the air 150 to 160 mph
To cover the greatest distance 210 to 215 mph
The manifold pressure for both is 35".

Detailed briefing for any long tactical overwater flight will be furnished you but become familiar with this ATC chart and you will find that long range cruise control is easy and simple to follow.

LONG RANGE CRUISE CHART A-26B-C

Continued

Legend

- **C.I.A.S.** — CALIBRATED INDICATED AIR SPEED — STATUTE M.P.H.
- **R.P.M.** — ENGINE REVOLUTIONS PER MINUTE
- **AVER. M.P.** — AVERAGE MANIFOLD PRESSURE — INCHES OF MERCURY
- **LBS/HR** — POUNDS PER HOUR — FUEL FLOW
- **T.A.S.** — TRUE AIR SPEED — STATUTE M.P.H.
- **TIME** — TIME THROUGH 2,000 LB. WEIGHT ZONE — HRS. & MINS.
- **O.A.T.** — OUTSIDE AIR TEMPERATURE — °C OR °F

Conditions

- **ENGINES:** P & W R-2800-71, 79
- **PROPELLERS:** HAMILTON STANDARD
- **CARBURETORS:** PT-13G5
- **FUEL GRADE:** 100
- AUTO LEAN MIXTURE
- COWL FLAPS CLOSED
- ALL GUNS REMOVED

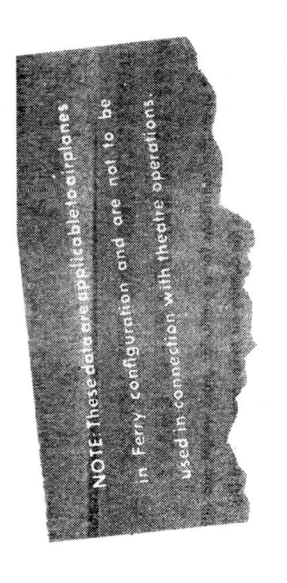

NOTE: These data are applicable to airplanes in ferry configuration and are not to be used in connection with theatre operations.

HIGH BLOWER — GROSS WEIGHT (LBS.) 26,000 TO 24,000

CIAS	RPM	AVER M.P.	LBS/HR	T.A.S.	TIME
182	1970	22.5	708	267	2.49
183	1950	23.0	699	264	2.52
184	2100	20.0	685	261	2.55
185	2020	20.5	675	258	2.58
186	1970	21.0	665	255	3.00
187	1900	21.5	657	252	3.02
188	1850	22.0	649	249	3.05
189	1820	22.5	640	246	3.07
190	1770	23.0	632	244	3.10
191	1720	23.5	624	241	3.12
192	1700	24.0	616	238	3.15
193	1650	24.5	610	236	3.17
194	1620	25.0	604	233	3.19
195	1570	25.5	597	231	3.21
196	1550	26.0	593	229	3.22
197	1520	26.5	589	226	3.24
198	1500	27.0	585	223	3.25
199	1500	27.5	583	221	3.26
200	1500	28.0	580	219	3.27
201	1500	28.5	578	217	3.27
202	1500	29.0	575	215	3.29
203	1500	30.0	574	212	3.29
204	1500	30.5	572	210	3.30
205	1500	31.0	571	208	3.30
206	1500	31.5	570	206	3.30

HIGH BLOWER — GROSS WEIGHT (LBS.) 28,000 TO 26,000

CIAS	RPM	AVER M.P.	LBS/HR	T.A.S.	TIME
182	2050	23.0	745	267	2.41
183	2000	23.5	735	264	2.43
184	1950	24.0	725	261	2.45
185	2100	20.7	711	258	2.49
186	2050	21.2	700	255	2.51
187	1970	22.0	690	252	2.54
188	1920	22.5	681	249	2.56
189	1870	23.0	672	246	2.58
190	1820	23.5	663	244	3.01
191	1770	24.0	654	241	3.03
192	1750	24.7	645	238	3.06
193	1700	25.2	637	236	3.08
194	1670	25.7	630	233	3.10
195	1620	26.2	623	231	3.12
196	1600	26.7	617	228	3.14
197	1570	27.5	614	226	3.15
198	1550	28.0	609	223	3.17
199	1500	28.5	606	221	3.18
200	1500	29.0	603	219	3.19
201	1500	29.5	600	217	3.20
202	1500	30.0	598	215	3.20
203	1500	30.7	596	212	3.21
204	1500	31.2	594	210	3.22
205	1500	31.7	592	208	3.23
206	1500	32.2	590	206	3.23

LOW BLOWER — GROSS WEIGHT (LBS.) 30,000 TO 28,000

CIAS	RPM	AVER M.P.	LBS/HR	T.A.S.	TIME
182	2100	23.5	787	267	2.32
183	2050	24.0	776	264	2.35
184	2000	24.5	765	261	2.37
185	1950	25.0	755	258	2.39
186	2100	21.2	737	255	2.43
187	2050	22.0	726	252	2.45
188	1970	22.5	715	249	2.48
189	1920	23.0	704	246	2.50
190	1870	23.7	694	244	2.53
191	1820	24.2	684	241	2.55
192	1800	25.0	675	238	2.58
193	1750	25.5	665	236	3.00
194	1720	26.0	656	233	3.03
195	1670	26.7	649	231	3.05
196	1650	27.2	642	228	3.07
197	1600	27.7	636	226	3.09
198	1570	28.2	632	223	3.10
199	1550	28.7	628	221	3.11
200	1500	29.0	625	219	3.12
201	1500	29.5	621	217	3.13
202	1500	30.7	619	215	3.14
203	1500	31.5	616	212	3.15
204	1500	32.0	614	210	3.15
205	1500	32.5	612	208	3.16
206	1500	33.0	610	206	3.17

LOW BLOWER — GROSS WEIGHT (LBS.) 32,000 TO 30,000

CIAS	RPM	AVER M.P.	LBS/HR	T.A.S.	TIME
184	2070	24.7	805	261	2.29
185	2020	25.0	794	258	2.31
186	1970	25.5	783	255	2.33
187	2100	22.0	761	252	2.38
188	2050	22.5	750	249	2.40
189	2000	23.2	739	246	2.42
190	1950	23.7	728	244	2.45
191	1900	24.5	717	241	2.47
192	1850	25.0	707	238	2.50
193	1800	25.7	697	236	2.52
194	1770	26.2	687	233	2.55
195	1720	27.0	678	231	2.57
196	1700	27.7	669	228	2.59
197	1650	28.2	662	226	3.01
198	1620	28.7	656	223	3.03
199	1570	29.5	651	221	3.04
200	1550	30.2	646	219	3.06
201	1520	30.7	642	217	3.07
202	1500	31.5	639	215	3.08
203	1500	32.0	635	212	3.09
204	1500	32.7	632	210	3.10
205	1500	33.2	629	208	3.11
206	1500	33.7	626	206	3.12

LOW BLOWER — GROSS WEIGHT (LBS.) 32,000 TO 30,000 (cont.)

CIAS	RPM	AVER M.P.	LBS/HR	T.A.S.	TIME
185	2070	25.5	835	258	2.24
186	2020	26.0	822	255	2.26
187	1970	26.5	810	252	2.28
188	2100	22.7	789	249	2.32
189	2050	23.5	776	246	2.35
190	2000	24.2	764	244	2.37
191	1950	24.7	751	241	2.40
192	1900	25.5	740	238	2.42
193	1850	26.0	729	236	2.44
194	1800	26.7	718	233	2.47
195	1770	27.5	708	231	2.49
196	1720	28.0	698	228	2.52
197	1700	28.7	689	226	2.54
198	1650	29.2	682	223	2.56
199	1620	30.0	675	221	2.58
200	1600	30.5	669	219	2.59
201	1550	31.2	664	217	3.01
202	1520	32.0	659	215	3.02
203	1500	32.5	654	212	3.03
204	1500	33.2	650	210	3.04
205	1500	33.7	646	208	3.06
206	1500	34.5	644	206	3.06

HIGH BLOWER — GROSS WEIGHT (LBS.) 34,000 TO 32,000

CIAS	RPM	AVER M.P.	LBS/HR	T.A.S.	TIME
185	2070	25.5	835	258	2.19
186	2020	26.0	822	255	2.21
187	1970	26.5	810	252	2.23
188	2100	22.7	789	249	2.27
189	2050	23.5	776	246	2.30
190	2000	24.2	764	244	2.32
191	1950	24.7	751	241	2.35
192	1900	25.5	740	238	2.38
193	1850	26.0	729	236	2.40
194	1800	26.7	718	233	2.43
195	1770	27.5	708	231	2.45
196	1720	28.0	698	228	2.47
197	1700	28.7	689	226	2.49
198	1650	29.2	682	223	2.51
199	1620	30.0	675	221	2.53
200	1600	30.5	669	219	2.55
201	1550	31.2	664	217	2.57
202	1520	32.0	659	215	2.58
203	1500	32.5	654	212	2.59
204	1500	33.2	650	210	3.01
205	1500	33.7	646	208	3.02
206	1500	34.5	644	206	3.02

HIGH BLOWER — GROSS WEIGHT (LBS.) 36,000 TO 34,000

CIAS	RPM	AVER M.P.	LBS/HR	T.A.S.	TIME
186	2100	26.5	862	255	2.19
187	2050	26.7	851	252	2.21
188	2000	27.2	839	249	2.23
189	2100	23.7	815	246	2.27
190	2050	24.5	800	244	2.30
191	2000	25.0	787	241	2.32
192	1950	25.7	774	238	2.35
193	1900	26.5	761	236	2.38
194	1850	27.2	750	233	2.40
195	1820	27.7	737	231	2.43
196	1770	28.5	726	228	2.45
197	1750	29.0	716	226	2.47
198	1700	29.7	708	223	2.49
199	1670	30.5	700	221	2.51
200	1620	31.2	692	219	2.53
201	1600	31.7	685	217	2.55
202	1570	32.7	679	215	2.57
203	1520	33.5	674	212	2.58
204	1500	34.2	668	210	2.59
205	1500	34.7	664	208	3.01
206	1500	35.2	660	206	3.02

INSTRUCTIONS FOR THE USE OF A-26 LONG RANGE CRUISE CHART

To obtain aircraft operating conditions for a particular gross weight and altitude:

1. Enter the temperature chart at the outside air temperature, point (A).
2. Proceed vertically to the pressure altitude, point (B). (Pressure altitude is read with altimeter set at 29.92" hg.).
3. Move horizontally, left or right, to proper gross weight bracket and read applicable aircraft operating conditions.
4. As gross weight decreases during flight, move progressively to lighter gross weight brackets to obtain proper operating conditions.
5. Check pressure altitude and outside air temperature periodically and move vertically, up or down, to new operating conditions, if required.

NOTES

For your altitude and weight bracket, set R.P.M. and maintain C.I.A.S. with M.P. A check on the M.P. can be made by adding to the chart values 0.7" hg. per 10° C. (18° F.) that O.A.T. is above the standard temp. at the pressure altitude being flown, (Subtract if O.A.T. is below standard temp.), and an additional 0.3" hg. for each 10° C. (18° F.) that carb. air temp. is above O.A.T. If it is impossible to obtain C.I.A.S. when at full throttle with the R.P.M. shown, increase R.P.M. until desired C.I.A.S. is obtained.

Airspeeds shown are *not* instrument readings, but are calibrated indicated airspeeds. Airspeed must be calibrated and correction may be obtained by flying airspeed calibration course.

This cruise chart was derived from flight testing unpainted A-26B-50-DL and A-26C-25DT airplanes without de-icer boots; with turrets in place, but all guns removed.

RESTRICTED

THIS PAGE INTENTIONALLY LEFT BLANK.

RESTRICTED

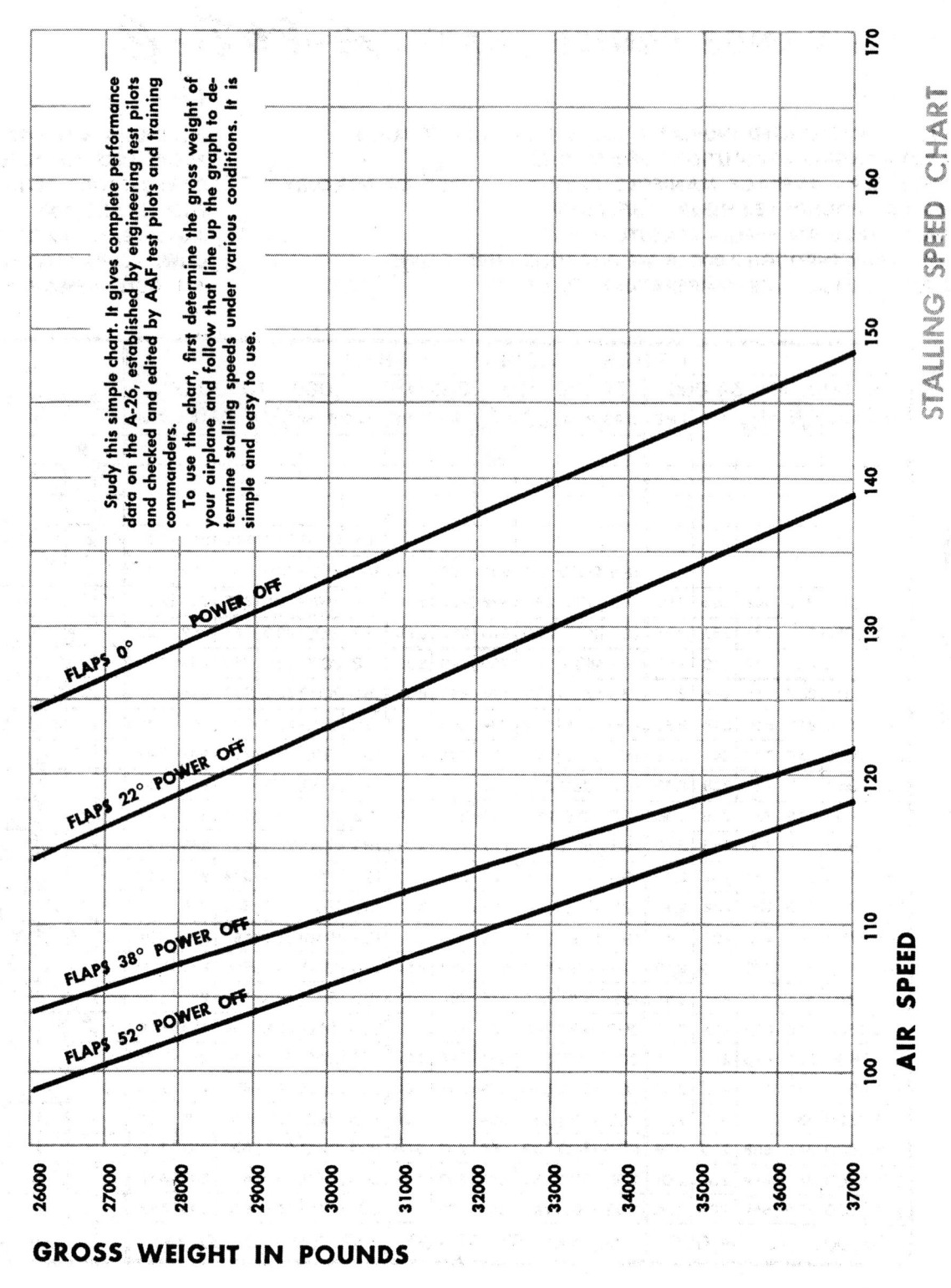

RESTRICTED

STALLING SPEED CHART

Study this simple chart. It gives complete performance data on the A-26, established by engineering test pilots and checked and edited by AAF test pilots and training commanders.

To use the chart, first determine the gross weight of your airplane and follow that line up the graph to determine stalling speeds under various conditions. It is simple and easy to use.

FLAPS 0° POWER OFF
FLAPS 22° POWER OFF
FLAPS 38° POWER OFF
FLAPS 52° POWER OFF

AIR SPEED

GROSS WEIGHT IN POUNDS

72

RESTRICTED

FLIGHT CHARACTERISTICS

The A-26 is a pilot's airplane. If you have not already flown it and discovered that for yourself, a description here of its handling abilities might read like superlative circus publicity. If you have flown the airplane you would find that same description inadequate to the point of understatement. In the meantime—ask the man who flies one.

Like all high-speed specialized aircraft, the A-26 has limitations you must observe strictly.

The following maneuvers are restricted:

a. All acrobatics.

Loops, spins, rolls and violent stalls are prohibited. The airplane has a wingloading of 60 lbs. per square foot normally loaded with flaps up. It was not designed for air circus maneuvers or student acrobatic training.

b. Vertical banks.

Remember that the A-26 has a high wingloading, and your stalling speed increases with your rate of bank. For example, at 31,000 lbs. gross in a 60° bank with the airplane clean and power off, your airplane stalls at 192 mph (42% higher in a 60° bank than in level flight).

All these maneuvers are prohibited chiefly because of the high wingloading of the airplane. Take the airplane designer's and your instructor's word for it. Don't experiment.

STALLING SPEEDS AT NORMAL LOADS (31,000 lbs.)

(See Performance Chart)

POWER ON (12")	125	CLEAN
POWER OFF	135	CLEAN
POWER ON (15")	100	WHEELS AND FULL FLAPS
POWER OFF	105	WHEELS AND FULL FLAPS

DIVING SPEED LIMITATIONS

The airplane accelerates rapidly when you dive it. As your airspeed builds up, the controls become more rigid. **Always allow more altitude for your pullout than you think you need.** Recovery from a high-speed dive is the only flight condition in which trim tab control is recommended to assist manual control. **Be careful. Use your elevator tab slowly and gradually.** At first there is little or no appreciable effect, but avoid overtrimming because control takes hold very quickly.

Anticipate the leveling out after pullout and crank forward the trim used to assist the pullout. Abrupt pullouts are dangerous in the A-26. It is possible to build up loads and stresses that the wings and tail section cannot stand.

When trimming out of a dive, handle the elevator trim wheel with great caution.

GROSS WEIGHT	DIVING SPEED LIMITATIONS
26,000	425 IAS
32,000	400 IAS
35,000	360 IAS

TIPS ON FLIGHT CHARACTERISTICS

To make a coordinated turn, lead with your aileron and, as you settle into your turn, follow through with the rudder. As you continue in the turn there is an increasing necessity for back pressure on the control column. This is caused by the non-servo trim tabs.

The A-26 stalls normally and has no tendency to drop either wing. The wing roots stall out first, giving a definite shuddering effect and plenty of warning before you reach the actual stall. When it stalls, the nose drops straight and rapidly.

Be a pig for altitude while getting acquainted with the A-26. Don't forget that it has an extremely high wingloading and needs plenty of room for recovery.

LANDING

The A-26 lands differently from any other airplane. Most airplanes, both tricycle and conventional gear land in a tail-low attitude.

The A-26 lands in an almost level attitude.

To help fix the difference in your mind, have a look at the B-25 and B-26 below.

Now look at the A-26 landing attitude. The A-26 lands in an almost level attitude with the nosewheel just off the runway. **Never land the A-26 in a tail-low attitude.**

B-25 LANDING ATTITUDE

B-26 LANDING ATTITUDE

ALWAYS LAND THE A-26 IN AN ALMOST LEVEL ATTITUDE

Here's Why:

RESTRICTED

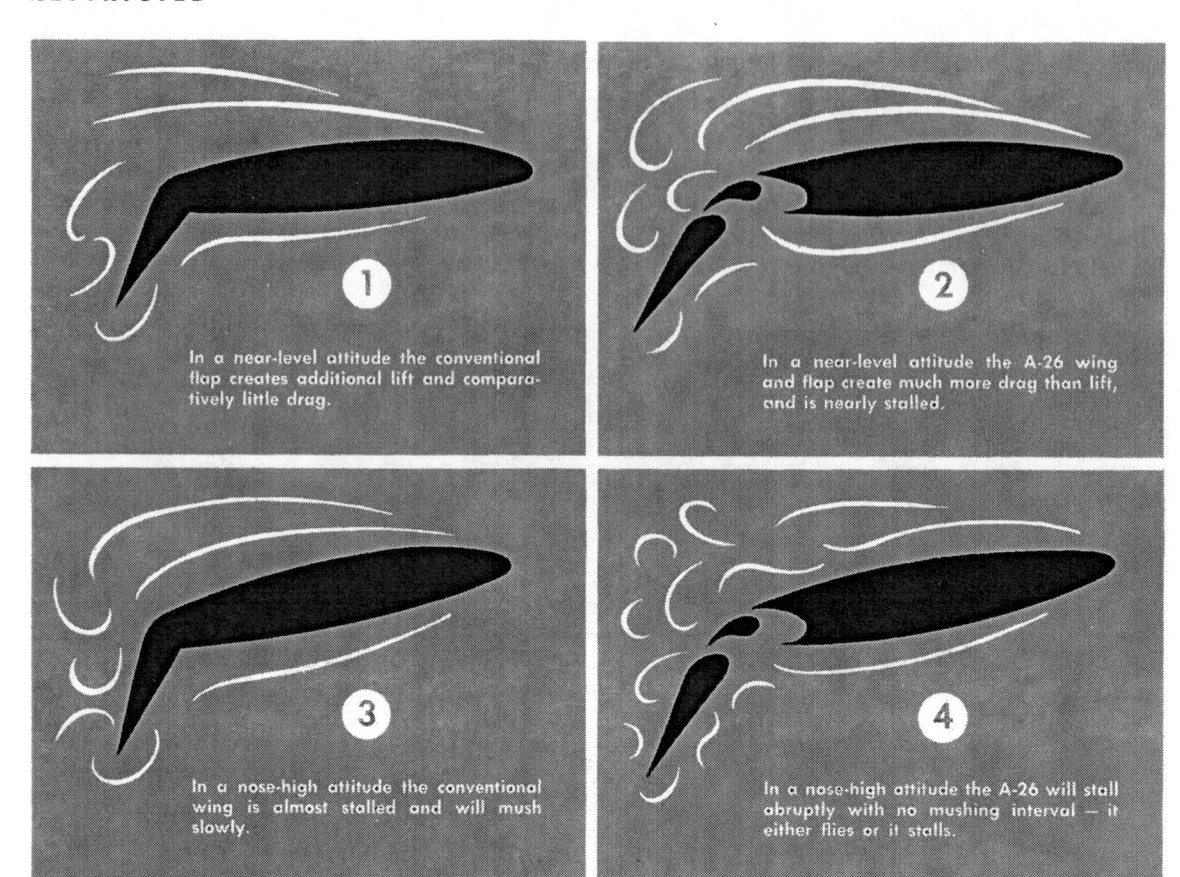

1. In a near-level attitude the conventional flap creates additional lift and comparatively little drag.

2. In a near-level attitude the A-26 wing and flap create much more drag than lift, and is nearly stalled.

3. In a nose-high attitude the conventional wing is almost stalled and will mush slowly.

4. In a nose-high attitude the A-26 will stall abruptly with no mushing interval — it either flies or it stalls.

Here's why: The conventional wing and flap will fly at slow speeds and, in a nose-high landing attitude, will mush and stall out slowly.

The Douglas high speed wing and double-slotted flap will not mush in a nose-high landing attitude but will stall out and slam the nosewheel on the runway. **Always land the A-26 in this almost level attitude.**

> **Nearly half the total A-26 accidents involve landing gear difficulties. These accidents occurred for a number of reasons. It is believed that hard landings are the largest contributing factor to these accidents.**

The A-26 normal landing is a full flap landing.

Actual contact with the runway is not landing but the last step of the landing procedure.

Your landing procedure starts with your initial radio call to the tower.

The tower tells you:
1. Wind direction and velocity.
2. Traffic pattern and field conditions.
3. Altimeter setting.

On your downwind leg of the traffic pattern, drop ¼ flaps for better visibility and to check them for proper operation.

Before landing make the following cockpit check:
1. Fuel supply..........Select fullest tanks
2. Mixture control............AUTO RICH
3. Props ....2400 rpm.
4. Boosters ....HIGH
5. Blower ....LOW
6. Hydraulic pressure.......850 to 1000 psi.

Turn on your base leg in accordance with local traffic regulations. On most traffic patterns you drop your wheels when the airplane is 90° to the runway (about ½ the width of the base leg).

To Lower Wheels

Move the landing gear lever to the DOWN position momentarily.

Leave the landing gear handle in the DOWN position.

After the gear has extended, make the following checks:

1. Landing gear indicator.
2. Warning light.
3. **Nose gear; make visual check through cockpit floor window.**
4. Hydraulic pressure gage.
5. Visual check of main wheels.

While turning on to your final approach, check your landing gear indicator and warning light for gear down and locked. As an added precaution, visually check all three wheels, as well as your hydraulic pressure gage.

Approach

Line up with the center of the runway as you roll out on the final approach and lower flaps. **Stay lined up with the center of the runway throughout the entire approach.** Adjust your throttles for a constant airspeed and rate of descent, and aim for a spot landing on the first 300 feet of the runway. Use power when necessary and establish a constant glide path during the first half of your approach. Make a normal approach with airspeed approximately 135 mph.

Trim the airplane to relieve excessive control pressures during the final approach.

Landing

A good landing depends on a good flare-out as well as a good approach. One without the other is useless. During final approach and landing always pick up a low wing with rudder. Break your glide smoothly and gradually until the airplane assumes a landing attitude. As you approach this landing attitude after breaking the glide, smoothly retard the throttles and at the same time put additional back pressure on the stick to make a smooth ground contact.

Always fly the airplane onto runway. Avoid a stall landing. If you let the airplane stall completely while it is still in the air it is impossible to hold the nosewheel off the ground.

Anticipate contact with the ground so that you can immediately apply back pressure to hold the nosewheel off.

After the airplane is on the ground and power is completely off, avoid holding the nosewheel too high; lower it onto the runway gently.

You can add drag to shorten the landing roll by putting the mixture controls in IDLE CUT-OFF, which allows the props to windmill. Do this only on short runways when absolutely necessary. Remember to return the mixture control to AUTO RICH before the props stop.

As soon as practicable, apply both brakes gently to test them. At the same time:
1. Turn booster pumps OFF.
2. Put propeller controls full forward.

Slow the airplane by applying pressure on both brakes.

Clear the runway as quickly as possible, and then complete this check:
1. Flaps .... UP
2. Oil cooler doors..OPEN or AUTOMATIC
3. Cowl flaps .... OPEN

Full-flap Landings

Under normal conditions **there is only one correct way to land the A-26, and that is with full flaps.** Remember that the A-26 is a new and advanced airplane. The laminar flow wing and the high-efficiency flap set up entirely new landing problems and a different feel.

The airplane is designed for full-flap landings. With their use and the resulting drag, the landing roll is normal and you need a minimum amount of brakes.

In a ¾-flap landing the airplane literally seems to scoot on the landing roll and excessive use of brakes is unavoidable. The visibility in a ¾-flap landing is restricted by the nose-high attitude. The last ¼-flap extension is all drag, and serves as an effective air brake.

The A-26 full-flap landing does not feel like an A-20 landing or a B-26 landing or like anything else you have ever landed. The high-efficiency flaps are literally air brakes of a totally new design. Remember that during your transition you have to develop a new landing technique.

When you set up your glide path, maintain your airspeed with power. Flare out in a level, not a nose-high, attitude. Fly onto the runway in this level attitude just before the stall occurs. Carry 10″ to 12″ Hg. of power until your main gear touches the runway. **Do not cut your power until you make contact.**

Continue on the landing run holding the nosewheel off the runway until you can ease it on gently.

Be alert. Use back pressure on the control column to keep the nosewheel off the ground until you have slowed down your landing run.

¾-flap Landings

Three-quarter flap landings do not differ much in feel from A-20, B-25, or B-26 landings.

During transition, while you are still making ¾-flap landings, notice the restricted visibility because of the nose-high attitude. Also, notice the airplane's tendency to scoot and not lose speed after making contact with the ground. To offset this, drop full flaps as soon as you have made contact with the ground. You'll be surprised at the extreme efficiency of these new flaps and how they materially shorten your landing roll even after you are on the ground.

Refer to the table showing stalling speeds. Learn and remember the stalling speeds at different loads and flap settings.

Full-flap (Power-off) Landings

Power-off full-flap landings require a higher airspeed, an extremely steep glide path, **and a more gradual flare-out.** You learn these after you have learned normal landings.

No-flap Landings

Your instructor will demonstrate no-flap landings, although under normal operating conditions you never land the airplane without flaps.

If, however, your flaps fail to work and a no-flap landing is necessary, plan your approach with extra caution and keep these things in mind:
1. Visibility is restricted because of the extreme nose-high attitude.
2. The airplane stalls at a much higher airspeed.
3. You need every inch of the runway for effective braking to slow the airplane.
4. Get the nosewheel on the runway as soon as possible to begin braking action.

DRAW TRAFFIC PATTERN OF YOUR FIELD ON THIS PAGE

GO-AROUND PROCEDURE

To land or not to land should never be a question. Either you are set up for a good landing or there are factors in traffic or in your approach that make go-around procedure wise.

It is obvious that if an airplane on the ground threatens to taxi into your landing path, precautionary go-around is absolutely necessary. There are times when go-around may not be absolutely necessary from a danger standpoint. When in doubt, always apply power and go around. If you are not absolutely sure you are set up for a good approach and landing, go around and set up another landing.

It doesn't embarrass seasoned pilots to apply power and go around when they are not completely satisfied with their approach, so don't let it embarrass you. Keep this in mind: **Unless you are set up for perfect landing—go around.**

Keep these two factors in mind on the go-around:

1. Decide early. Don't hold a lengthy debate with yourself about whether to go around. The longer you wait the more critical your position becomes.

2. Be airspeed conscious. Get those throttles on and pick up single engine airspeed as quickly as you can. Know and be deliberate in your procedures.

Procedure

1. Increase power.
2. Raise landing gear.
3. Raise flaps to ¾ extended as soon as possible. Then bring your flaps on up as soon as you have sufficient airspeed and altitude.
4. Reduce power to normal climb setting as soon as flaps are up and you have obtained critical single engine speed.
5. Adjust your cowl flaps and oil cooler doors as necessary.

> As you advance your throttles and raise your gear and flaps the trim changes considerably. Fly the airplane. Then trim if necessary.

If you decide to make your go-around early enough, you may not require full power and thus won't need to change your propeller controls. However, the important factor is airspeed. Never sacrifice airspeed for power.

STOPPING ENGINES

WHEN YOU TAXI TO A STOP BE SURE THE NOSEWHEEL IS TRACKING STRAIGHT AHEAD BEFORE STOPPING THE ENGINES.

There is a logical reason behind the following sequence for stopping engines. Follow it:

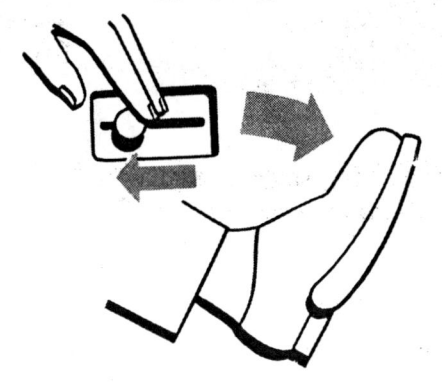

1. Set parking brakes.

2. With engine idling at 1000 rpm, pull right mixture control to IDLE CUT-OFF.

3. Open bomb bay doors—check hydraulic pressure.

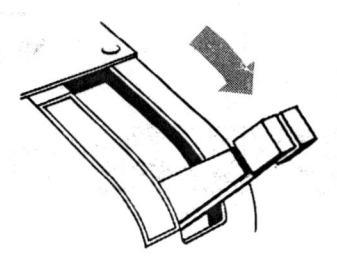

4. Pull left mixture control to IDLE CUT-OFF.

5. Slowly advance throttles full open while props stop turning.

6. After props stop turning, cut all switches, including the radio.

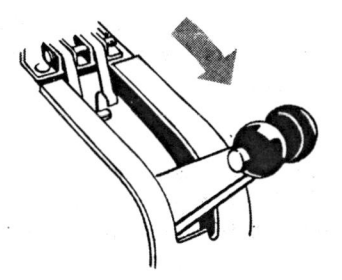

7. Close the throttles and lock the controls.

8. As soon as chocks are in place, release the parking brakes. (If the brakes are hot, leaving the parking brakes on may cause the brakes to warp or freeze.)

9. Complete the Form 1 and 1A.

YOUR FLIGHT IS NOT OVER UNTIL FORMS 1 AND 1A ARE PROPERLY FILLED OUT

NIGHT FLYING

Your ability to fly at night is directly related to your ability as an instrument pilot. It consists of being alert, knowing your cockpit, and relying on your instruments.

Your check for night flying is the same as in the daytime, with this exception: **You must check all your lights for proper operation before you taxi out.**

Night Takeoff

Check your flight instruments carefully before takeoff. **Be sure your landing lights are fully retracted before takeoff.** They set up a violent aileron flutter if they are extended at all. Night takeoff is practically the same as instrument takeoff. Rely on your flight instruments as soon as you leave the ground.

Keep your altimeter going up and your rate of climb on a good, steady climb indication. Check your artificial horizon for wings level. Establish a steady climb and keep power on until the landing gear is up. Then reduce the power and retract the flaps.

Your airspeed picks up rapidly and you will be well over single engine flying speed. Continue your climb at normal power settings.

Never drop the nose to gain airspeed. Too many pilots have flown back into the ground this way.

Don't attempt to fly half contact and half instruments. Stay on instruments until you reach safe altitude.

Night Approach and Landings

Your approach and landing procedure is much the same at night as it is in the daytime, except that after calling the tower on the downwind leg, you extend your landing lights and then return switch to the OFF position. This leaves your lights extended and ready for use when you switch them on before landing.

Use a little more speed on the night approach. Turn on your landing lights when you are near the ground.

When making a night landing at a strange field, watch carefully for obstructions. Ask the tower for complete information.

The general tendency is to undershoot at night, so aim your glide path to allow for this.

Test your brakes soon after landing and start to slow up immediately. It is difficult to judge the end of the runway at night.

Tips

Carry a flashlight. Have it handy in case of an emergency.

Clean your windshield.

Use the landing lights only as much as necessary while taxiing.

Taxi slowly and be doubly alert for other airplanes and obstructions.

Keep all unessential lights turned off.

Turn your cockpit lamps down so there is no glare.

EMERGENCIES

SINGLE ENGINE FLIGHT

If you know what to do and how to do it, A-26 engine failure merely means single engine flight and not an emergency at all.

Single engine flight has long been one of the most kicked-around subjects in the AAF. Hangar pilots have been the great experts; they have reached many important decisions. The only trouble with their decisions is that in most cases they are not true. Actually there is nothing unusually complicated or dangerous about A-26 single engine flight or emergencies **if you follow orderly procedure:**

A. Maintain single engine airspeed.
B. Maintain directional control.
C. Be positive and deliberate in your procedure.

Engine failure on a 2-engine airplane is considered an emergency, but if you know what to do and how to do it, engine failure merely means single engine flight and not an emergency at all.

For a green pilot, almost everything unusual that happens in the air is an emergency. For a seasoned pilot almost everything that happens in an airplane can be overcome by an orderly procedure, and the actual emergency stage is seldom reached.

To become proficient in single engine flight, you practice simulated engine failure.

RESTRICTED

Single Engine Flight

In the A-26 there are 11 operations in single engine procedure. Follow these 11 steps. Do not deviate from them.

1. Throttle back slowly on bad engine.
2. Depress feather button on bad engine.
3. Put mixture control in IDLE CUT-OFF on bad engine.
4. Trim rudder.
5. Increase rpm on good engine (if necessary).
6. Increase throttle on good engine (if necessary).
7. Put mixture control into AUTO RICH on good engine (green zone).
8. Vacuum selector valve on good engine.
9. Close cowling and oil cooler doors on bad engine.
10. Cut magneto switch on bad engine.
11. Turn fuel selector valve to bad engine OFF.

After you complete the foregoing procedure, watch operating temperatures of good engine.

Trim the plane to the needle-ball and maintain a cruising attitude to keep airspeed as high as possible.

In cruising flight you will have an IAS of approximately 250 mph when starting single engine practice. The airplane is easy to control at this speed.

After several simulated single engine flights, cut the airspeed down to 150 mph and slowly reduce one throttle to note the great difference in rudder pressure necessary to keep the plane straight and level at lower speeds. By this you can realize how much more rudder pressure it would take if you lost an engine on takeoff with maximum power setting. Therefore, keep in mind that airspeed and engine power are the factors governing the controllability of the airplane while on single engine.

Practice shallow single engine turns both away from and into the dead engine **only if you have single engine airspeed or above.** However, when at lower airspeeds always turn into the good engine.

Never make a quick movement on the controls or change power settings on the good engine in a turn at these low speeds.

Starting Engines in Flight

When starting the engine again, remember to treat it like a cold engine that you are first starting in the morning (determine by cylinder-head temperature).

1. Prop control—Low rpm (back).
2. Open throttles ¼.
3. Turn mag ON.
4. Hold down red feathering button until the prop turns over 800 rpm, and then release it.
5. Push mixture control to AUTO RICH.
6. Set throttle to about 15"; with prop control clear back you will have about 1200 rpm. When cylinder-head temperature rises, increase prop to 1500 rpm and throttle to 33". Then slowly return to normal cruising power after reaching 100°C cylinder-head temperature. Tip: To help increase cylinder-head temperature slow the airplane down to about 160 IAS.
7. Adjust cowl flaps and oil cooler doors as necessary.
8. Trim the airplane while performing the foregoing procedure.

Engine Failure on Takeoff

Engine failure on takeoff requires cool, quick thinking plus correct procedure. If your engine cuts out before you are airborne, cut your power immediately and stop the airplane.

If you are off the ground and it is possible to hold the airplane in the air, your old familiar A B C procedure still holds.

A. Get single engine speed (135 mph) as quickly as possible. (This may mean lowering the nose, even at low altitudes. But get that airspeed up at all costs.)

B. Maintain directional control.

C. Start your procedures immediately. Every single engine emergency happens under slightly different circumstances. While you're learning single engine procedure in the A-26, rehearse in your own mind what you would do if your engine cut on takeoff.

The No. 1 job, of course, is to maintain what airspeed you have and to increase it as rapidly as possible until you reach 135 mph.

The No. 2 job is to get directional control.

No. 3 is to begin orderly procedure to continue single engine flight. It requires split sec-

RESTRICTED

ond decisions and good pilot technique, but **most of all it requires cool thinking!** Don't get rattled. If you lose an engine on takeoff you have your hands full, but if you use your head and know your procedures you won't get hurt.

The most common mistake is reaching for everything in the cockpit in one mad scramble, which often results in feathering or cutting the good engine instead of the bad engine.

If you lose an engine at a critical point during takeoff or climb, don't hesitate to reduce power on the good engine if necessary to maintain directional control. Next, don't hesitate to sacrifice altitude in order to maintain or gain single engine speed. **Do not feather a bad engine if you are getting some power out of it—at least, not until you have passed the critical stage.**

Single Engine Landings

Single engine landings in the A-26 do not differ greatly from normal landings. For single engine landings:

1. Fly your pattern larger and make your turns shallow.

2. Do not lower landing gear until you are sure you will make the field.

3. Make your approach slightly higher to avoid any need of adding a big burst of power at the last moment. Maintain an airspeed of 150 mph on your single engine approach.

4. Use full flaps. But before you drop full flaps make sure the landing is in the bag.

5. Trim as you need to on final approach. You can easily override remaining trim after flare-out.

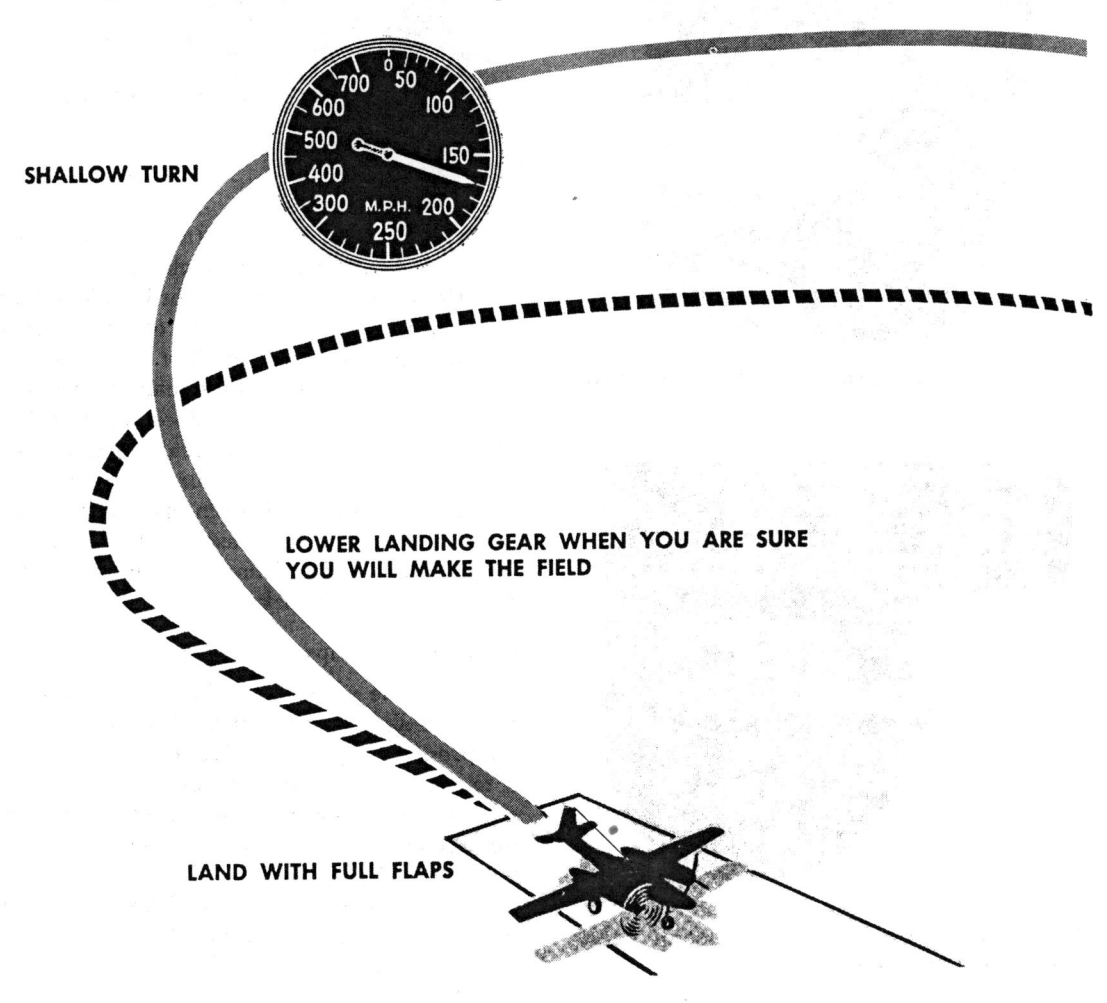

SHALLOW TURN

LOWER LANDING GEAR WHEN YOU ARE SURE YOU WILL MAKE THE FIELD

LAND WITH FULL FLAPS

RESTRICTED

HYDRAULIC SYSTEM FAILURE

The A-26's hydraulic system is well-designed and dependable in operation. But as long as aircraft fly, some hydraulic emergencies will occur, and in the war theaters flak will continue to puncture lines and tanks. So study the diagram and know the hydraulic system.

If you know the system and how to use it, you will find that most hydraulic emergencies are not real emergencies at all.

If the main system fails, be sure of what you are doing. First figure out what your trouble is and then act to correct for it.

To Lower Landing Gear With Emergency System

1. Put the main gear lever in DOWN position.

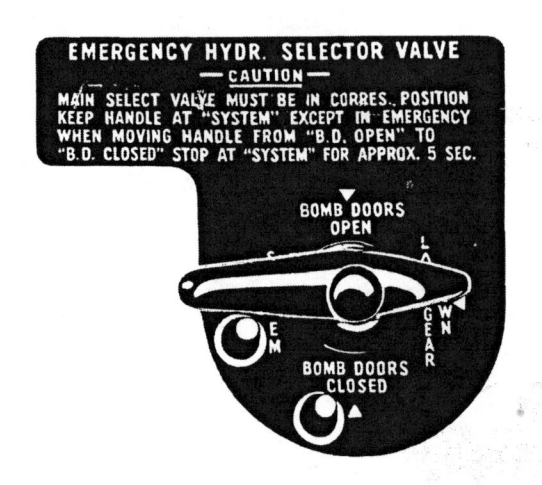

2. Turn emergency hydraulic selector valve to LANDING GEAR DOWN.

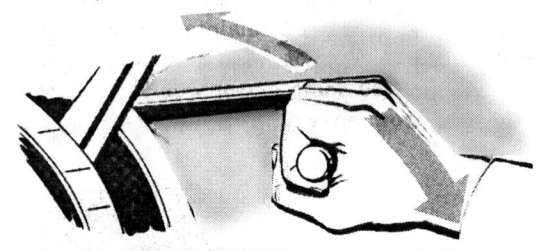

3. Operate hand pump (about 170 strokes are needed to extend and lock the gear).

4. Return emergency selector handle to SYSTEM until you require some other operation.

Your main gear extends first. The nose gear does not start down until the main gear is down and locked. If the nose gear does not start down within 6 strokes after the main gear locks, it indicates insufficient pressure to release the up-lock pin. Release this pin manually by pulling the up-lock pin release on the left side of the pedestal, and continue to pump until nose gear is down and locked.

Landing Gear Tips

If you lose your hydraulic pressure and the gage still shows sufficient fluid in the reservoir, the pressure regulator valve may be stuck. Tap it to see if the vibration frees the poppet valve and allows normal hydraulic pressure to build up. Keep your hydraulic selector valve on SYSTEM.

If your gear does not extend because of fluid loss resulting from a broken line, put all your hydraulic controls in NEUTRAL position.

RESTRICTED

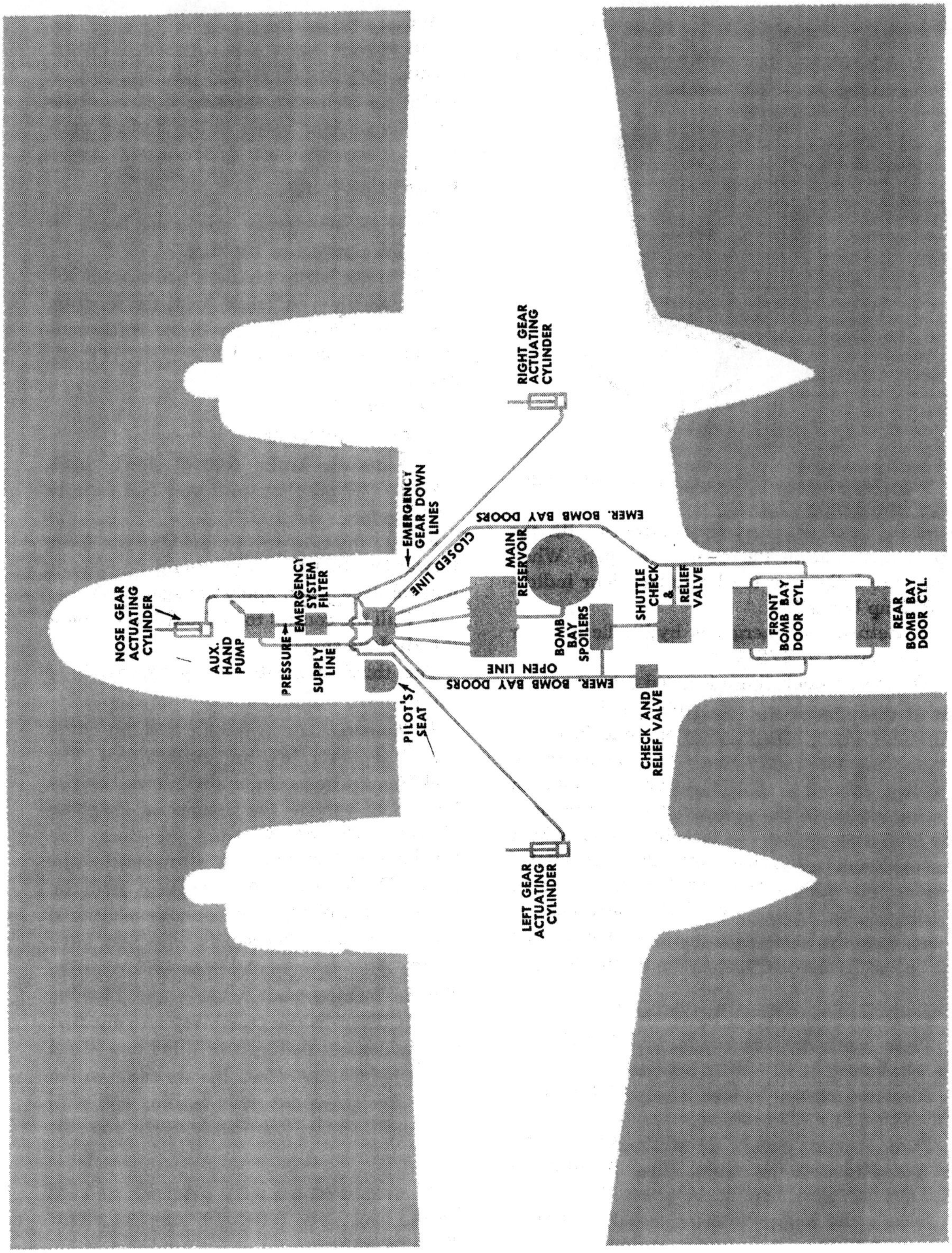
NOSE GEAR ACTUATING CYLINDER
AUX. HAND PUMP
PRESSURE
SUPPLY LINE
EMERGENCY SYSTEM FILTER
PILOT'S SEAT
EMERGENCY GEAR DOWN LINES
CLOSED LINE
OPEN LINE
RIGHT GEAR ACTUATING CYLINDER
LEFT GEAR ACTUATING CYLINDER
EMER. BOMB BAY DOORS
MAIN RESERVOIR
BOMB BAY SPOILERS
EMER. BOMB BAY DOORS
SHUTTLE CHECK & RELIEF VALVE
CHECK AND RELIEF VALVE
FRONT BOMB BAY DOOR CYL.
REAR BOMB BAY DOOR CYL.

Emergency Opening of Bomb Bay Doors

1. Place bomb bay door switch (or handle on earlier models) in OPEN position.

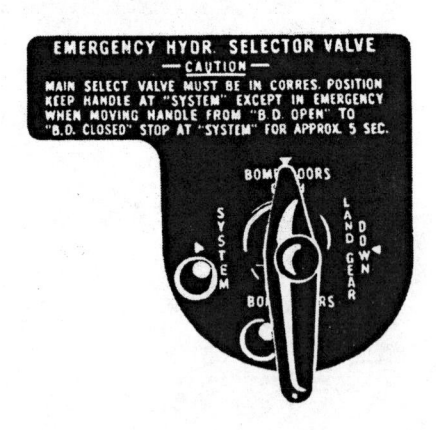

2. Place emergency hydraulic selector valve in DOORS OPEN position.

3. Pump approximately 60 strokes with the hand pump until the doors are open. When they are fully open the bomb bay door indicator lamp burns red.

4. Return the emergency hydraulic selector valve control to SYSTEM.

On most models there is a red salvo knob in front of the pilot at the bottom of the instrument panel which, when pulled, quickly opens the bomb bay doors and salvos the bombs in the bomb bay, as well as wing bombs or tanks on the wing racks. In the gunner's compartment there is also an emergency salvo switch which opens the bomb bay doors and salvos the bombs. However, the gunner's switch does not salvo the wing racks. In case of electrical failure, you can open the bomb doors by an emergency lever below the fire extinguisher in the cockpit.

Emergency Closing of Bomb Bay Doors

1. Place bomb bay door handle (or switch on some airplanes) in CLOSED position.

2. Place emergency hydraulic selector valve in DOORS CLOSED position.

3. Pump approximately 60 strokes on the hand pump to close the doors. When they are closed the indicator lamp burns green.

4. Return the hydraulic selector valve control to SYSTEM.

Important: When operating emergency hydraulic selector valve from DOORS OPEN position to DOORS CLOSED position, stop at SYSTEM for at least 5 seconds, then continue moving the selector valve to the desired position.

Hydraulic Brake Failure

There is an emergency air brake bottle in the A-26 for emergency braking.

The air brake bottle carries a pressure of 450 to 575 psi, which is sufficient for three separate braking applications. The air brake bottle control has three positions: RELEASE, NEUTRAL, and ON.

To use:

1. Break safety wire.

2. Ease the air brake control slowly back toward the ON position until you feel definite braking action.

3. Release the pressure by pushing the lever forward to RELEASE position and the wheels will roll free. Then apply air again and release.

4. Pull the control to ON **and leave it on until the airplane stops.**

The third application is your last braking action.

There is enough air in the air braking bottle for three separate braking applications. The first two applications are to slow down the airplane and to reduce the danger of snapping off the nosewheel or blowing the tires. The third and last braking action is to stop the airplane. Don't forget that an airplane skids on the rim of a blown tire and creates additional fire and crash hazards. That's why you must make the first two applications with caution and avoid locking your wheels and blowing your tires. There is the possibility on your first brake application, that you will find one wheel crabbing before the other. If this happens, let your air straighten out your landing roll with rudder and throttle. Cautiously apply your air again.

AFTER STOPPING DO NOT ATTEMPT TO TAXI BACK TO THE LINE WITHOUT BRAKES. WAIT FOR THE TOW TUG.

FUEL SYSTEM FAILURE

The A-26 fuel system is dependable and well-designed to supply fuel to either engine in case of operating or combat emergency.

The difference between fuel system failure and a critical emergency lies in your knowledge of the fuel system and your ability to picture the system mentally and to take the proper steps to offset the trouble.

It is absolutely necessary that you memorize the fuel flow diagram (page 34).

Study the chart. Set up and solve fuel system failure in your mind.

For example:

QUESTION

You have dropped your bombs, and coming from the target your left main tank, hit by flak, is leaking. Assuming you have used all your fuel except that in the left and right main tanks, what procedure would you follow?

ANSWER

1. Turn crossfeed bomb bay selector valve . . . . . . On Crossfeed
2. Switch left booster pump . . . On HIGH
3. Turn left tank selector valve . . On LEFT MAIN
4. Turn right tank selector valve . OFF
5. When the left main tank is down to 50 gallons: Switch right booster pump . . On HIGH
6. Turn right tank selector valve . On RIGHT MAIN
7. Turn crossfeed bomb bay selector valve . . . . . . OFF

   THEN: When left main tank is completely dry, fuel pressure will drop and the left engine will cut out.

8. Turn crossfeed bomb bay selector valve . . . . . . On CROSSFEED
9. Turn left tank selector valve . . OFF

ALWAYS TURN OFF BOOSTER PUMPS IF NOT NEEDED

RESTRICTED

There are only three points to bear in mind:

1. Study the diagram on page 34. Know your fuel system so well that you carry a picture of it in your mind for any emergency.

2. When failure occurs, locate the source of trouble quickly. Check to determine whether it is a broken line, a punctured tank, or a faulty engine-driven pump.

3. Set your selector valve properly and use your tank booster pumps as needed.

Remember

When using your crossfeed selector valve you are cutting out your bomb bay tank supply and feeding fuel from the tanks on one side of the airplane to the engine on the other side.

FUEL CAN BE SUPPLIED

TO EITHER OR BOTH ENGINES

FROM ANY ONE TANK.

Engine-driven Pump Failure

In case of engine-driven fuel pump failure, don't forget that you have five booster pumps, one for each tank, that (on HIGH boost only) direct an adequate supply of fuel wherever you want it.

These boosters force fuel from the tank through the selector valve and strainer to the faulty engine-driven pump. As pressure builds up and is unable to pass through the faulty engine pump, a bypass valve operates and passes the fuel directly to the carburetor.

ELECTRICAL FAILURE

Partial or even complete electrical failure does not constitute a serious emergency in the A-26 during daytime flight unless you are on a tactical mission.

Complete electrical failure causes failure of:
1. Guns.
2. Bomb release (except manual salvo).
3. Radio.
4. Compass.
5. Flaps.
6. All lighting equipment.
7. Electrical instruments.
8. Cowl flaps and oil cooler flaps.

Complete electrical failure is rare. If it happens, select the nearest available field with a long runway and make a no-flap landing.

Aside from combat emergencies most electrical failures are caused by an overloaded circuit or a weak connection which pops the corresponding circuit breakers or protectors.

You cannot repair electrical failure in flight but you can insure temporary electrical operation by re-setting the circuit breakers in the cockpit. Once you re-set them in they may stay, or it may be necessary to hold them on for such necessary electrical operation as lowering your flaps, keeping the radio alive, or operating your landing lights.

Check your circuit breakers before takeoff. Check your voltage and amperage. With these checks you will find that the A-26 is virtually free of all electrical system failure.

RESTRICTED

PROPELLER FAILURE

Hydromatic propeller failure rarely occurs. If you follow the checklist and engine run-up faithfully, you probably never will have propeller trouble.

Athough rare, these two troubles can happen:

1. Runaway prop because of congealed oil in the dome. This occurs only in cold weather and is the direct result of pilot error. Guard against it by:

    a. Proper oil dilution.

    b. Proper run-up procedure and prop check before takeoff.

2. Faulty propeller governor lines or mechanical failure.

If propeller failure occurs, retard throttle and alternately press and release the feathering button. If this fails to control the overspeeding propeller, try the prop control at different settings. One of these operations usually brings the propeller under control.

If there is a mechanical failure which you cannot overcome by use of the foregoing procedures, feather the propeller. If the prop does not feather, use the throttle to keep the propeller turning fast enough to avoid drag, continue single engine flight, and land at the nearest field.

Feathering Button Failure

When feathering a propeller, if the feathering button fails to pop out when the prop reaches the full-feathered position, pull it out by hand. Otherwise, the blades go right through the feathering cycle and start to unfeather. Pull out a stuck feathering button quickly if the propeller starts to unfeather; otherwise, you risk engine overspeeding and possible damage.

FEATHERING CIRCUIT IS NOT FUSED. IF THERE IS NO FEATHERING ACTION WITHIN 90 SECONDS, PULL OUT THE FEATHERING BUTTON QUICKLY.

BAILOUT–DITCHING–CRASH LANDING

When emergencies arise in the air you have little time to think out the action you wish to take. You must know beforehand exactly what to do and how to do it so that you react instinctively and without hesitation.

Practice your emergency procedures on the ground regularly.

Drill your crew until the time element for each procedure is reduced to a minimum.

Plan ahead for emergencies even though your engines are purring smoothly and your airplane is functioning normally. There is no substitute for preparation—ask the oldtimers.

Don't keep a secret! Use your interphone when emergency occurs. Notify your crew at once of the procedure to be used.

If there is **any** indication of an emergency condition arising, it is only fair to warn your crew in advance so they may be well prepared. If possible, keep them informed at frequent intervals of what is going on, and particularly, of impending impact on crash landing and ditching. Conversation, if used in a normal manner, relieves the tenseness of the situation and promotes clear thinking.

BAILOUT

Pilot Procedure

1. Sound three short rings on alarm bell. Call crew on interphone to "adjust parachute and stand by." Have crew members acknowledge.
2. Turn on IFF. Reel in trailing antenna (if used).
3. Gain as much altitude as possible (if flying low level). Slow airplane to 150 mph.
4. Open bomb bay doors and salvo bombs or torpedoes (to clear exit for rear gunner).
5. Lower one-half flaps to put plane in tail-high attitude.
6. Feather both props (to prevent possible injury to bombardier bailing out through nose exit).
7. Trim airplane for level flight or steady rate of descent at 150 mph.
8. Slide seat back.
9. Lift cockpit escape hatch by pulling emergency handle down hard.
10. Call crew on interphone. Give bailout order. Turn alarm bell on. Hold on firmly as you climb out of seat to prevent blast from blowing you out prematurely.
11. Exit through cockpit escape hatch after other crew members have jumped. Dive flat head first out on to the trailing edge of the wing. The downward flow of air passing over the trailing edge of the wing will force you down and under the horizontal stabilizer with no danger of becoming entangled in any part of the tail section.

> If your airplane is spinning or out of control below 5000 feet, bail out immediately. Always jump toward the inside of the spin.

Crew Procedure

Rear Gunner—Face direction of flight. Bail out head first through bomb bay.

Bombardier—Bail out through bombardier's nose hatch, only if bomb bay doors are closed. (Alternate—Bail out same as pilot).

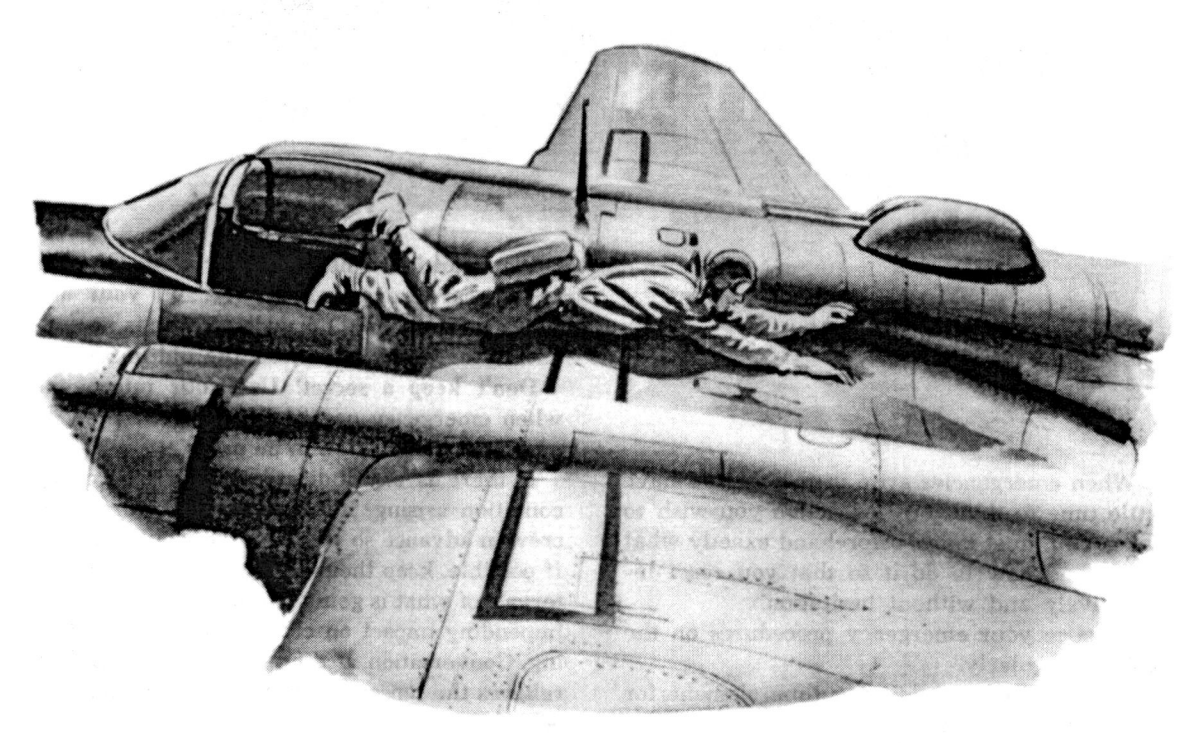

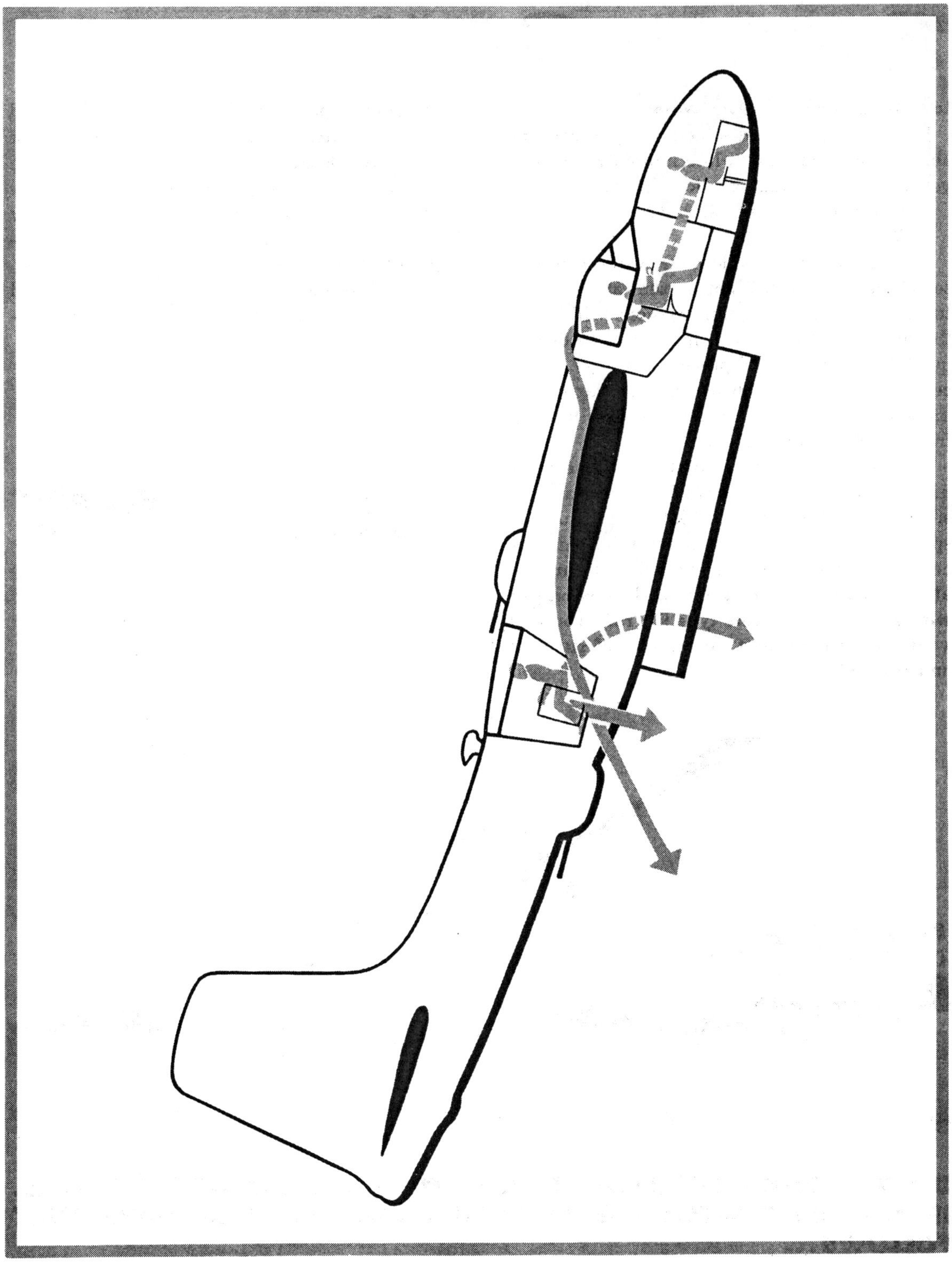

RESTRICTED

Bailout or Ditch?

Low Altitude Bailout Over Water

If your airplane is disabled and you are unable to continue flight while flying over water, you will have to make a quick choice:

a. Will I pull up and bail out?
b. Will I ditch?

Bailout at low altitude over water presents some hazards that are not present at high altitudes. Since many of your missions will be on the deck over water, you may have to decide quickly which survival procedure to use. Make certain your crew is drilled and rehearsed for immediate action if your decision is to pull up from the deck and bail out.

If you decide in favor of bailout, use your high airspeed to gain as much altitude as possible before levelling off and killing off your airspeed as recommended in normal bailout procedure. **If your crew is well drilled in low altitude bailout over water, and is equipped with one man parachute type life raft, you and your crew have a first rate chance of survival and rescue.**

Whenever possible, bailout is recommended instead of ditching. The A-26 does not ditch effectively. Because of its inherent design, the airplane is nose heavy when it stalls in a normal runway landing. On water, this nose heavy tendency often means quick submersion, making survival extremely hazardous. At best, NACA tests show that the A-26 when ditched perfectly stays above water only 30 to 60 seconds.

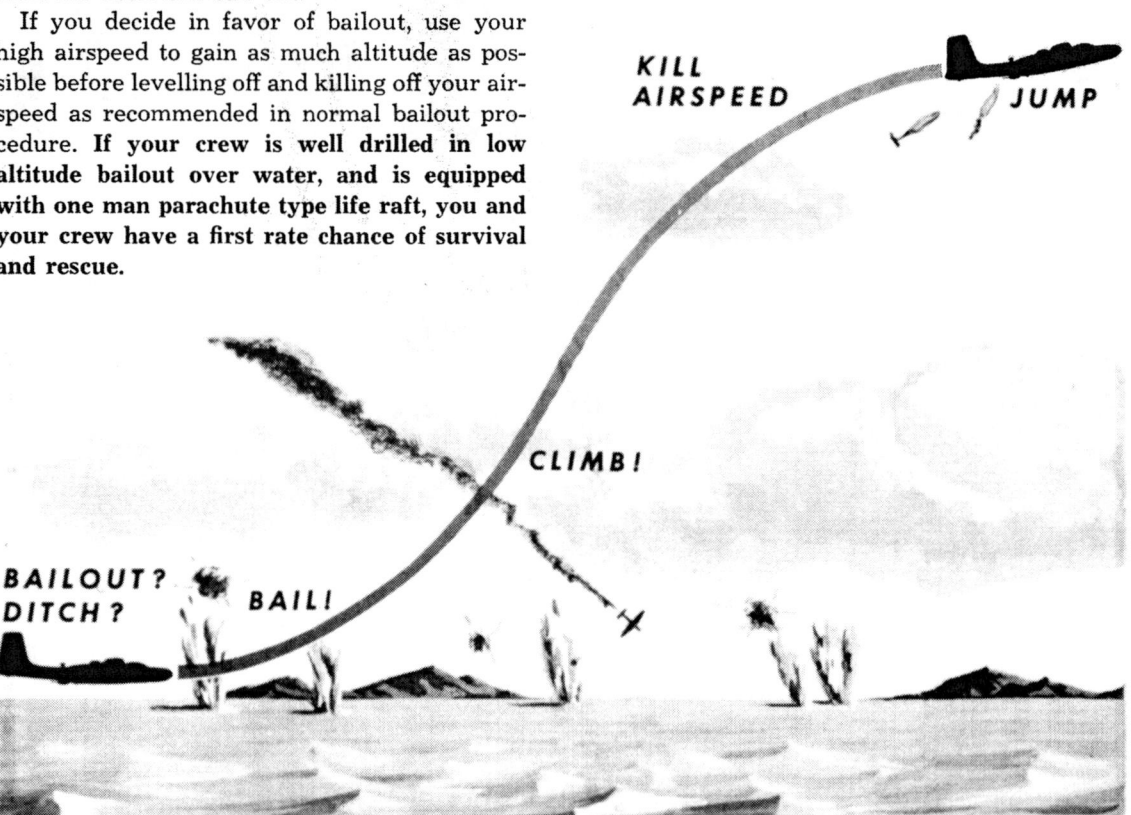

DO NOT DITCH THE A-26 UNLESS YOU HAVE NO OTHER CHOICE. IF YOU MUST DITCH THE AIRPLANE, USE THE PROCEDURE THAT FOLLOWS...

RESTRICTED

DITCHING

Ditching an airplane presents a series of problems which vary under different conditions. The chance of survival in ditching an A-26 is good only if the pilot has drilled his crew so often that each member knows his specific duty in case of emergency. **The safety and survival of your crew depend on you. Make ditching drill a must.**

There may be swells but no wind.

The wind may be blowing across, rather than with the swells. A high wind produces large waves and an extremely rough sea.

Follow this general rule: If you see white crests ditch your airplane in the trough of the waves or swells.

If you see streaks of foam or spray blowing off the tops of the waves ditch directly into the wind.

Approach and Touch-down

Plan your approach and touch-down just as if you were picking out a smooth pasture for a belly landing. Make your actual touch-down in the trough of the waves if the winds are 35 miles per hour or less.

Touch-down directly into the wind only if the surface wind appears to be over 35 miles per hour or if there are no swells.

Remember, you still have to be rescued from the water after you have safely ditched your airplane.

When flying over water ask yourself these questions:

1. Where is the nearest land?
2. Is the wind blowing toward the land?
3. Is the wind blowing with or across the swells?
4. Chances of rescue (after bailout or ditching) by surface ships in the search area?
5. Rough sea—better to have crew jump?

HOW TO DETERMINE WIND VELOCITY

A few white crests ... 10 to 20 mph.
Many white crests ... 20 to 30 mph.
Streaks of foam .... 30 to 40 mph.
Spray from crests .... 40 to 50 mph.

CREW POSITIONS FOR DITCHING

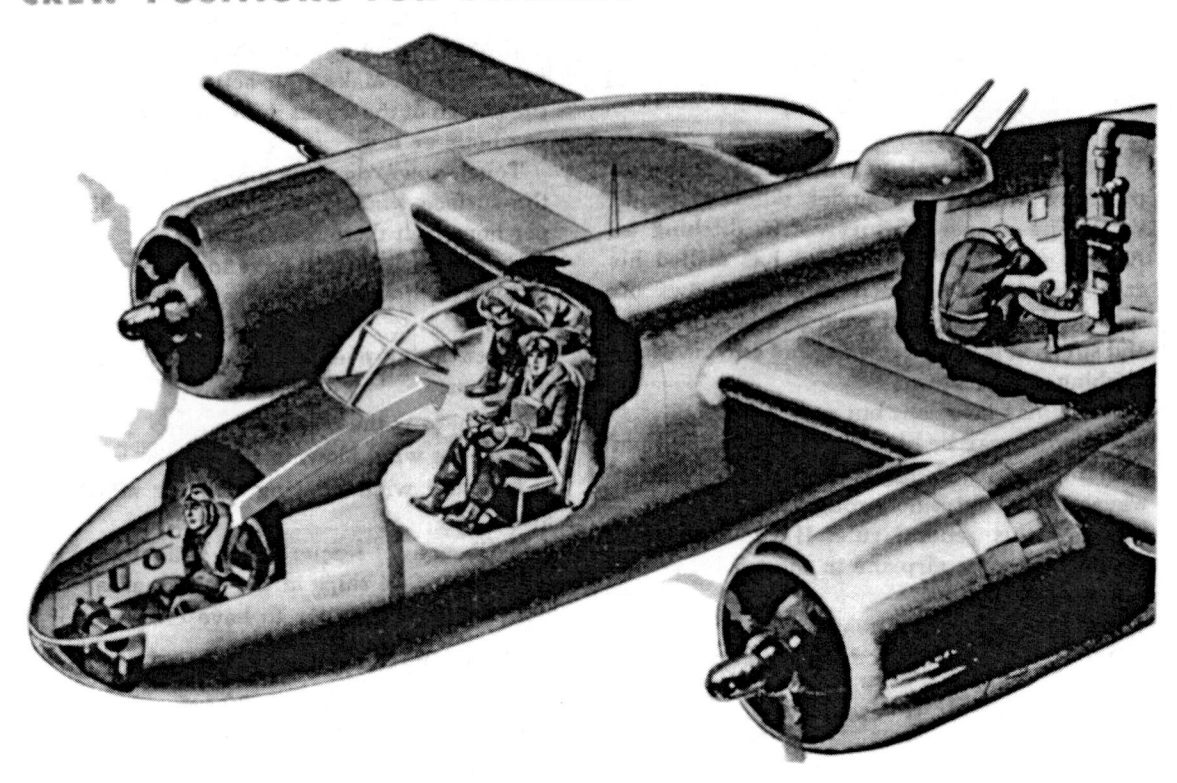

Caution

If the airplane alights in the proper (slightly tail-down) attitude, there is a slight impact as the aft fuselage section strikes the water. This is followed by a severe impact with sudden deceleration. (If the landing has been made too fast, a bounce occurs.) As the airplane comes to rest, the nose submerges.

Use of Flaps

The amount of flaps you will need will be determined by the amount of power available. **Remember you are trying to make a normal landing.** That is, a minimum safe forward speed with a minimum rate of descent. **Do not use more than ¾ flaps in any case.** Always try to ditch your airplane while you still have some power available and touch down on the water just as you would on a runway—in a normal landing attitude.

DITCHING PROCEDURE

Pilot

1. Call crew on interphone: "Prepare for ditching." Have crew acknowledge. (6 short rings on the alarm bell.)
2. Switch on emergency IFF transmitter. Brake safety wire on VHF control box toggle. Turn ON transmitter.
3. Unbuckle parachute.
4. Tighten safety belt and shoulder harness.
5. Salvo bombs. Close bomb bay doors.
6. Slide seat back but still maintain rudder control. (Use seat cushion for face and chest crash pad.)
7. Just before impact sound one long ring on

alarm bell. Call crew on interphone: "Brace for impact."

8. Have bombardier pull emergency lever to jettison cockpit hatch just before touch-down. (If no bombardier, do it yourself.)

9. Settle airplane onto water as gently as possible with tail only slightly down. **Maintain flying speed until contact.**

10. Pull life raft release handle. (On earlier airplanes the life raft is not self-expelling and must be released by the gunner.)

11. Exit through escape hatch. Inflate Mae West. Proceed to raft.

The airplane can be expected to float for a maximum period of 1 minute. You and your crew must act quickly.

Rear Gunner

1. Lock upper turret guns in aft position at a 45° angle.
2. Lock sighting station in aft position.
3. Release the escape hatch.
4. Unbuckle parachute.
5. Sit on floor facing aft in the right forward corner of the compartment with back against sloping bulkhead.
6. Brace self with hands and feet and listen on interphone.

Always wait for final impact before moving out of this position.

7. When airplane has come to rest pull emergency life raft release handle. (On earlier airplanes the life raft is stowed in the gunner's compartment and the gunner must release the raft and push it out the gunner's escape hatch on the right side of the airplane.
8. Exit through escape hatch and inflate your Mae West.

Bombardier

1. Take position on jump seat beside pilot.
2. Unbuckle parachute.
3. Tighten safety belt.
4. Pull emergency lever to release cockpit escape hatch (on signal from pilot).
5. Place arms in front of face just before impact.
6. Assist pilot from his seat and exit through hatch opening.
7. Inflate Mae West. Proceed aft.

Use of Radio in Emergencies

Each theater has its own definite radio procedure for emergencies. You will be briefed before each mission on the exact procedure to follow.

Below is a typical radio procedure for bail-out over water or ditching. Your first job is to transmit as calmly and lucidly as possible. There have been a number of airplanes lost at sea needlessly because the pilot yelled his instructions excitedly and the receiving station was unable to get the necessary information for rescue.

If possible try to gain altitude, especially if you are below 5000 ft. This increases the range of your transmission and helps Air/Sea Rescue to get a good fix. How quickly you are rescued—or whether or not you are rescued will depend on the accuracy of the fix the receiving station is taking on you:

1. Notify wingman that you are in trouble.
2. Turn on IFF EMERGENCY.
3. Transmit "Mayday" (3 times). Give call sign of airplane 3 times.
4. If you have plenty of time the first transmission will be on the assigned air ground frequencies. If you are unable to quickly establish contact with your station, break radio silence and use any frequency you need.
5. If time permits give the following information to your receiving station:
    a. Estimated position and time.
    b. Heading and speed.
    c. Altitude.
    d. Intention of pilot:
        "I am ditching." "I am bailing out." "I am crash landing."
    e. Before ditching, bailing out, or crash landing break the safety wire on your VHF control switch flick the switch to transmit position and leave it on.

When trouble comes, your wingmen or flight members, when they hear your call on operation channels, will orbit the spot and will continue to transmit for help after you have ditched, crash landed, or bailed out. One wingman will follow you down while another remains high and continues to transmit signals.

CRASH LANDING

Pilot

1. Call crew: "Prepare for crash landing." (Have crew acknowledge.)
2. Switch on emergency IFF radio transmitter.
3. Unbuckle parachute.
4. Tighten safety belt and lock shoulder harness.
5. Salvo bombs or rockets. Close bomb bay doors.
6. Make a normal approach. Use full flaps. Always make a wheels-up landing.
7. Slide seat back but still keep rudder control. (Place cushion between chest and control column.)
8. Have bombardier pull emergency lever to release cockpit hatch when airplane is just off the ground.
9. Mixture controls to IDLE CUT-OFF.
10. Turn battery and master ignition switches to OFF.
11. Tank selector valves to OFF.
12. Exit through upper hatch opening.

Rear Gunner

1. Lock upper turret guns in aft position at a 45° angle.
2. Lock sighting station in aft position.
3. Release upper escape hatch by pulling emergency release handle.
4. Unbuckle parachute.
5. Sit on the floor facing aft in the right forward corner of the compartment with back firmly against sloping bulkhead.
6. Brace self with hands and feet.
7. Exit through escape hatch opening.

Bombardier

1. Sit on jump seat beside pilot.
2. Unbuckle parachute.
3. Tighten safety belt.
4. Pull upper emergency escape hatch release (on signal from pilot).
5. Lean well forward with hands behind head and protect head and face.
6. Exit through upper hatch opening.

RESTRICTED

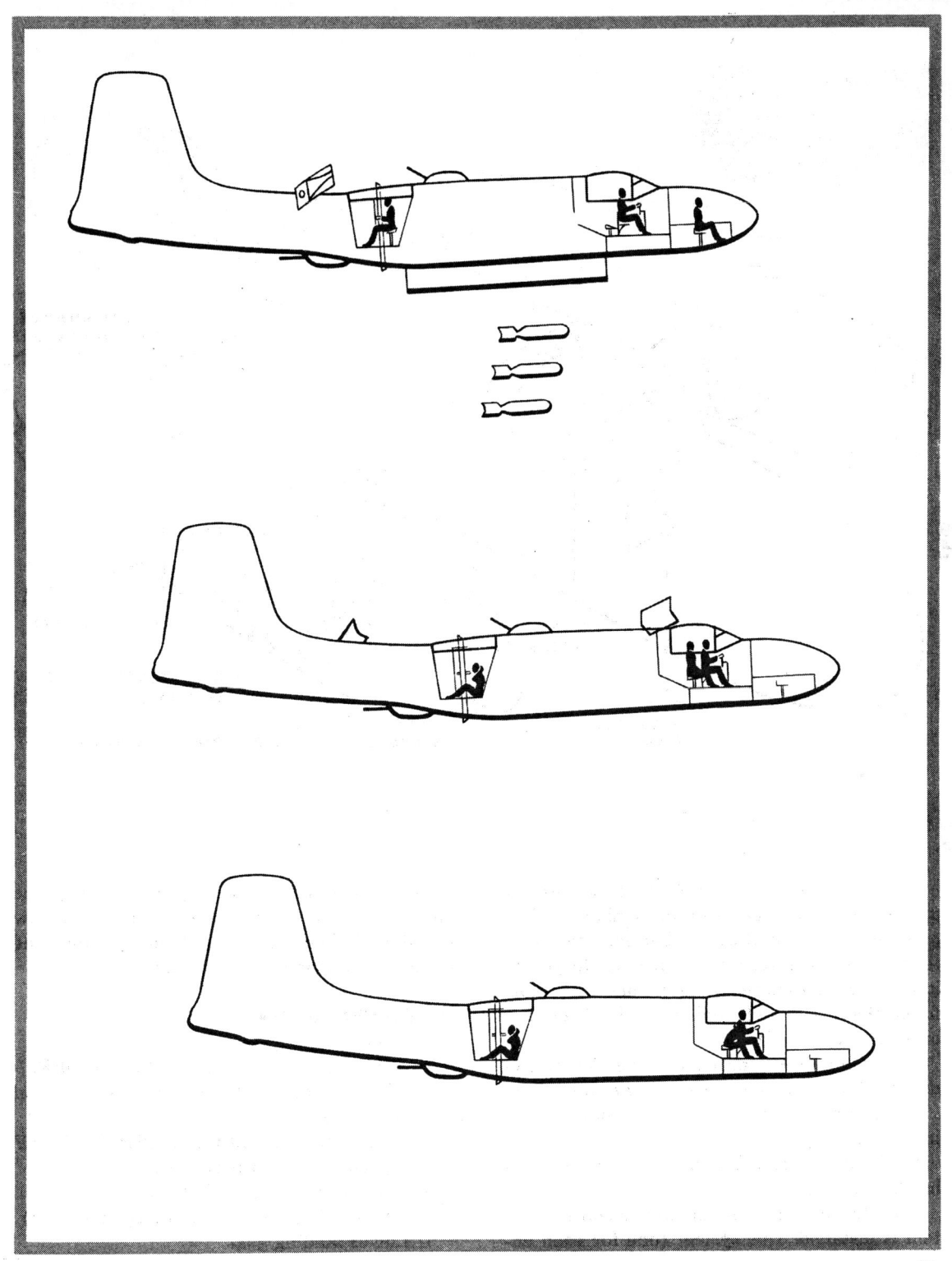

RESTRICTED

99

FIRES

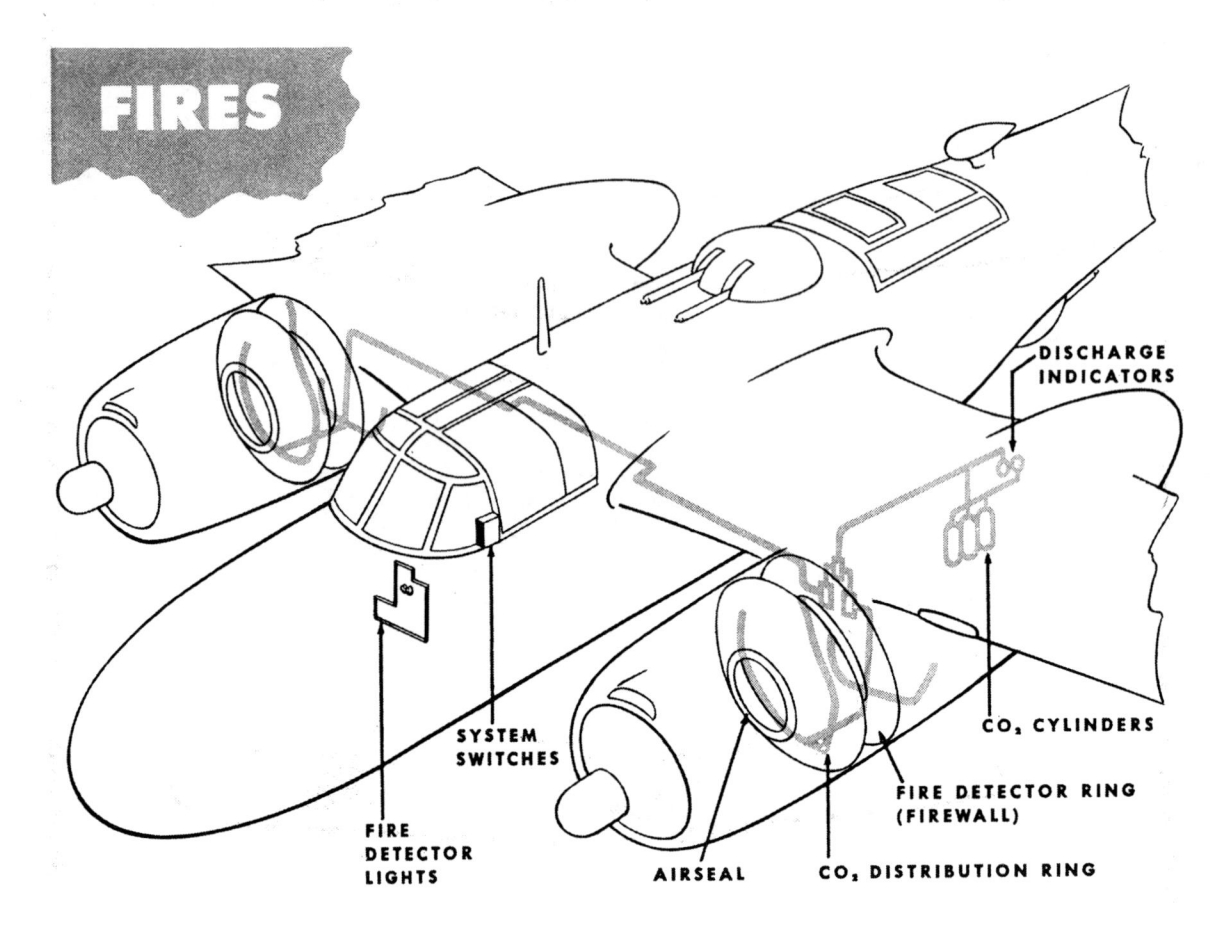

Labels on diagram: DISCHARGE INDICATORS, SYSTEM SWITCHES, FIRE DETECTOR LIGHTS, AIRSEAL, CO_2 DISTRIBUTION RING, FIRE DETECTOR RING (FIREWALL), CO_2 CYLINDERS

ENGINE FIRE EXTINGUISHER SYSTEM

The fire hazard in the A-26 is no less or greater than in other medium bombers. While most fires are caused by combat emergencies a few still occur in training, so it is up to you to know your procedures perfectly and to be able to use them accurately and correctly. There are only two types of fires:

a. **Engine Fires**—caused by fuel, oil or hydraulic fluid coming into contact with hot metal.

b. **Electrical Fires**—caused by a short circuit in your wiring.

Of the two, engine fires are more serious and harder to control.

On later airplanes an engine fire control system is installed. This system (one for each engine) consists of a CO_2 ring surrounding the engine and a single switch which stops the flow of all fuel, hydraulic liquid and oil into the engine area. Engine fire procedure is:

ON BURNING ENGINE
1. Open cowl flap.
2. Turn fuel selector and boost pump OFF.
3. Close engine and hydraulic oil switch (on later airplanes only).
4. Feather prop (mixture to IDLE CUT-OFF by prop feathering procedure).
5. Turn mag switch OFF later.
6. Release CO_2 system (later airplanes only).
7. Lower landing gear.

ALWAYS SLIP AWAY FROM THE FIRE!!

If you have plenty of altitude slip the airplane away from the fire.

Electrical fire unlike engine fire is slow in starting and if the short circuit is anywhere near the cockpit you may detect the fire early by smelling or seeing smoke.

Your only procedure in case of an electrical fire is to cut off all battery and gear switches and slip the airplane away from the fire. DO NOT CUT OFF YOUR ELECTRICAL SYSTEM UNTIL YOU ARE CERTAIN THAT YOU WILL NOT HAVE TO FEATHER A PROP. Don't forget that your prop feathering motor is on your electrical circuit.

Cockpit Fire

In case of cockpit fire while in the air, close all windows and shut off vents and heaters then spray the base of the fire with the CO_2 hand extinguisher located in the cockpit. Most electrical cockpit fires burn very slowly and are easily detected before any great amount of damage is done.

ENGINE FIRE EXTINGUISHER CONTROL PANEL— PILOT'S RIGHT

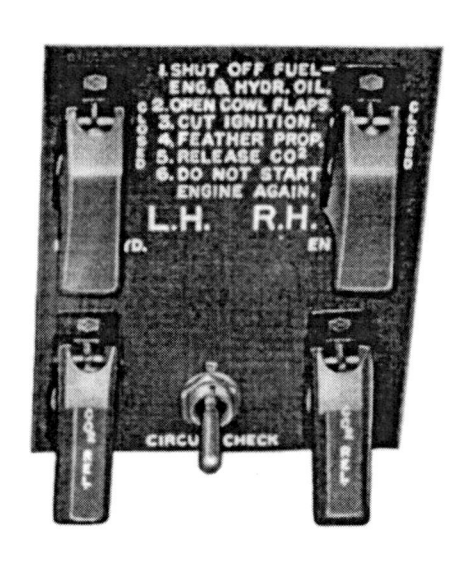

USE OF THE AIRPLANE

AIRPLANE COMMANDER

When you are assigned an A-26 crew, you are much more than just a pilot. You hold a command post and all the responsibilities of a unit commander.

You now have an airplane and a 2-man or 3-man crew for which you are responsible, not only when you are flying or on the flight line, but for 24 hours of the day. Because you have a smaller crew than the medium or heavy bomber, you may think that you have less responsibility. **This is not true.** Actually, your responsibilities are greater, since you have only one or two other men to assist in the care of the airplane. This means that you must know and understand maintenance and operation of each unit in the airplane.

Know the capabilities and shortcomings of each of your crew members. Know their backgrounds, their personalities, and their individual problems. This knowledge enables you to assist and guide them in the training still required to make them specialists in their field.

See that every man is not only thoroughly trained in his own job but understands the other crew members' responsibilities. This develops the harmony demanded of all combat teams.

Be concerned for your crew's welfare. Check to see that they are fully equipped with necessary and modern flying gear. Go to bat for your crew, make sure their parachutes fit, that their Mae Wests are in order, and that they have all the G.I. flying equipment they need.

You cannot over-emphasize the morale effect of neat appearance. Insist on it.

It isn't your job to check the morals and personal behavior of your crew members. But, when lack of sleep or over-indulgence begins to impair their efficiency, it becomes your job.

Remember, your crew depends on you for survival. This means that you must be an expert in every operation of the airplane. As an expert, you will have complete confidence to cope with any situation. Confidence is contagious. When you have confidence, your crew members will not only have confidence in you, but will develop confidence in themselves. Don't forget that confidence should always **follow,** not **precede** knowledge.

Now, about the subject of military discipline.

You are the absolute boss. Use your authority wisely. Don't be a "swell guy pushover." Don't be a Simon Legree. Just be fair—and your crew will respect you and work with you.

REMEMBER

Respect cannot be demanded ... It must be earned

FORMATION FLYING

In one year of training in a medium bombardment training unit, the requirements for formation flying have been increased from 5 hours to 30 hours. This means that about 30% of all 2nd-phase training is devoted to formation.

When you consider the amount of bombing, gunnery, instrument work, and navigation to be accomplished, you can see that formation flying is the most important phase in training.

After you arrive in your theater of action, you probably will spend more time learning how to fly formation before you go on your first mission.

If any doubt still exists in your mind about the importance of formation flying, question any combat pilot on the subject.

You have a man-sized job to do. Besides actually flying the airplane you need to check your fuel supply, change tanks, check engine instruments, and maintain radio contact with the lead airplane.

If you have another crew member in the pilot's compartment, by all means teach him to observe the engine instruments and fuel supply. But remember, the final responsibility rests with you. Depend on no one but yourself.

RESTRICTED

Basic Formation

When a squadron is briefed for a particular mission, a basic formation is selected, depending on the size and shape of the target. Any other type of formation used on the mission evolves from this basic formation.

THE BASIC FORMATION IS THE ONE RESUMED WHEN THE ROCK WINGS SIGNAL IS GIVEN.

FORMATION SIGNALS

FLUTTER AILERONS: Repeated and comparatively rapid movement of ailerons.

ATTENTION: Used on the ground or in the air to attract attention of all pilots in the formation. Stand by for radio message or further signal. When on ground and in proper position to take off, this signal will normally mean "Ready to take off."

FISHTAIL OR YAW: By rudder control during flight, move the tail of the airplane alternately and repeatedly right and left.

OPEN UP FORMATION: Where applicable, this may be used to order a search formation.

Keep Your Eye on Your Commander

SERIES OF SMALL DIVES AND/OR ZOOMS

PREPARE TO LAND: An order to each pilot in the formation to prepare to land. In the absence of further signals the landing will be made in the normal landing formation of the unit, which should be predetermined. Any change in formation for landing will be ordered by supplemental signal by radio.

DIP RIGHT (LEFT) WING:

From any formation other than echelon go into echelon of flights to the right (left).

Being in an echelon of flights to the right (left), go into echelon of individual airplanes to the same side. Being in an echelon of individual airplanes, if wing is dipped on the side to which airplanes are echeloned, form echelon of flights to the same side. Being in an echelon of flights or individual airplanes, if wing is dipped on the side away from the echelonment, form same echelon to the opposite side.

ROCK WINGS
Slow, repeated, rocking motion of airplane about longitudinal axis, by gradual use of ailerons. Wing movement to be slower and of greater amplitude than in "Flutter ailerons."

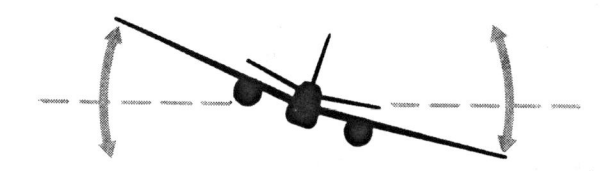

ASSUME NORMAL FORMATION:
From any other formation, go into the normal closed-up formation for the unit concerned. This formation is to be prescribed in each group and/or squadron.

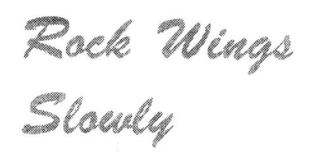

Rock Wings Slowly

Briefing

Never attempt to fly formation until you have been properly briefed. Be attentive at the briefing session. Ask questions regarding anything that is not clear to you. Some small point may be clear to everyone in the room but you. Don't sit in a daze. Don't be satisfied to "almost understand." One bonehead can ruin the entire formation and endanger the success of the mission. Be sure that's not you!

The formation commander tells you everything you should know to complete your mission. Do not leave the briefing session until you know:

1. The basic formation.
2. The number of the lead airplane.
3. Order of command within the formation.
4. Your position and number of the airplane you follow.
5. Number of aircraft in formation.
6. Signals to be used.
7. Route and ETA at destination.
8. Taxi, takeoff, and landing system to be used.
9. Instrument procedure.
10. Time to start engines and time of takeoff.
11. Emergency procedures.
12. Number and location of the spare airplane.

Know these things and keep them clear in your mind.

Takeoff and Assembly

You are given a takeoff interval during briefing. Understand clearly when and how to time this interval. Don't jump the gun. It makes your own assembly more difficult and messes up the timing of all the planes behind you.

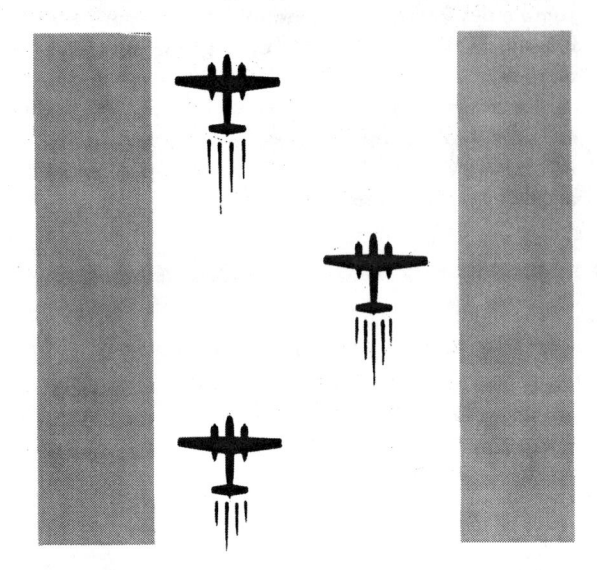

Alternate in the use of the runway.

The first plane takes off on the downwind side, the second on the upwind side, and the third directly in line with the first. This is done to help cut down the effect of prop wash.

The leader takes off and climbs straight ahead for a period of time determined by the number of the formation. Individual planes in the formation take off at 20-second intervals. Each succeeding pilot begins his turn 10 seconds after the airplane ahead of him has started to turn. Your formation leader maintains a constant ½ needle-width turn, a constant airspeed and rate of climb. Knowing these (you were told at briefing) you can govern your own airspeed so as not to overtake him too suddenly or join too far behind.

Plan to head him off as he comes out of his turn. **Aim for where he will be, not where he is.**

Do not attempt to shorten your flight path so much that you approach him at a 90° angle. This is dangerous.

Always keep the lead airplane in sight. If you know his speed to be 170, don't join the formation at 200—you will overrun him.

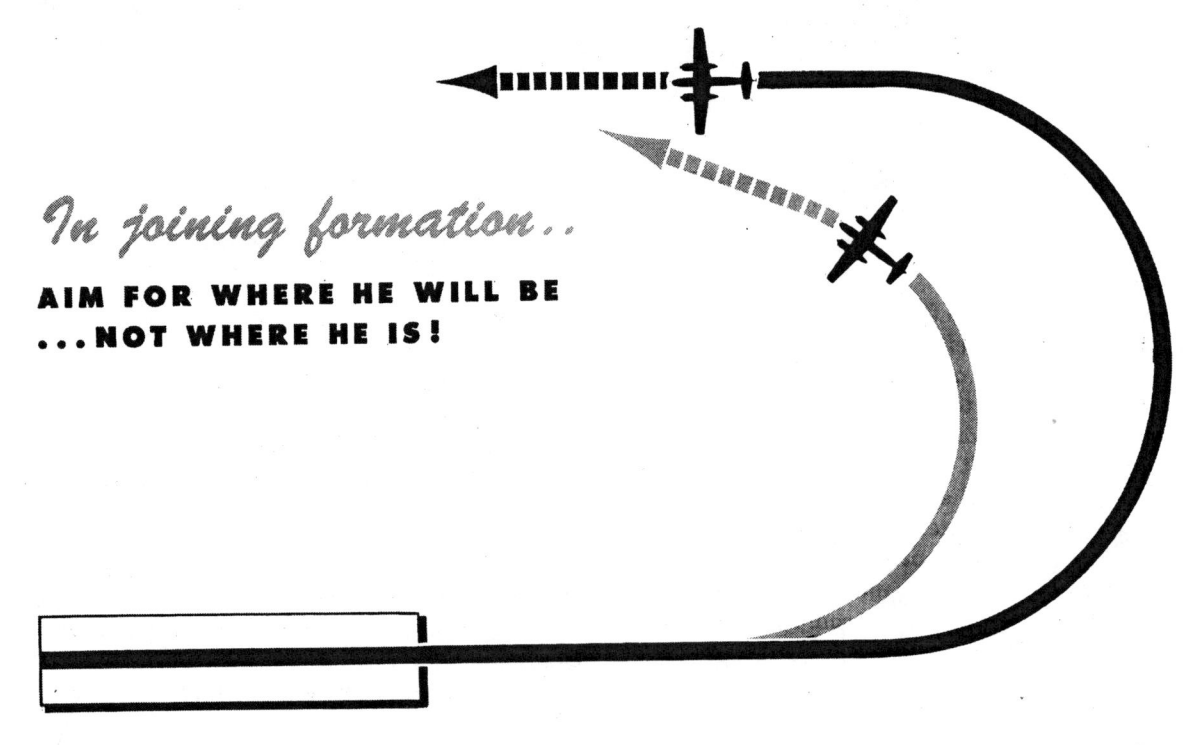

In joining formation...
AIM FOR WHERE HE WILL BE ...NOT WHERE HE IS!

FORMATION TAKEOFFS

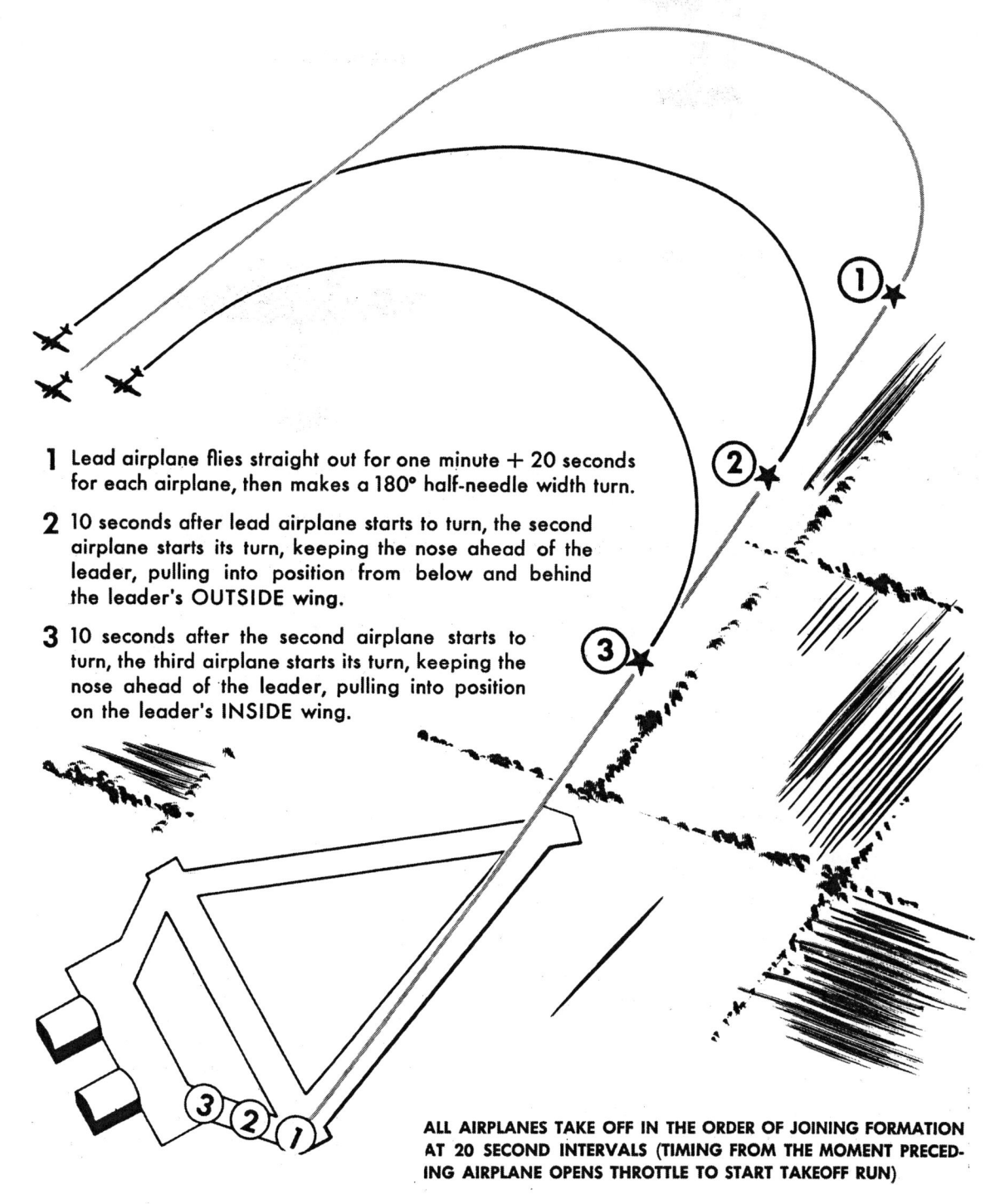

1. Lead airplane flies straight out for one minute + 20 seconds for each airplane, then makes a 180° half-needle width turn.

2. 10 seconds after lead airplane starts to turn, the second airplane starts its turn, keeping the nose ahead of the leader, pulling into position from below and behind the leader's OUTSIDE wing.

3. 10 seconds after the second airplane starts to turn, the third airplane starts its turn, keeping the nose ahead of the leader, pulling into position on the leader's INSIDE wing.

ALL AIRPLANES TAKE OFF IN THE ORDER OF JOINING FORMATION AT 20 SECOND INTERVALS (TIMING FROM THE MOMENT PRECEDING AIRPLANE OPENS THROTTLE TO START TAKEOFF RUN)

ONE-HALF WING SPAN

ONE-HALF FUSELAGE LENGTH

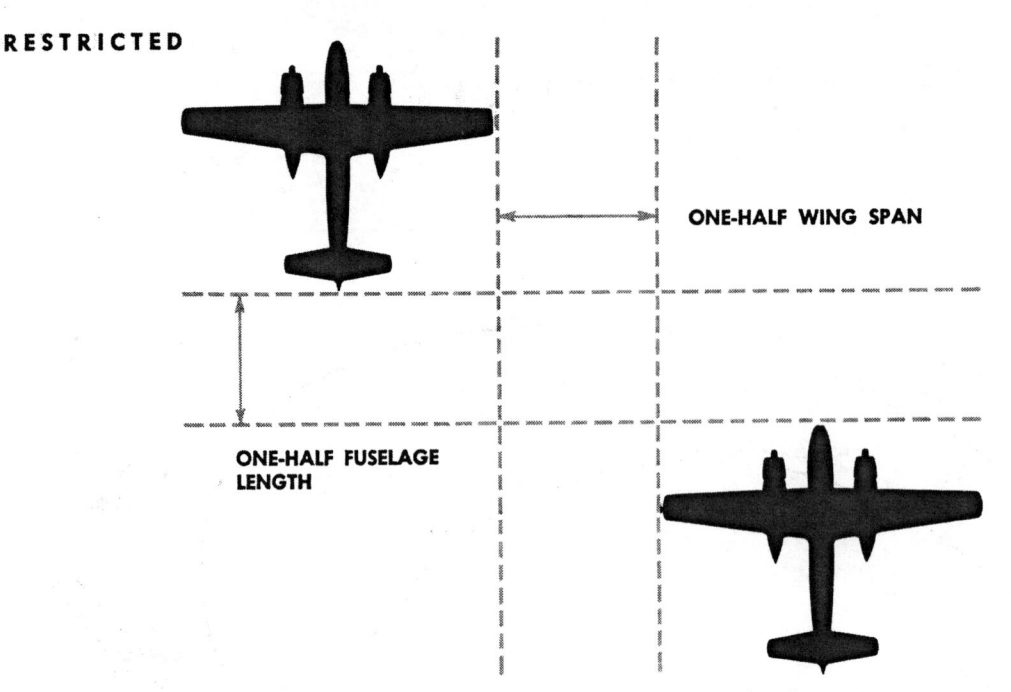

Position in Formation

Your position as wingman in close formation is ½ wingspan out from your leader and ½ fuselage length back from your leader. Fly just low enough so that your engine nacelle does not block clear vision of the lead airplane.

After you have established this position, hold it. To hold good position:

1. Be alert.
2. Anticipate your action to stick with your leader. This means:
   a. When your leader turns into you, reduce power momentarily to hold position and re-apply as needed.
   b. When your leader turns away from you, promptly apply power as needed.
   c. When your leader starts a climb, be alert. Increase rpm and manifold pressure.

Don't straggle. The lessons you learn now may save your life in combat. The enemy waits for stragglers.

Common Errors of Wingmen

Check yourself against these common errors:
1. Making throttle adjustments too radically.
2. Applying trim improperly.
3. Failing to anticipate the movements of the leader.
4. Flying with one wing low.
5. Taking eyes off the leader for too long a period of time. (Glance at one instrument at a time. Don't keep your head in the cockpit.)
6. Using too high an rpm setting for continuous cruise. (Use higher rpm only when maneuvering in formation.)
7. Failing to remember signals.
8. Being too tense.
9. Continuing too far out on cross-under.

Cross-Under

Do not take the term "cross-under" literally. You never actually cross under another airplane; you drop down and back slightly to clear the other airplane safely.

In moving into echelon formation, retard your throttle momentarily and drop down (about 50 feet) below your leader and back far enough to clear the wingman safely, keeping your leader and the wingman in sight at all times. As you make a coordinated bank to move into the echelon position, anticipate the need for additional power. **Always know the position of the other planes near you.**

Always make cross-unders with smooth, deliberate movements.

Formation Landing

The leader lands on one side of the runway, and each succeeding airplane lands on the opposite side from the plane in front of it. This eliminates prop wash.

Each succeeding flight repeats this procedure.

The success of formation landing depends upon exact timing and constant airspeed. Any errors you make along the way are transmitted and magnified back to the last airplane to land.

Critique

In combat the critique is the detailed review of the entire mission, success over the target, the number and types of enemy fighters encountered—in short, all information of the mission.

The critique is also the bitch session. This is where the boys let you have it. Everybody honestly airs his questions and gripes. Be attentive! Prove that you can take it. You learn plenty in critiques. It is important in that it helps eliminate future mistakes.

Formation Leader

Leading a formation is a great responsibility. The success of an entire mission is in your hands. Remember, your wingmen can be no better than you are.

Good formation depends on good leadership; good leadership depends on smooth, precise flying.

To be a good leader:

1. Follow the briefing instructions exactly. If you are to climb your flight at 200 mph at 500 feet per minute, **do so exactly**. This gives your wingmen confidence in your leadership.

2. Make all your turns smooth and constant.

3. Make your signals definite, but don't overdo them.

4. Demand and insist upon strict radio discipline. Your radio transmissions must be clear and brief. Tolerate no needless radio chatter.

5. Always consider your wingmen's problems. They must constantly change throttle settings in maneuvering, and consequently their fuel consumption is higher than yours.

IT IS A WELL-KNOWN FACT THAT THE COMBAT GROUPS WITH THE FEWEST LOSSES FLY THE BEST FORMATIONS.

DRAW YOUR OWN FORMATION LANDING PROCEDURE HERE

BOMBING

The A-26 carries a bomb load equivalent to that of a medium bomber. The design of the airplane and the all-purpose nose signify the different types of bombing this plane is equipped to do. Since you have a complete description of the bombing equipment in the armament section, this section adheres to operating instructions and procedures.

The pilot drops the bombs except when the bombardier nose is installed. Therefore, you must not only understand the bombardier's problems, but you must know how to operate all the bombing equipment yourself.

Loading the bombs plays a big part in a successful bombing mission. One faulty bomb station, or one that is only half cocked, may prevent all of the bombs from being dropped. It is your responsibility to check each bomb station by running through the racks before loading the bombs.

Do this:

1. Turn on battery switches.
2. Turn on BOMB CIRCUIT MAIN POWER switch.
3. Open the bomb bay doors.
4. Put racks on SELECT.
5. Put FRAG-DEMO switch in desired position.
6. Cock each station.
7. Turn on rack switches.
8. Set intervalometer in SELECT or TRAIN and for number of stations to be fired.
9. Then fire each station by the bomb release button while your gunner watches the stations.

Also check the indicator light panel for burned-out bulbs or defective wiring while checking the stations. Each light on the panel represents a bomb station. When the station is cocked, the light burns if the panel light switch is held on and the bomb bays are open. These

Warning Never hold panel light switch on during actual release or bombs will be dropped SAFE. (Some airplanes do not have indicator light panels.)

lights go out as their respective stations are fired.

Then Check the Intervalometer:

1. Put racks in the TRAIN position.
2. Set large intervalometer dial to desired spacing of releases.
3. Set the small dial to the number of bombs to be dropped.
4. Set intervalometer switch to TRAIN.

Be sure that the bomb bay doors are opened fully (note indicator lamp) before making a rack selection of SELECT or TRAIN. After cocking the stations, push the bomb release button once and the intervalometer fires all the stations.

5. Turn off battery and all bombing switches.

When you are satisfied that the stations of each bomb rack are operating O.K., cock the stations again. Then proceed to load the bombs. If heavy bombs are used, you need the bomb hoist equipment stowed in the right nacelle. You can use this equipment to load either the bomb bay or wing racks.

Releasing Bombs

If you are flying a plane with the bombardier nose, your bombardier releases the bombs. However, it is your responsibility to have the pins pulled, the bomb bay doors open, and the racks set in the position required.

Select

If you are flying wing position and dropping on the lead plane in single releases, it's your responsibility to:

1. Have pins pulled (before takeoff).
2. Make sure (by indicator light) that bomb bay doors are fully opened (with lead plane).
3. Set racks on SELECT.
4. Set arming selector switch on ARM position.
5. Set nose and tail selector as desired (not necessary on practice bombs).
6. Select DEMO or FRAG position.

Train

For bombing in train the same operations must be followed, except that you set the racks in TRAIN position instead of SELECT position, and you set the intervalometer before takeoff for spacing between bombs, number to be released, and the TRAIN position. It may be necessary to change interval dial setting as changes of ground speed may be encountered. Know the position of each switch so that you can complete these operations while keeping formation.

Bombing Tips

Know which of these operations you can complete on the ground without danger on takeoff.

When bombing in TRAIN, these two switches must be:

1. Rack switch on TRAIN for FRAG bombs.
2. Intervalometer switch on TRAIN.

Salvo

The other method of releasing bombs is salvo, and you usually use it in emergency. Salvoing is done on some of the early series by means of the bomb bay door lever by the pilot's left leg. First pull it back to the OPEN position. As soon as the doors are open, pull it farther back to the SALVO position. This mechanically releases the bombs in the bomb bay and on the wing racks. You also can salvo wing bombs by an electrical wing salvo switch. On later-series airplanes you can open the bomb bay doors by an electric switch on the upper right corner of the indicator light panel. The bombs are salvoed mechanically by pulling the red plunger on the bottom of the panel directly in front of the pilot.

Types of Bombing

Synchronous bombing is usually done in the A-26 at altitudes from 7,000 to 15,000 feet. This kind of bombing requires the utmost cooperation of the pilot and bombardier and cannot be successful until the pilot understands the problems of the bombardier.

The two most important pilot responsibilities of the bombing run are:

1. First and most important is **constant airspeed**, which is agreed upon during briefing.
2. Next in importance is constant altitude, also agreed upon during briefing.

KEEP ALTITUDE AND AIR SPEED CONSTANT

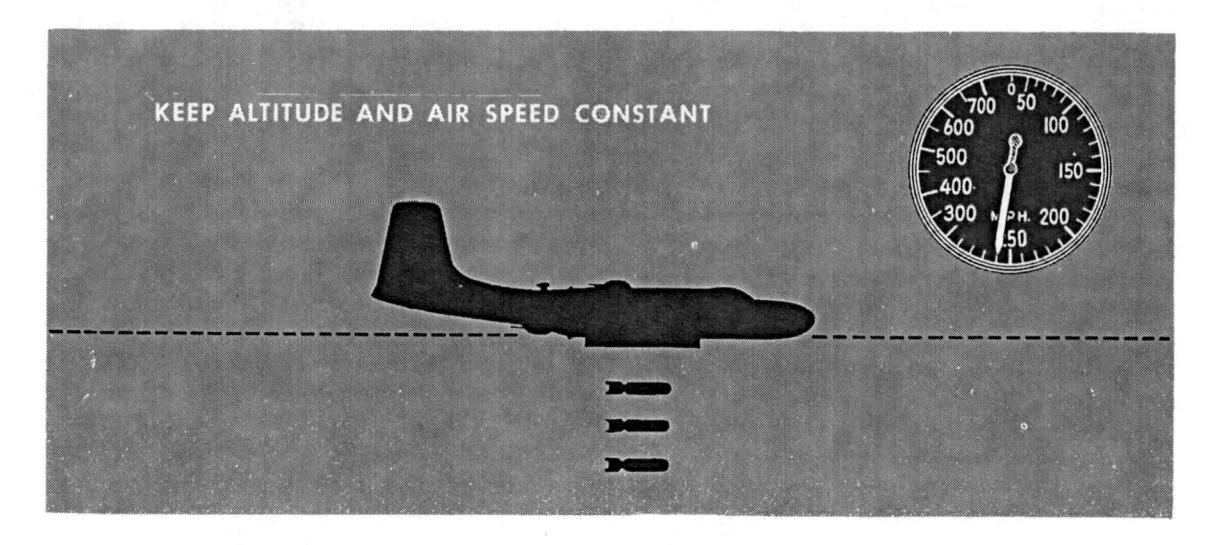

With these two factors known, the bombardier can pre-set his trail into the bombsight. Trail is the distance the bomb lags behind the airplane at the time of impact. Flying at an altitude of 10,000 feet, if you are flying 5 mph faster than the prearranged airspeed for which the bombsight is set, the bomb falls almost 200 feet short of target. A difference of 100 feet too high, even though the airspeed is correct, would cause the bomb to hit about 65 feet beyond the target. From these examples you can see that airspeed is the most important factor, and altitude is next in importance. It is easy for a good pilot to keep them both exact.

With altitude and airspeed being held constant, the next problem is deflection, or course.

Pilot's Directional Indicator

The pilot's directional indicator (PDI needle) tells the pilot the course correction set in the bombsight by the bombardier. Keeping the needle in the center means keeping the plane on the bombsight course. The changing of the needle to one side doesn't necessarily mean a correction by the bombardier; it may mean that you are letting the plane point off the true course.

Another factor which affects your course is crosswind, which causes the bomb to drift after it has been dropped. This is corrected by the bombardier by flying a parallel course on the upwind side of the target. This correction for drift effect is known as **cross-trail.**

It is the pilot's responsibility to fly the airplane straight, level, and steady at the point of bomb release. Lurching or skidding of the plane throws the bomb several hundred feet off.

Bombing Run Procedure

Many dry runs are caused by misunderstanding the signals between you and your bombardier. Your procedure should be the same on

KEEP THE PDI ON

all runs so that all operations can be anticipated. Plan ahead with your bombardier so that you understand when the bombardier wants his different levels and corrections.

When turning from the initial point (IP) help the bombardier by leveling out on a straight line to the target. Practice this until you can recognize and kill drift. Your bombardier can be no better in his job than you are in yours.

When leaving the IP and starting your run:

1. Open the bomb bay doors and maintain constant bombing airspeed and altitude.

2. The bombardier immediately requests "Stabilizer level." Hold the plane in a straight and level attitude. This **absolute level** of the plane is extremely important, because if the leveling bubble is off even half a bubble it causes a larger error than faulty altitude or airspeed. Acknowledge bombardier's request for level **only when plane is level,** not when it's almost level or when you think it soon will be.

3. Hold this level until the bombardier says "Level complete." Check your course again and give the bombardier "On course," which he acknowledges.

After that you get your first PDI correction. The first corrections are the largest. The PDI is extremely sensitive. From center to full right or left means only a 5° turn indicator change of course. Make these first corrections smooth and coordinated, with never more than a 10° bank. After you have the course straight with PDI centered, note the heading on the turn indicator. Hold this heading. At the same time, constantly refer to the PDI needle for further corrections.

If the PDI needle moves to the right, bring it back to center by a small correction to the right. Hold the new turn indicator heading. Continue these corrections until your bombardier is fat, happy, and on course.

All during this run you have been holding a constant airspeed and altitude, and you now have a true course. Approximately 10 to 15 seconds before the bomb is released, the bombardier calls for another level. Check for level flight. Make certain the airplane is level, and acknowledge at this time. Your bombardier is taking a bubble level which sets the bombsight gyro level. Again he says "Level complete," and you acknowledge with "Back to PDI."

Soon after this the bomb is released, so don't make large corrections. When the bomb is dropped the bombardier calls "Bombs away." After caging his gyro, the bombardier advises "O.K. to turn." Do not turn off before this O.K. It may cause material damage to the delicate bombsight.

The foregoing procedure seems long, but it can be accomplished in 40 seconds with practice. The first runs take as long as 2 minutes, but familiarization and anticipation reduce this time to a minimum.

Take into consideration your wind drift so you can set up an initial course that requires little PDI correction. Always check with the bombardier so that he does not clutch in the sight until he has the course hair lined up. If there is a crosswind that you have already corrected for, and he clutches in the sight before lining up the course hair, he takes your drift correction out to set the course hair on the target. Then he has to turn it back again to set in a new crab. This is done within the bombsight itself and causes a reverse correction on the PDI.

ALWAYS HAVE THE BOMBARDIER LINE UP THE COURSE HAIR BEFORE CLUTCHING IN THE BOMBSIGHT.

To use this method successfully, you must line up the plane within 10° of bombing course.

Bombing From Wing Plane

Bombing from wing position in the A-26 means a dual job for the pilot. You must fly a good formation, and also release the bombs.

Memorize the position of all the bombing switches so you can operate each one as you hold your position in formation. Set the intervalometer before takeoff.

You must accomplish the following in formation:

1. Turn on BOMB CIRCUIT MAIN POWER switch.
2. Open bomb bay doors at the same time the lead ship's doors open.
3. Set racks (either SELECT or TRAIN position).
4. Arming selector in ARM position.
5. Type bomb switch either FRAG or DEMO.
6. NOSE AND TAIL switch set as desired.

Then concentrate on lead plane so that you can drop bombs instantaneously with it. Be ready to operate bomb bay doors at the same time as the leader to make formation position easier to maintain.

Skip Bombing

Successful skip bombing depends on flying skill and knowledge of setting the dropping angle in the N-9 gunsight. This angle is set according to airspeed and altitude, computed on a chart used with the N-9 sight. Skip bombing is usually done at altitudes from 50 to 300 feet. Contrary to popular belief, skip bombs should be dropped for direct hits, preferably the base of the target—for example, the waterline of a ship. Remember: Unlike synchronous bombing, altitude is a more important factor than airspeed in skip bombing.

Line up with the target and go in extremely low, with evasive action if necessary. About 5 seconds before releasing the bomb, bring the plane to proper altitude and hold on straight and level course (check needle-ball). It is necessary to keep the airplane in this position for only a few seconds before bomb release. Looking through the sight the circle and dot pass over the surface and over the target. Anticipate actual pressing of the bomb release button to reduce the personal lag error. A large error results if the plane is diving or climbing at instant of release. Always lead a moving target slightly.

Here are examples of the importance of altitude in skip bombing. The sight is set for 250 mph and 100 feet altitude.

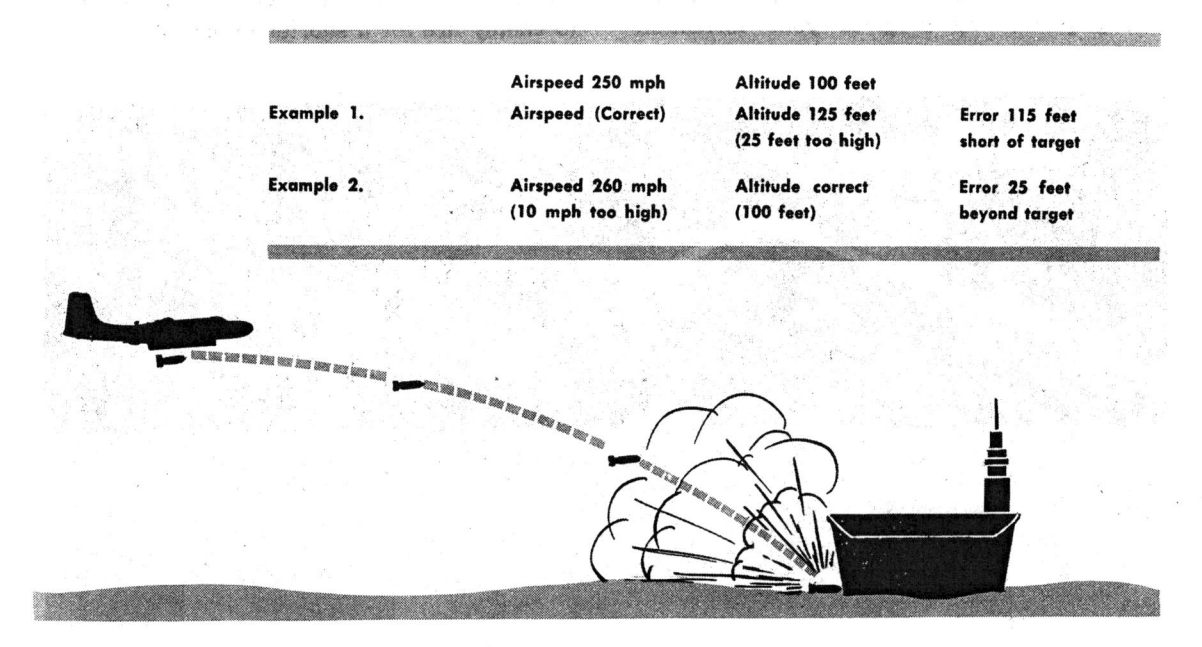

	Airspeed 250 mph	Altitude 100 feet	
Example 1.	Airspeed (Correct)	Altitude 125 feet (25 feet too high)	Error 115 feet short of target
Example 2.	Airspeed 260 mph (10 mph too high)	Altitude correct (100 feet)	Error 25 feet beyond target

Combat Bombing

Combat bombing, usually done in formation, is divided into two types:

Precision pattern bombing, and area bombing.

Precision bombing means placing the bomb on a specific target by a precise synchronous sighting operation.

Area bombing means placing a number of bombs in a given area and probably will not be used much in the A-26.

Evasive Action

When you gotta zig . . . you gotta zag!

The purpose of evasive action is to prevent the anti-aircraft gunner from predicting the position of your airplane at the time his projectile reaches its point of detonation. To avoid being a cold turkey you must understand the anti-aircraft gunner's operations. It takes approximately 15 seconds for the ack-ack gunner to estimate your altitude and airspeed, and cut fuses to get his projectile into the air. It takes one second for each 1000 feet of travel through the air. Knowing this, you can see why it's advisable to hold a straight course for approximately 10 seconds, then change course. This causes the enemy gunners to set up a predicted aiming point, and it gives your formation enough time to move to a new heading before the projectile reaches point of detonation. When flying evasive action, consider the men trying to stay in formation with you.

1. Make your changes in course a smooth maneuver but in plenty of time to get the rest out of range.

2. Make these turns not over a 15° bank, but make at least a 30° change of course.

3. The change of altitude is almost as effective as the change in course, so coordinate the change in course with the change in altitude all during evasive action.

Where Evasive Action Is Not Used

Under certain conditions evasive action is sometimes impractical.

At the discretion of the theater commanders, evasive action may or may not be used. It has been found that in certain heavily defended areas where the enemy anti-aircraft tactics are to lay a solid curtain of flak, losses are lighter when the formation uses no evasive action, but bores right through the anti-aircraft fire in straight and level flight.

The reason for this is that the formation enters and passes through the heavily defended area more quickly, and consequently is exposed to enemy fire for a shorter period of time.

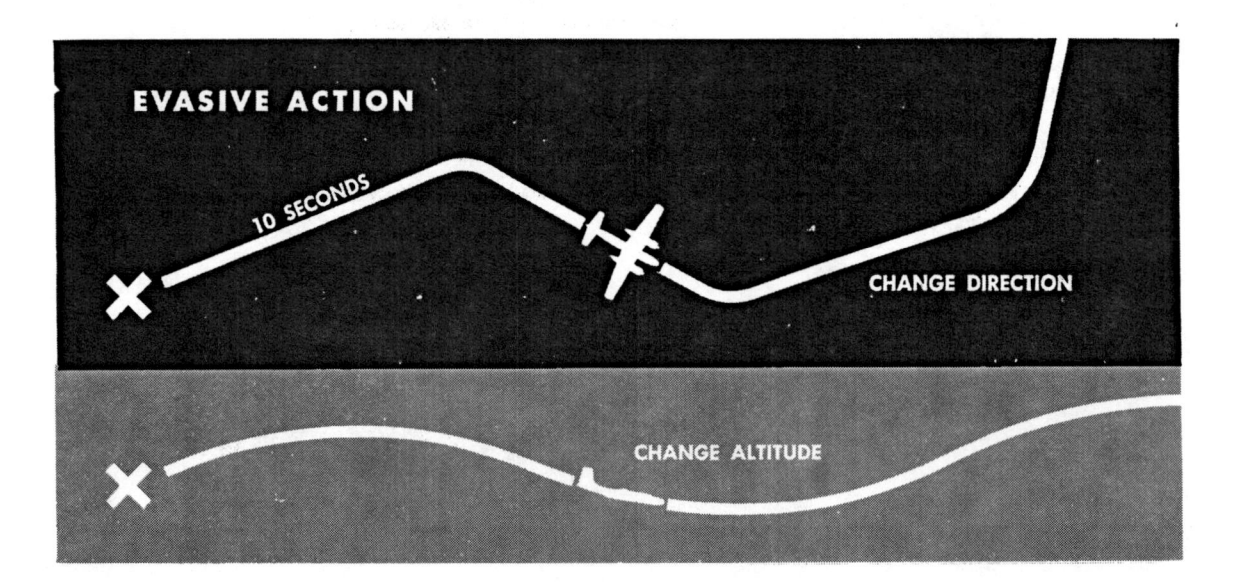

EVASIVE ACTION

10 SECONDS — CHANGE DIRECTION

CHANGE ALTITUDE

GUNNERY

No other plane in the Army packs the forward firepower of the A-26. It is designed, among other uses, for low-level attack and strafing. You must know the location of all your gun switches, how to load your guns, and the principle of air-to-ground gunnery.

Later airplanes have pneumatic gun chargers with which you can charge your guns in flight.

On earlier airplanes all the guns must be loaded and charged while on the ground.

See your armament officer for complete information.

When you charge your guns, be certain that the airplane is pointed where there is absolutely no danger of hitting anything or anyone in case of an accidental firing (preferably a gun abutment).

Cookoff

Cookoff or uncontrolled firing of your guns may occur after prolonged bursts. To prevent overheated guns from cooking off, flick the gun charger switch to OPEN and then hold back switch to ON. The breeches of the guns will then remain open with no danger of self firing until the trigger is again pressed. Always operate this gun-charging switch immediately after firing and you will never be the kind of ace who shoots his own wingmen.

Air-to-ground Gunnery (Fixed)

For air-to-ground fixed gunnery, considerable skill is required. Here are some points:

1. Know and abide by all the range rules.
2. Have good radio contact and guard the range control throughout the entire mission.
3. Set your rpm at about 2200 and use throttles as needed to hold airspeed.
4. Turn on your gunsight and adjust it.

RESTRICTED

5. On your fire control panel, switch your top switch on GUN AND CAMERA.

Now set up your pattern, which in most cases is an ordinary rectangular pattern at 1,000 feet. Make a few dry runs on the target with your actual approach path at about a 40° angle with the ground. On these passes, trim your plane up so that at the time you normally would be firing (1000 to 500 feet from the target), the needle and ball are centered exactly. Your airspeed at the time of firing will be between 260 IAS and 280 IAS. From the accompanying illustration, you can see why it is necessary to center the needle and ball.

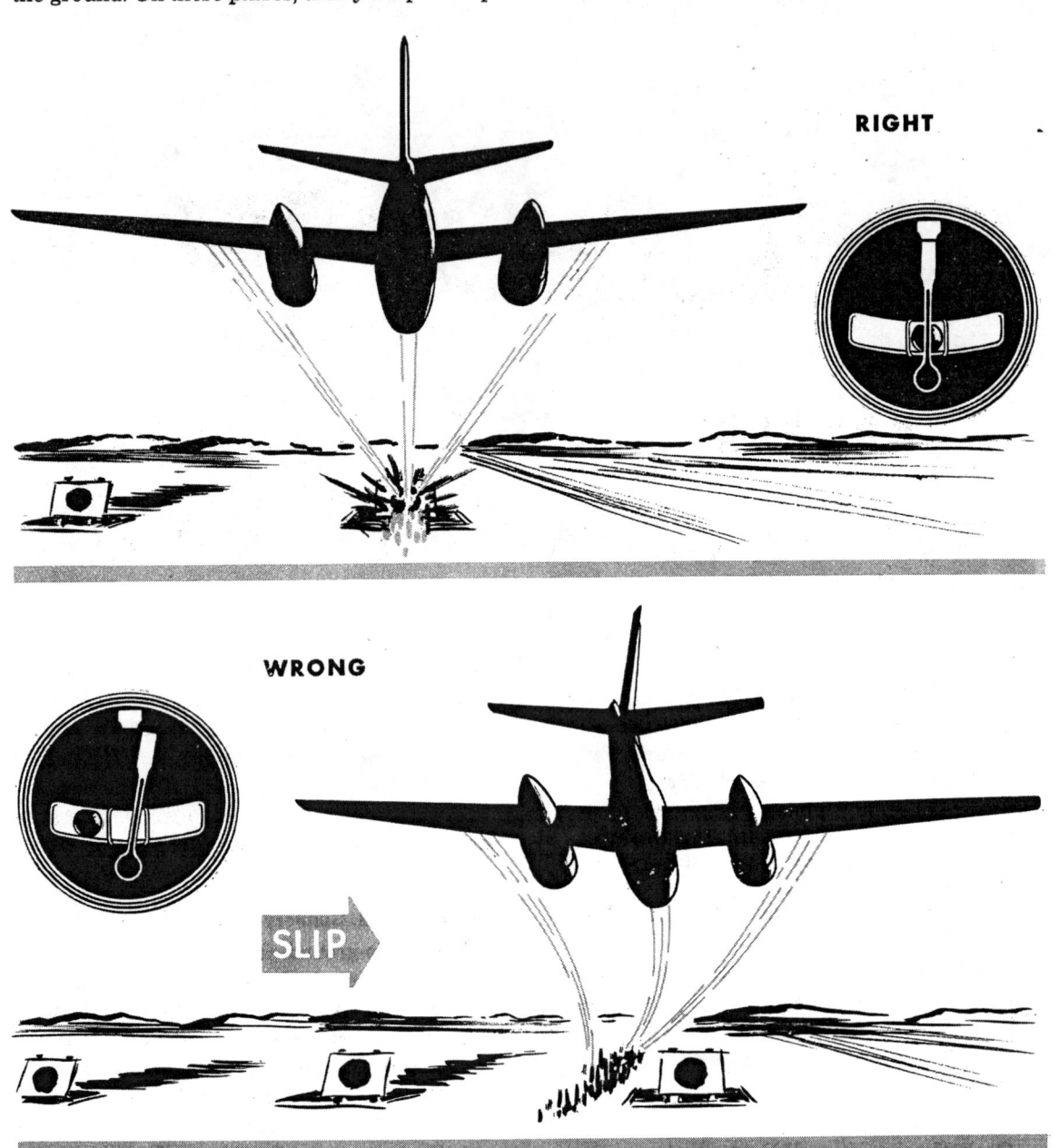

RIGHT

WRONG

SLIP

When using the gunsight, keep both eyes open. When you have accomplished the foregoing procedure, you are ready to fire. Do not turn on the FIRE CONTROL switch on the fire control panel until you have rolled out of your last turn and are lined up with the target.

Then put the bead on the target with coordinated use of stick and rudder. Once the bead is on the target, freeze on the rudder and make last little corrections with the aileron. Above all, hold the rudder steady while you are actually firing. Fire short bursts of no. more than 20 continuous rounds per gun.

Correct for wind drift by dropping a wing into the wind, but keep the ball in the center.

Pull out well over the target, because bullets and dirt ricochet and may possibly come back through the windshield.

As you chandelle up off the target, your first duty is to turn off the FIRE CONTROL switch on the fire control panel.

Don't be afraid to make plenty of dry runs, and don't waste ammunition.

Air-to-ground Strafing

Strafing differs from target gunnery in that you fly to your target at a low level and pull up and dive on the target to strafe. Make no effort to keep the ball in the center or to hit any one particular target.

The firing procedure is the same, but you use the sight for range only. As you fire, take your eyes off the sight and watch the targets.

Gently fan your rudder enough to cover the width of the targets with your fire. Here again, make your bursts as short as possible.

Do not make your approach too flat, or your bullets tend to go over the target.

Flexible Gunnery

During your fixed gunnery, the only person over whom you had to exert control was yourself. In flexible gunnery you control your fire through the rear gunner. This means that you need the ultimate in air discipline.

Instill this into your gunner. Insist that he wear his headset at all times. Make your radio and interphone communications as brief and concise as possible. Never take off until your gunner understands his duties thoroughly and is fully briefed on how the mission is to be run.

Learn your gunner's problems by having a bull session upon the completion of each mission.

Air-to-ground Flexible Gunnery

Fly your pattern to give your gunner good, clear shots.

Air-to-air Flexible Gunnery

Proficiency in air-to-air flexible gunnery is your insurance against enemy fighter opposition. Air discipline and teamwork is the secret.

Have the gunner call off the position of the other plane in terms of the clock system, "3 o'clock low," "6 o'clock high," etc. Camera guns are used in air-to-air gunnery to check your gunner's marksmanship, and your job is to follow your leader in good formation while the "enemy" planes make passes.

On every mission you and your gunner must be constantly searching the sky for other aircraft. Get into the habit of calling their position off to one another at all times during flight. The gunner should track these "enemy" aircraft, with empty guns only, to gain proficiency.

NAVIGATION

The importance of your ability as a pilot-navigator cannot be over-emphasized in the A-26. In the models with a bombardier nose, your bombardier doubles as a navigator, but even then you need to be a good navigator yourself. Navigation is not the tough problem it's cracked up to be. It amounts to only two things: Preparation and procedure.

Preparation PLOT AND PLAN YOUR FLIGHT IN DETAIL

KNOW: Distances • Headings • Altitudes
Alternate destinations • Time of departure •
Estimated time of arrival • Methods of
navigation • Fuel consumption •

MOST NAVIGATION BALL-UPS ARE CAUSED BY

INSUFFICIENT PREPARATION.

Know Your Weather

Take the initiative. Ask the weather man. Know the winds aloft, and immediate and forecast conditions along your route.

Have Your Equipment

Do not try to navigate without all necessary navigational aids. Be sure you have:
Time and distance computer.
Sectional and regional maps.
Radio facilities chart.
Pencils.
Log forms.

Procedure

There are three types of navigation:
1. Pilotage.
2. Dead reckoning.
3. Radio navigation.

Depending on the type of your mission, you lean heavily on one of the three main methods of navigation. **But you seldom use one type to the exclusion of all others.**

Always check yourself while navigating by using all three types of navigation.

Pilotage

In combat zones, where there are few radio aids, most of your navigation depends on pilotage and a combination of pilotage and dead reckoning. Over-all terrain features become increasingly important in a fast airplane. Learn to recognize outstanding terrain features quickly and accurately.

Make certain that before you take off you have plotted your course and have clearly marked your check points at regular mileage intervals. Log your time of departure accurately; approximate your ETA to your first check point and watch closely for it. This way you can determine your groundspeed and accurately figure ETA's for each succeeding check point. Figure and write down your groundspeeds at each check point. **It is easy to forget—but it's easier to write it down.**

As you progress on your course, observe to

which side of course you are drifting. Correct for drift immediately before large drift corrections are necessary. You must be doubly alert on low-level missions. Flying at high speed at low altitude is a challenge to your pilotage. You've got to be on the ball all the time.

Watch your fuel gages even more closely during low-level navigation. Treetop level is not the place to run a tank dry.

Dead Reckoning

Dead reckoning is the backbone of navigation. It depends on the accurate use of your magnetic and directional compass. The same cardinal rule holds in dead reckoning as in all other types of navigation. Before takeoff, prepare—prepare—prepare!

The procedure is simple. Hold your heading and altitude constant. Fly out your ETA. Remember altitude and temperature when computing true altitude and airspeed. Check every range station for winds aloft at your flight altitude.

Don't fight with your airplane. Keep it trimmed so it flies hands-off and you have plenty of time to make log entries and plot fixes. Watch your fuel consumption carefully.

Contact every range station, giving your position and asking for weather along your route. If you get into trouble Flight Advisory Service will call you and advise a way out. Don't wait for this emergency call based on your failure to arrive at your destination or your failure to check in at the range stations en route. Call Flight Advisory Service through your nearest range station if you are in any difficulty and they will, within a few minutes, find the answer to your question, whatever it may be.

While flying dead reckoning, don't neglect to make necessary drift corrections every time you make a change in course.

Radio Navigation

Outside combat theaters, radio navigation is your most important aid in navigation of the A-26. It is possible to navigate an entire training mission on radio alone, but it is wise to cross-check yourself with pilotage and dead reckoning.

Preparation is still the most important factor. In addition to noting weather, check points, and danger areas, make certain you have the latest corrected radio facilities chart.

Always remember that you cannot always depend on radio navigation. Violent electrical disturbances or radio failure make your log on dead reckoning and pilotage important. In bad weather, when you need your best navigation, your radio is the first to desert you.

There are four basic methods of using the radio compass. In any case, turn the jackbox marked VOICE, RANGE, BOTH to the BOTH position. Turn the other jackbox for maximum volume. Turn the selector switch on your jackbox to the radio equipment you want to use (in this case to the COMP position).

While you fly your course you will want to take radio fixes to determine your exact position. Fixes can be taken with either compass or loop.

Compass Fixes

Fixes are established by taking three bearings. Select three nearby stations with at least one on each side of your course. Look up their frequencies in the radio facilities chart and tune in your first station, writing down the time you take your first bearing. Make certain you are holding a constant heading as you follow the procedure given here.

COMPASS FIX PROCEDURE

1. With radio compass on ANT, tune up the station until you can positively identify it by its call letters.

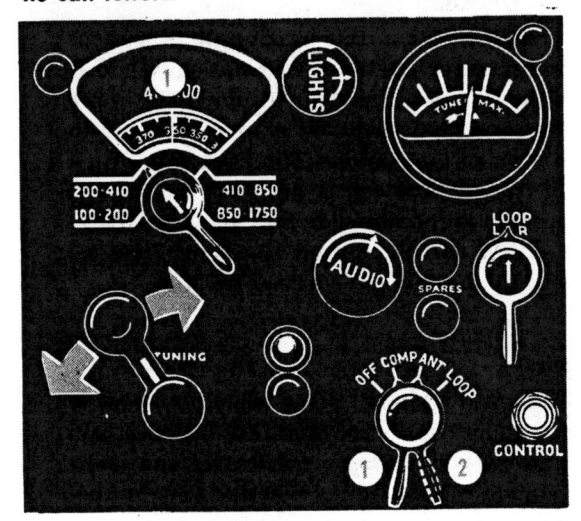

2. Switch your radio compass to the COMP position. (The needle on the dial points to the station you have tuned.)

3. As your needle points to the station, take a reciprocal reading (the opposite end of the needle). Add your reciprocal reading to the true heading of the airplane. This is your station-to-plane bearing.

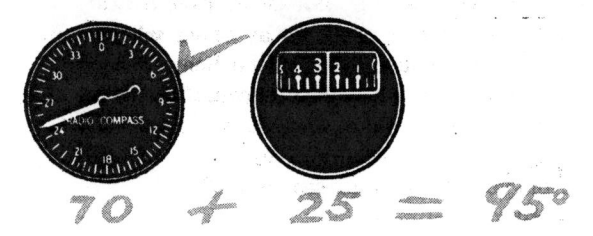

70 + 25 = 95°

Important: If the sum of the compass reading and the true heading of the airplane is more than 360°, subtract 360° from that total to arrive at the station-to-plane bearing.

4. Write this bearing down and repeat Steps 1 through 4 for the other two stations. These three bearings give you a position fix.

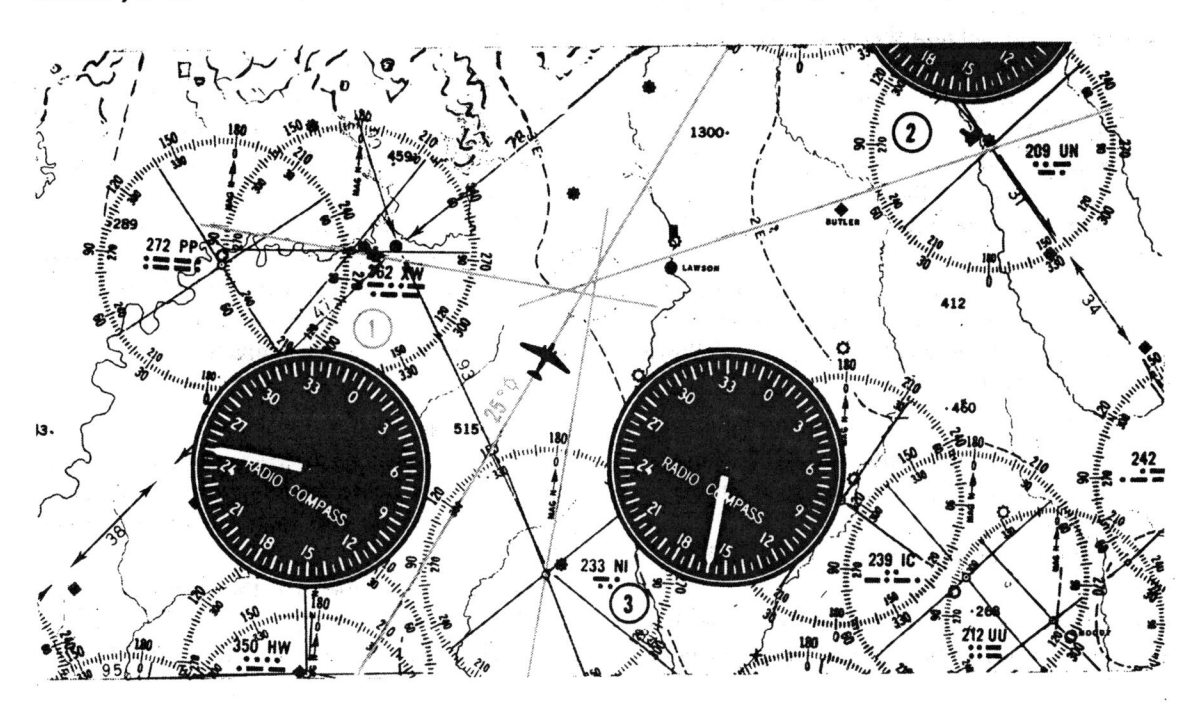

Take all three bearings quickly but accurately and remember that you must hold a constant heading while you are taking your bearings to establish a true fix.

When you have the three station-to-plane bearings, plot them on your map. They will form a small triangle, the center of which is your position, or fix, **at the time you took your first bearing. Allow for time elapsed on course. Always think of your fix as being where you were when you took your first bearing, instead of where you are when you complete all three.**

The faster you take accurate bearings the less error (smaller triangle) you have. At 240 mph you travel approximately 8 miles in only 2 minutes.

Loop Fixes

During extreme static conditions it is almost impossible to control the sensitivity of the needle while on COMP. When these conditions prevail, use the LOOP position on your radio compass to take bearings and establish your fix. This loop method is known as an aural null fix.

You can recognize this null by the complete fade in signals, the narrowness of the signal in degrees on the dial and the fact that you get an aural null, or fade, at 180° reverse positions. You follow the same procedure in the LOOP aural null fix.

Pick three stations with at least one on each side of your course. Be certain that you hold your heading accurately while you are taking your bearings.

Look up the frequency of the stations in the radio facilities chart and always write down the time you take your first bearing. Work quickly and accurately.

Procedure:

1. With the radio compass on ANT, tune up the station until you can identify it by its call letters.

2. Switch your radio compass to the LOOP position.

3. Rotate the loop until you get a complete fade (aural null) in the station. Write this compass reading down.

4. Add this compass reading to the true heading of the airplane. This may be the station-to-plane or the plane-to-station bearing.

Important: If the sum of these two readings is more than 360°, subtract 360° to get the correct bearing.

5. Make a note of this bearing. Repeat Steps 1 through 5 for the other two stations. Do this quickly and accurately. Then plot these three bearings on your map and extend the lines on both sides of the stations. The lines will form a small triangle, the center of which is your fix, or position at the time you took your first bearing. Allow for the proper lapse of time on course to estimate your actual position.

Homing

There will be many times when you want to home on your radio compass. For instance, you may know your position accurately and know the station is a few miles ahead of you, but because of poor visibility you have trouble locating it. You can home with your radio compass on COMP or LOOP position.

Procedure

1. Tune up and identify the desired station on ANT position.

2. Switch the radio compass to the COMP position. The compass needle will point toward the station.

3. Turn the plane to whatever direction the needle is swinging and keep the needle centered until you arrive at the station. Control the sensitivity of the needle with the compass knob on the face of the radio compass.

Loop Homing

When static conditions are so severe that you cannot accurately home by following the compass needle, home on the loop and orient by aural null:

1. Tune up and identify the desired station on ANT position.

2. Switch the radio compass to the LOOP position.

3. Turn the airplane until you hear a complete fade (aural null) of the signals.

4. Make a note of your magnetic heading to maintain this null.

5. Turn 90° to the right and fly this heading for 5 minutes.

6. Then turn to the left until you obtain the aural null again.

7. If your magnetic compass heading is less than the first one, the station is ahead of you. Continue to fly your aural null until you reach the station.

8. If your magnetic compass heading is more than the first one, the station is behind you. Make a 180° turn, pick up the aural null and fly until you reach the station.

Hints About Using Radio

When flying a beam problem on the command set, tune the volume on the jackbox as high as it will go and control your volume with the volume control on the command receiver.

Always have your headset on when taking a fix.

The foregoing description of how to use the radio compass for navigation is necessarily brief. For more details study your 30-100 Series T. O.'s. These T. O.'s describe all your radio navigation methods in detail. Study them. Learn them. The day will come when you need to know all there is to know about radio navigation.

INSTRUMENT FLIGHT

The knowledge of instrument flying is a pilot's best life insurance. There is no halfway point in instrument flying. A pilot who just gets by on instruments is far worse off than the old-fashioned seat-of-the-pants pilot. Instrument flying is not difficult, but it requires knowledge and delicate, exact procedures. It requires physical coordination, plus the ability to relax, physically and mentally, and to have absolute faith in your instruments.

It is your job to know that the instruments are in proper condition for instrument flight. Know how to determine faulty instruments.

Make an instrument cockpit check before every flight on which there is a possibility of instrument conditions.

Develop the habit of cross-checking the full panel of flight instruments until you are able to recognize correct or incorrect operation subconsciously.

INSTRUMENT COCKPIT CHECK

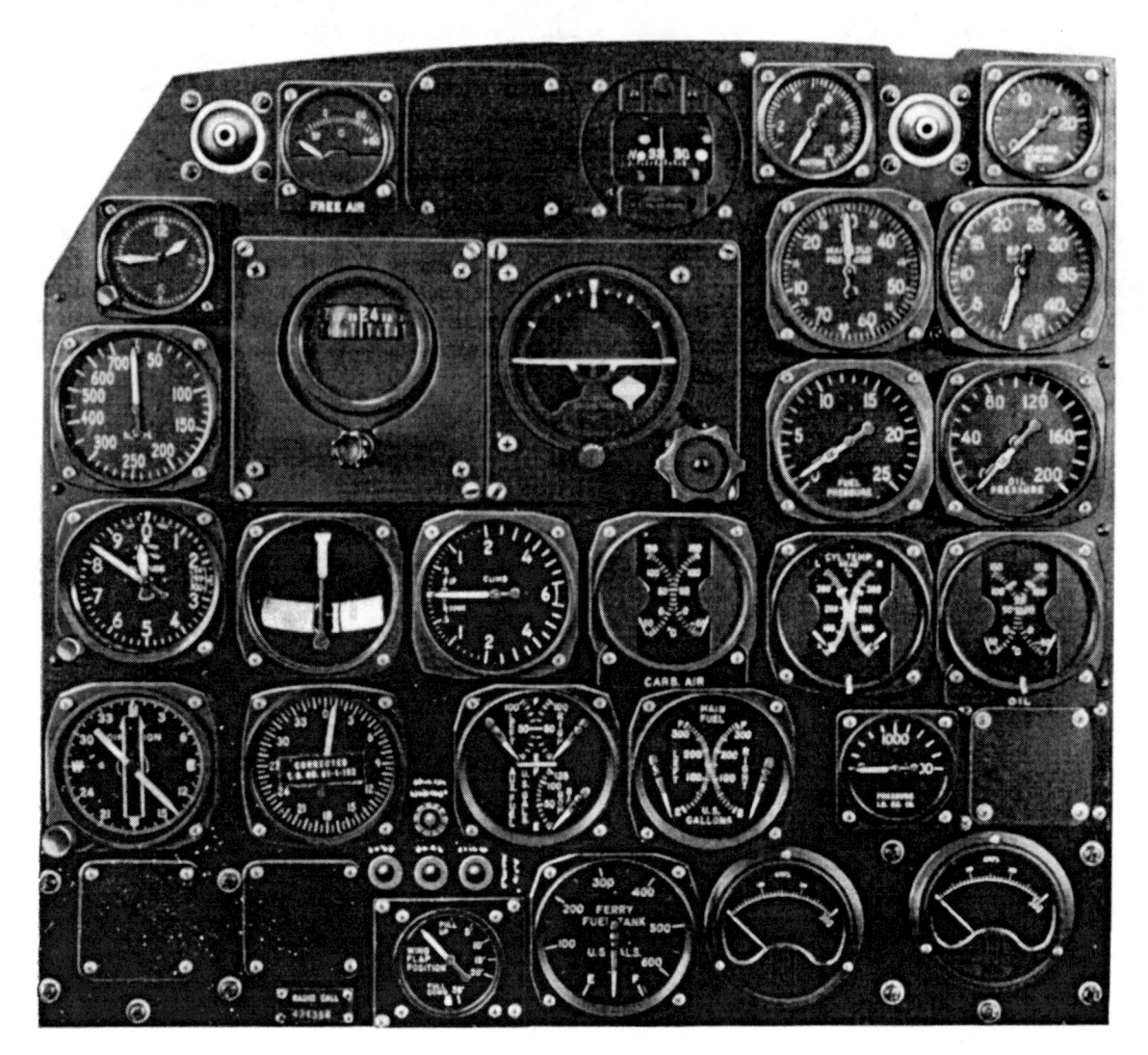

1. Airspeed Indicator

Re-check to see that pitot covers are off. Turn the pitot heat switch ON for 5 seconds and have someone feel the head to make sure it heats up properly.

If it doesn't heat up, check the forward junction box to see that the circuit protector has not popped out.

Note any deviations which are listed on the airspeed compensation card.

2. Altimeter

Set your altimeter to the station altimeter setting and note the indicated altitude. It should indicate the field elevation. If there is any difference between the altimeter indication and the actual field elevation, it indicates a scale error in the instrument. Allow for this during flight. If the scale error is greater than 50 feet, return to the line and have the instrument repaired or replaced.

3. Remote Indicating Compass

The compass itself is behind the gunner's compartment and relays its reading electrically to the pilot. This is a magnesyn type compass. Turn the plane to some known direction, parallel to a runway or on a compass rose. The needle should turn while the airplane turns and finally indicate the runway heading.

If there is a difference between runway heading, or compass rose, and needle indication, check when compass was last swung.

If the needle does not turn at all, check the circuit protector.

Be sure your compass is accurate. Your navigation can be no better than your compass.

4. Vacuum Selector Valve

Turn the vacuum selector valve, directly behind the pilot's head, to each engine and see that both pumps are operating properly.

Check the suction gage for a reading on each engine of between 3.7" and 4.7" Hg. The vacuum pumps should deliver normal pressure with the engines at idling speed.

5. Rate-of-climb Indicator

Check the rate-of-climb indicator to see that the needle is at zero. If it isn't, tap the instrument casing and check to see if the needle returns to zero. If not, have the instrument replaced.

6. Artificial Horizon

See that the artificial horizon is uncaged **before** you start the engines.

Adjust the miniature aircraft to neutral as indicated by the horizon bar. Allow sufficient time for the rotor to gain speed (5 minutes at approximately 4" Hg.). If the horizon bar descends quickly to the horizontal and remains at the correct position for the attitude of the aircraft, the instrument is operating normally.

In the A-26 the horizon bar may remain in a tilt even after the engines have been running for some time. If this happens, slowly cage the gyro and then uncage it. It should then remain in the correct position. If the horizon bar even temporarily departs from the horizontal after the rotor speed is obtained, the instrument is not operating properly.

Check to see if the horizon bar tips while making taxiing turns. Tipping indicates that the instrument is not operating properly. If it tips, have it replaced.

7. Turn Indicator

After the engines are started, cage the instrument and then twist the caging knob, and at the same time pull it out sharply. If the card spins after the knob is pulled out, the instrument is unreliable.

Set gyro to the magnetic compass reading before taxiing out. Re-check the relationship between the two immediately before takeoff. If there is any great difference, the instrument is not operating properly.

In flight, re-set your gyro with your magnetic compass heading frequently.

8. Bank-and-turn Indicator

Ground Check

While taxiing, turn the plane to the right and left. Note the reaction of the turn needle. If its indications are not positive, or if the needle is sluggish and does not return to zero promptly when the turn is stopped, the instrument is not operating properly.

Flight Check

Establish straight and level flight at 200 mph. Make coordinated single needle-width turns, left and right. Check the degree of bank on the artificial horizon. If the degree of bank is approximately 25° at 200 mph, the turn indicator is operating properly.

If your indicator is out of adjustment, write it up in Form 1A.

9. Carburetor Heat

Operate carburetor heat controls for momentary rise in temperature, then turn carburetor heat OFF and watch for temperature drop.

10. Alternate Source

Before takeoff, switch from STATIC to ALTERNATE and check your altimeter for fluctuation. This indicates that your alternate source is working.

> ## *Instrument Flight*
>
> Make the 30-100 Series of T. O.'s your bible of instrument flying.
>
> These T. O.'s provide the best single source of information for instrument flying that has ever been written. Read them thoroughly and carefully.

The A-26 has the fatigue range of a medium bomber, but unlike other long-range airplanes there is no copilot to help you fly instruments. In other words, you do all the work all the time.

The lag of flight instruments is great because the airplane is extremely fast. Plan well ahead of the airplane and make your corrections small but definite.

Always use full panel instruments under actual conditions. **Don't save any of your instruments for the Saturday night dance!** Keep your eyes constantly moving from one instrument to another and correct each one immediately. This eliminates any necessity for large corrections.

Your mental attitude is of the utmost importance while flying instruments. Don't fight the airplane. Relax and trim your plane in the normal manner.

Use trim for climb, descent, and straight and level flight. Do not trim off the back pressure which you have to apply in turns. Even in steep turns in the A-26 you can hold all the necessary pressure with one hand. By trimming this pressure off you destroy the feel of the airplane.

Never make more than a 30° bank while on instruments; the possibility of a diving spiral becomes too great. If you do get in a diving spiral, roll out of the turn and then apply back pressure to stop the dive. Watch for the zoom as you recover, and do not overcontrol.

Don't be lazy or over-eager in making instrument turns. Make your movements definite and sure. Use your altimeter, airspeed, and artificial horizon to maintain constant altitude in turns. The rate-of-climb indicator is of no practical value while in turns. Ignore it—its lag is too great.

When flying contact, practice rolling in and out of turns, noting rudder pressures necessary to keep the ball centered. You soon get the feel of the required rudder pressure necessary to roll in and out of turns during instrument conditions.

Predetermined Power Settings

The rate of climb or descent is governed by the use of power and airspeed. Predetermined power settings help you establish the proper rate of climb and descent. Individual airplanes with different load conditions cause the exact settings to vary slightly.

DESIRED PERFORMANCE	POWER SETTINGS
1. Level flight at 170 IAS	22" Hg. and 2100 rpm
2. Level flight at 160 IAS (wheels down)	28" Hg. and 2300 rpm
3. Climb at 170 IAS (500 feet per minute)	28.5" Hg. and 2300 rpm
4. Descent at 160 IAS (500 feet per minute, wheels and ½ flaps)	28" Hg. and 2300 rpm

Instrument Takeoff

Instrument takeoff procedure differs little from normal takeoff. Set the turn indicator and hold it constant until you are 500 feet in the air. Your directional gyro is your directional guide. Your airspeed indicator is your bible for climb.

Use your artificial horizon to keep your wings level.

For instrument takeoff, always double check the cockpit.

Entering an Overcast

Before entering an overcast, level off while still on contact and allow your instruments to stabilize. Check and set them for proper operation; then you're ready to enter the overcast.

Instrument Letdown

Know how to make instrument letdowns clean (with wheels up) and with wheels down and ¾ flaps. In either case the go-around is not critical. Give the wheels plenty of time to come down and lock so you have time to square off for a good approach.

When less than 1500 feet above the ground never descend on instruments at a rate exceeding 500 feet per minute. Drop ¾ flaps on the final approach to the runway. When your wheels touch the runway, drop the remainder of your flaps immediately and put the nosewheel on the ground so you can apply brakes quickly.

CARBURETOR ICE

The A-26 engines are as trouble-free from icing as any engines used in the Air Force. However, your missions may take you into weather conditions that are far from usual and on any possible instrument flight you should be alert for carburetor ice.

There are three types of ice which can form in your induction system:

1. Impact Ice

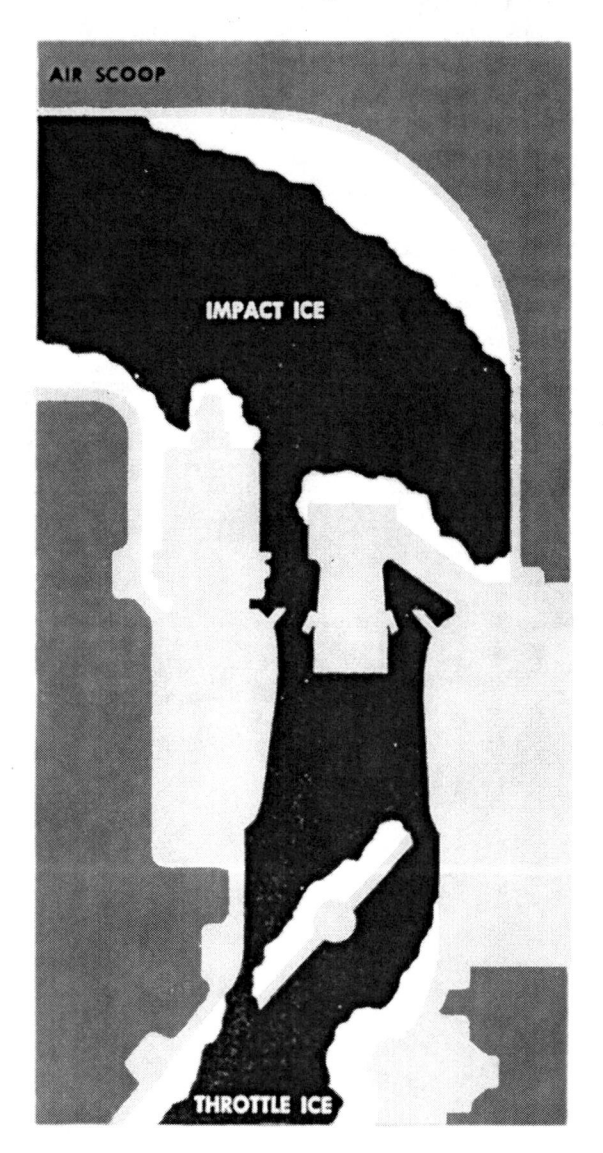

Impact ice forms when water which existed originally as snow, sleet, or super-cooled water strikes a surface which is colder than 0°C. Impact ice occurs only when visible moisture is present and the outside air temperature is less than 15°C. If carburetor intake screens are used, they quickly become clogged by the impact ice, cutting off the airflow. If no screens are installed this ice clogs up the area around the carburetor metering elements and also chokes off the airflow. Make this a rule: **When you fly through clouds or freezing rain, keep your carburetor air temperature above 5°C.**

2. Throttle Ice

Throttle ice forms when damp air flows through a restriction (venturi tube) and is therefore quickly cooled below the freezing point. Remember that throttle ice can form even though outside temperatures are above freezing. This type of ice occurs only when the throttle butterfly valve is less than 45% open and only when visible moisture is present and the outside temperature is 5°C or less. Throttle ice accumulates rapidly, first causing the butterfly valve to stick and finally choking off air passage entirely.

To avoid throttle ice, take the following precautions:

Avoid descents through overcasts at low temperatures with throttles nearly closed.

Vary throttle settings often to prevent the throttle from sticking.

3. Fuel Evaporation Ice

Fuel evaporation ice forms when the mixture cools because of evaporation. This type of ice is unusual on the A-26 because of the design of the fuel discharge spinner ring.

Tips on All Carburetor Ice

Carburetor ice is dangerous. The best guard against it is to be on the alert and to prevent its forming by maintaining the proper temperatures. Remember, too much heat is better than not enough.

Your first indication of carburetor ice is a drop in manifold pressure. Ice can form quickly under ideal temperature and moisture conditions.

TO REMOVE ALL CARBURETOR ICE TURN CARBURETOR HEAT FULL ON

COLD WEATHER OPERATION

Cold weather operation of the A-26 calls for special equipment and procedures.

De-icer boots and arctic equipment may be installed.

Besides the regular preflight inspection for normal operation, you must perform the following steps if the temperature drops below 0°C:

1. Preheat the engine. As much as 2 hours may be required to heat the engine when the temperature is extremely low.

2. Preheat the oil. Oil should be heated to a temperature of approximately 95°C just before starting the engine.

3. Check all fuel selector valves for proper operation.

4. Check the Y and oil pump drains for ice and congealed oil.

5. Check for proper operation of the de-icer, anti-icer, defroster, and heating equipment.

6. Remove **all** frost, snow, ice, and water from the wings, tail, and control surfaces.

7. Check pitot tube for ice or stoppage.

Starting Engines

If you have preheated the engine properly, start it in the normal manner. If the engine is cold, more priming is necessary.

Do not use the battery for initial starts except in emergencies. If it must be used, store the battery in a warm place until just before you need it. A warm battery produces much more energy than a cold one.

After the engines are running, idle them at 1000 rpm until the oil pressure is normal.

Operate the bomb bay doors and flaps to their fullest extent to remove any ice that may have formed.

Cold Weather Takeoff

Always keep your cowl flaps at least slightly open, regardless of the cold. Close or nearly close the oil cooler doors to prevent the oil from congealing. Use some carburetor heat when you are climbing in a cold rain, snow, or sleet, or when visible wing icing exists.

After takeoff operate your gear several times to prevent freezing in the up position.

Cruising

Watch your oil temperature closely. Oil congeals quickly, and when it does, the oil temperature goes up rapidly and the oil pressure drops off. If your oil congeals and closing the oil doors does not help, then increase your rpm to free the congealed oil.

Limit your airspeed to 300 IAS when the de-icers are operating and 350 IAS when they are not operating.

Approach

Make all approaches power-on in cold weather to prevent the engines from cooling off too much.

Use extreme caution when you apply your brakes after landing on a slippery runway.

TAXI WITH EXTREME CAUTION ON ICY SURFACES

Correct Procedure for Oil Dilution

Anticipated Lowest Outside Air Temperature   **Dilution Time**

4°C to —12°C.................................... 4 minutes

—12°C and lower............................... Dilute 4 minutes and use heat before next start.

If more dilution is necessary, shut off engines, allow to cool and start again to re-dilute.

WHEN STOPPING ENGINES IN COLD WEATHER ALWAYS CLOSE THROTTLES

Never dilute longer than 4 minutes.
1. Idle the engine at 800 to 900 rpm.
2. Make sure oil temperature is below 50°C and oil pressure remains above 20 psi.
3. Booster pumps OFF for oil dilution.
4. Hold the oil dilution switches in the ON position for the desired length of time. (A drop in fuel and oil pressure occurs if the dilution is normal.)
5. Advance the throttles to 1200 rpm.
6. Depress the feather button and hold it until the propeller runs through its complete feathering cycle at least twice.
7. When dilution time has elapsed, stop the engines in the normal manner.
8. Do not release dilution switches until engines stop.
9. Turn boosters on HIGH and be sure that fuel pressure returns to normal. (This indicates that oil dilution switches are not stuck.)

On the Ground

When you park the airplane on snow or ice, place a layer of fabric, grass, straw, or other insulatory material under the wheels. If you don't do this, large hunks of rubber will be pulled from the tires when you move the airplane from its frozen position.

UNUSUAL OPERATING CONDITIONS

In Hot Weather

Your takeoff run is longer.
Don't overheat on the ground.

Taxiing on Soft Ground

Do not taxi over soft ground until the area has been thoroughly checked for soft spots and muddy holes. **Your prop clearance is only 15".**

Know your best path of travel and keep moving steadily, keeping the nosewheel as straight as possible.

If the nosewheel gets mired, it will probably cock. **Under no circumstances try to blast it out with throttles.** Stop your engines and have the airplane towed out.

Takeoff on Rough or Soft Terrain

Consider the weight of airplane, the velocity of the wind, and attitude of the field before you attempt takeoff.

Use up to ½ flaps if necessary.

After you apply full takeoff power, pull the nosewheel slightly off the ground as quickly as possible. This relieves the weight on the nose during the takeoff run.

Make normal landings on soft terrain.

When flying in the rain, visibility is extremely restricted and you are on instruments most of the time. Avoid landing in the rain whenever possible. When landing on a wet runway, use extreme caution when applying the brakes.

Index

	PAGE
Airplane Commander	102
Armament	51-55
Armor	8
Autopilot	44-47
Blowers	16-17
Bomb Bay Doors	31
Bombing	111-116
Brakes	30
Parking	30
Capacities and Limitations	9-10
Carburetor Ice	129-130
Climb and Cruise	67-72
Long Range Cruise	70
Cold Weather Operation	130-132
Compass Fix Procedure	123
Cowl Flaps	17
Detonation	14-15
Douglas Wing	7
Electrical System	18-22
Control Panels	20-21
Gunner's Relay Box	22
Emergencies	83-101
Bailout	92-94
Crash Landing	98-99
Ditching	95-97
Electrical Failure	90
Fires	100-101
Fuel System Failure	89-90
Hydraulic System Failure	86-88
Propeller Failure	91
Single Engine Flight	83-85
Emergency and Miscellaneous Equipment	48-49

	PAGE
Engines	11-17
Limitations	13
Operation	14
Flaps	7
Flight Characteristics	73-74
Formation Flying	103-110
Landing	109
Signals	104-105
Takeoff	106-107
Fuel System	33-36
Pumps	36
Selector Valves	34
General Description	5
Go Around Procedure	80
Gunnery	117-119
Hydraulic System	23-32
Bomb Bay Doors	26
Brakes	25
Emergency	32
Landing Gear	24
Inspections and Checks	56-64
After Starting	61
Before Takeoff	64
Inside	59
Magnetos	64
Outside	57-58
Runup and Check	63
Starting Engines	60
Instrument Flight	125-129
Introduction	3
Landing	75-79
Landing Gear	28-30
Main	28

	PAGE		PAGE
Nose	29	Radio Equipment	41-43
Navigation	120-125	Stopping Engines	81
Night Flying	82	Takeoff	65-66
Nose Section	6	Taxiing	62
Oil System	37-38	Unusual Operating Conditions	132
Propellers	39-41	Water Injection	11
Feathering	40-41	Weight and Balance	50

WARSHIPS DVD SERIES

AIRCRAFT CARRIER MISHAPS
SAFETY AND TRAINING FILMS

-PERISCOPEFILM.COM-

NOW AVAILABLE ON DVD!

Aircraft At War DVD Series

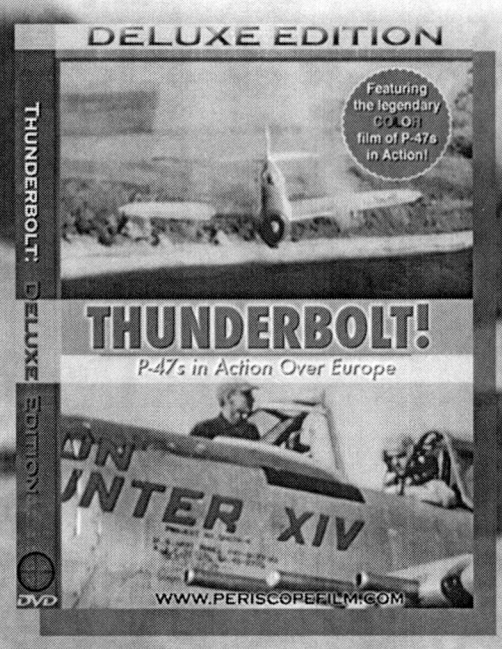

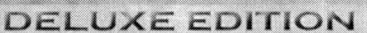

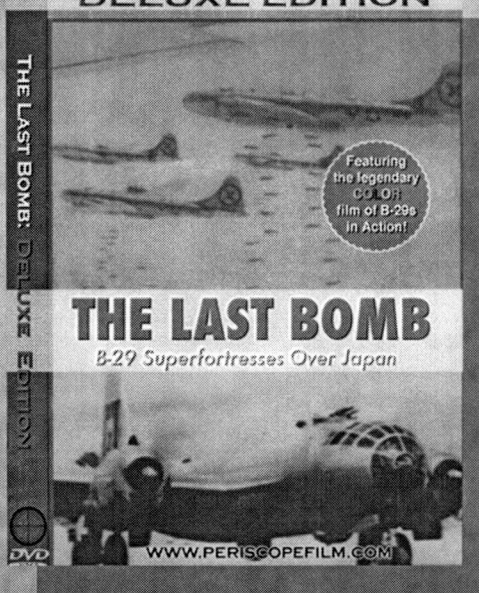

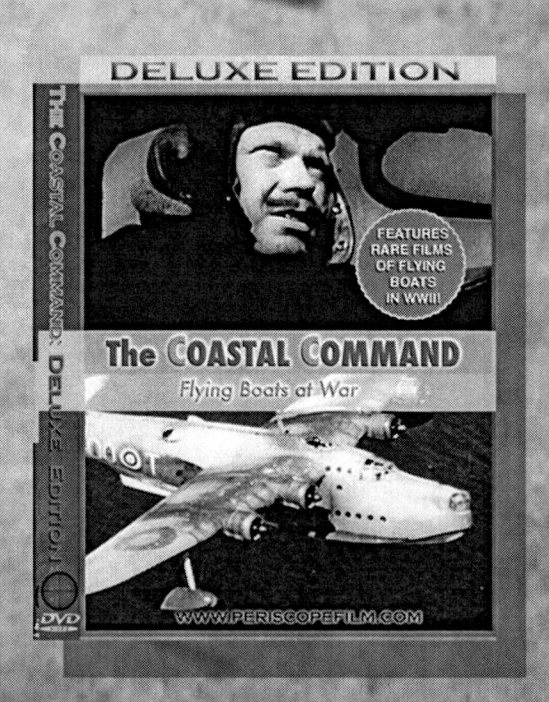

Now Available!

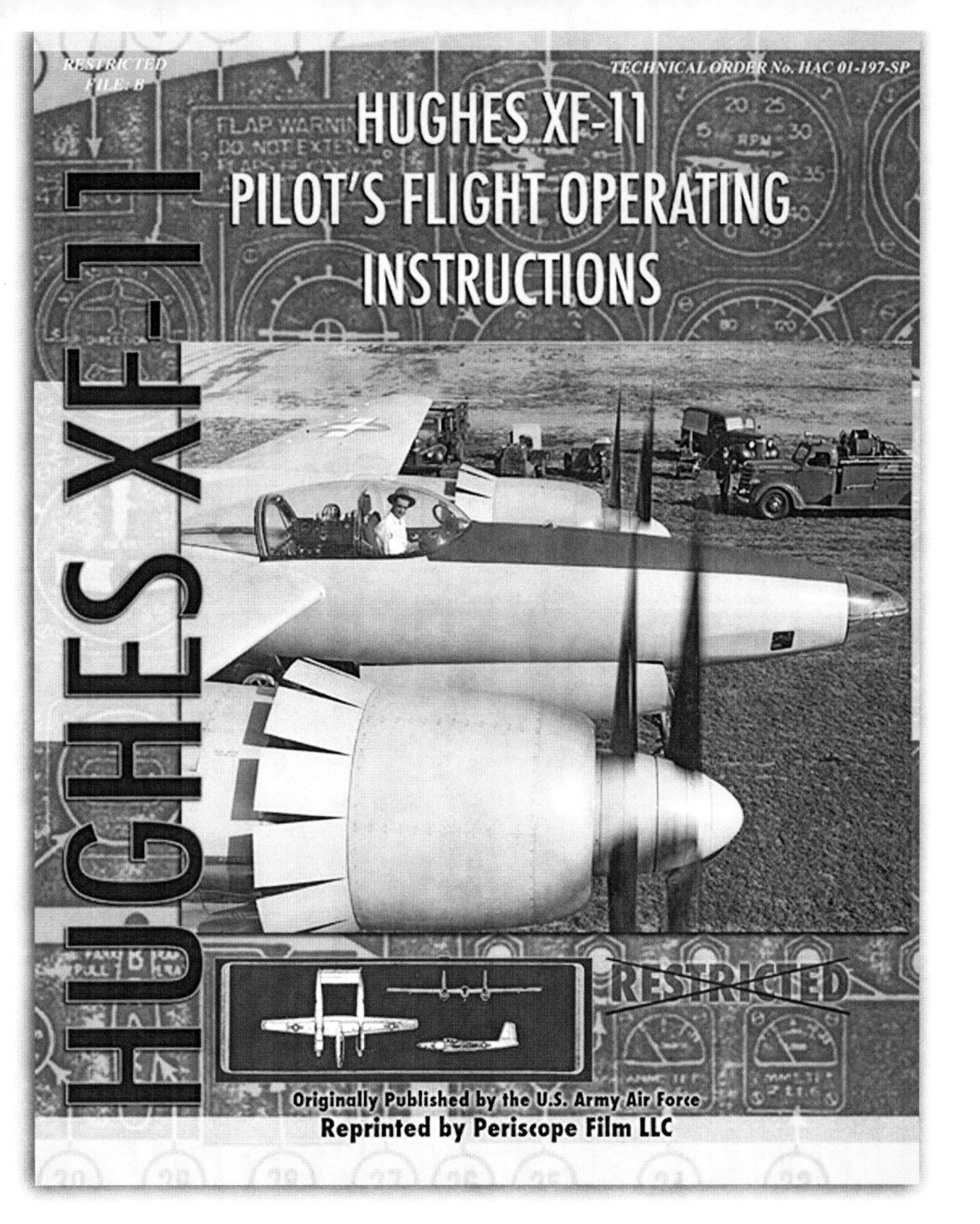

HUGHES XF-11 PILOT'S FLIGHT OPERATING INSTRUCTIONS

TECHNICAL ORDER No. HAC 01-197-SP

Originally Published by the U.S. Army Air Force
Reprinted by Periscope Film LLC

NOW AVAILABLE!

SPRUCE GOOSE

HUGHES FLYING BOAT MANUAL

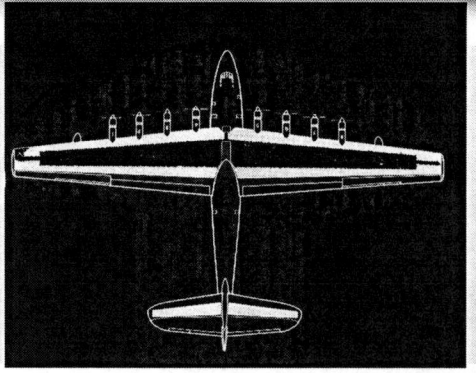

~~RESTRICTED~~

Originally Published by the War Department
Reprinted by Periscope Film LLC

NOW AVAILABLE!

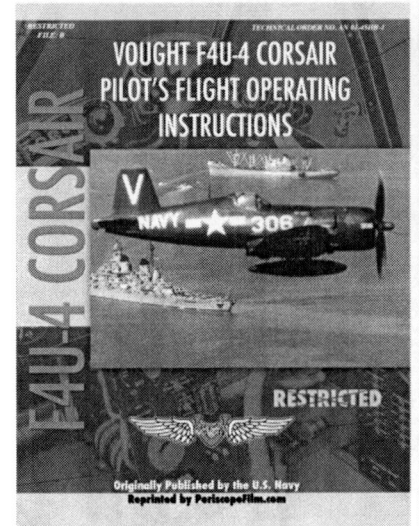

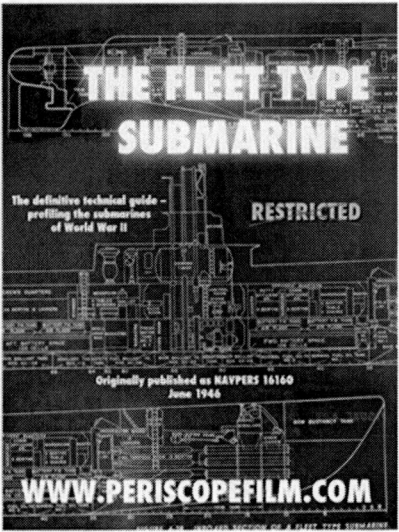

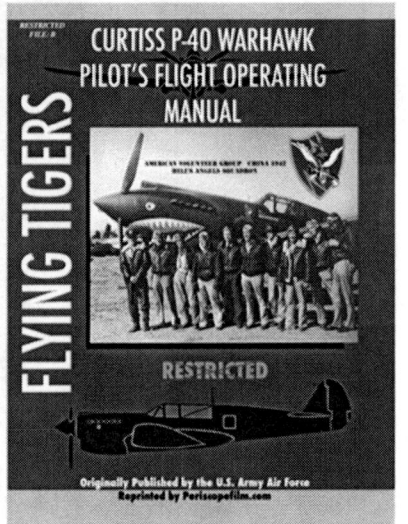

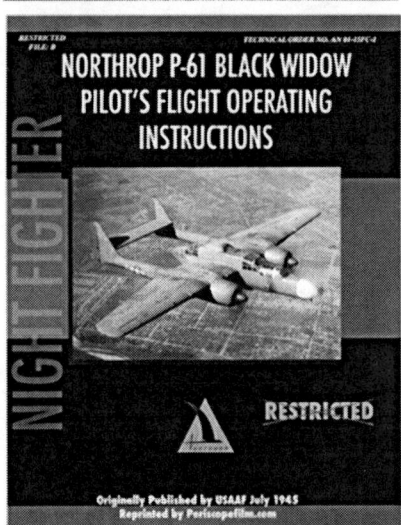

ALSO NOW AVAILABLE FROM PERISCOPEFILM.COM

©2008-2010 Periscope Film LLC
All Rights Reserved
ISBN #978-1-935700-03-6
www.PeriscopeFilm.com

CPSIA information can be obtained at www.ICGtesting.com
Printed in the USA
BVOW05s0834271113

337501BV00001B/3/P